Sustainable Urban Development in Southern Africa

Fortune Mangara • Nirmala Dorasamy

Sustainable Urban Development in Southern Africa

Disaster Risk Reduction and Economic Resilience

palgrave
macmillan

Fortune Mangara
Department of Public Management
Durban University of Technology
Durban, South Africa

Nirmala Dorasamy
Department of Public Management
Durban University of Technology
Durban, South Africa

ISBN 978-3-032-08285-5 ISBN 978-3-032-08286-2 (eBook)
https://doi.org/10.1007/978-3-032-08286-2

This Palgrave Macmillan imprint is published by the registered company Springer Nature Switzerland AG.
The registered company address is: Gewerbestrasse 11, 6330 Cham, Switzerland

Foreword

The Southern African region stands at a crossroads of urban transformation and climate vulnerability. As cities expand rapidly amid deepening socio-economic inequalities and growing exposure to natural hazards, the urgency for integrated planning and risk-informed development becomes undeniable. This book, *Sustainable Urban Development in Southern Africa—Disaster Risk Reduction and Economic Resilience*, arrives at a pivotal moment. Dr. Fortune Mangara and Professor Nirmala Dorasamy have produced a timely and insightful volume that synthesises critical theory, empirical case studies, and regional policy analysis. With clarity and academic rigour, the book bridges the longstanding divide between urban planning and disaster risk reduction fields that have too often operated in isolation. By grounding its arguments in the lived realities of cities such as Harare, Maputo, Lusaka, and Durban, the book illuminates the structural barriers and innovative practices shaping the region's urban future. What sets this book apart is its insistence on contextual relevance. It does not merely apply global frameworks to local challenges; it interrogates and localises them, offering a Southern African voice to global debates on resilience and sustainability. In doing so, it provides a roadmap for inclusive, equitable, and adaptive urban governance that resonates far beyond the region. Whether you are a policymaker, planner, academic, or development practitioner, this book will sharpen your understanding and inform your interventions. I commend the authors for their depth of analysis, clarity of purpose, and unwavering commitment to social justice and sustainable development.

This is a book that does not simply describe the risks our cities face—it equips us with the tools to transform them.

Department of Public Management and Economics
Faculty of Management Sciences
Durban University of Technology (DUT)
Durban, South Africa

Fortune Mangara
Nirmala Dorasamy

Preface

In an era of rapid urbanisation and mounting climate-related threats, integrated and forward-thinking urban planning has become essential. Southern Africa, endowed with rich natural resources and cultural diversity, stands at a critical juncture. Its cities are vibrant and full of promise, yet they also face significant vulnerabilities stemming from poor infrastructure, socio-economic inequalities, climate risks, and governance challenges. *Sustainable Urban Development in Southern Africa: Disaster Risk Reduction and Economic Resilience* responds to this complex reality, offering a comprehensive approach to reimagining urban spaces that are sustainable, resilient, and inclusive. This book is the product of extensive academic research, practical fieldwork, and deep engagement with the urban development issues that define the Southern African context. Cities across the region grapple with the combined pressures of informal expansion, service delivery backlogs, and environmental shocks. However, amid these challenges lies the potential for pioneering solutions integrating disaster risk reduction (DRR) into every facet of urban planning.

Our work positions DRR not as a separate discipline but as a strategic entry point into sustainable urban development. By examining land use management, resilient infrastructure, climate adaptation, and governance reforms, we present practical frameworks grounded in theory and experience. The case studies, ranging from Maputo's flood-risk settlements to Johannesburg's land use reforms, illustrate how locally rooted innovations can drive transformative change. What distinguishes this book is its emphasis on the interlinkages between resilience, economic development, governance, and social equity. It contributes to the global pursuit of the

Sustainable Development Goals, particularly Goal 11: Sustainable Cities and Communities, by demonstrating how localised DRR strategies can achieve a lasting impact. Southern Africa's unique socio-political legacies, environmental uncertainties, and urban dynamics offer lessons that extend beyond the region. By centring the voices and experiences of communities, policymakers, and practitioners within the region, this book contributes to a more inclusive discourse on urban resilience, which is often dominated by narratives from the Global North. We hope this work inspires urban planners, policymakers, academics, and citizens alike to rethink how cities are built and governed. The journey towards sustainable urban development in Southern Africa is ongoing. Still, through collaboration, innovation, and community empowerment, the region can shape cities that thrive amid uncertainty and lead by example in a rapidly changing world.

Durban, South Africa
June 2025

Fortune Mangara
Nirmala Dorasamy

Blurb About the Book

This book provides a critical examination of how disaster risk reduction (DRR) strategies can be systematically integrated into urban planning processes to enhance resilience in rapidly growing cities across Southern Africa. Grounded in interdisciplinary research and real-world case studies from countries such as Zimbabwe, Mozambique, and South Africa, the book offers an in-depth analysis of urban vulnerability, governance constraints, infrastructure challenges, and climate-induced risks. It explores key themes, including land use management, resilient infrastructure, institutional reform, and policy integration, framed within the context of Sustainable Development Goal 11 and the Sendai Framework for Disaster Risk Reduction. This volume advances a unique regional perspective, highlighting both the structural barriers and innovative local responses to urban risk. It synthesises theoretical and applied insights to present actionable strategies for mainstreaming resilience across planning systems. Emphasising the interconnectedness of social, economic, environmental, and institutional factors, the book demonstrates how cities can transition towards more inclusive, risk-informed development trajectories. A valuable resource for researchers, practitioners, urban planners, and policymakers, this book contributes to global debates on urban resilience and sustainability by centring the experiences of Southern African cities. It will appeal to scholars in disaster risk studies, urban and regional planning, climate change adaptation, and public governance, as well as professionals working in urban development across the Global South.

Contents

About the Authors

Fortune Mangara is a Post-doctoral Research Fellow in the Department of Public Management and Economics at the Durban University of Technology (DUT). He holds a PhD and an M.Sc. in Urban and Regional Planning from North-West University. Dr. Mangara's research centres on spatial and urban resilience, focusing on key areas such as disaster risk studies, disaster resilience, disaster risk governance, urban disaster risk, and social and economic geography. His work also explores urban policy, urban governance, transport planning and mobility, and spatial transformations in African cities. Dr. Mangara has presented his research at international conferences and actively participated in discussions at both national and global forums. He has also contributed to academic research through local and international publications.

Nirmala Dorasamy is a Full Professor in the Department of Public Management and Economics at the Durban University of Technology (DUT). She lectures in the undergraduate and postgraduate programmes at DUT. The focus area of her research is ethics and public sector management, with an emphasis on enhancing the effectiveness and efficiency of public service delivery, underpinned by a strong sense of governance within a democratic dispensation. She has successfully supervised and graduated several Master's and Doctoral students, while being recognised as a local and international examiner for postgraduate research. She has co-authored textbooks for senior secondary learners, books for higher education purposes, and she has published in local and international journals as well as presented papers at national and international conferences.

Acronyms

BRT	Bus Rapid Transit
CBO	Community-Based Organisation
CCA	Climate Change Adaptation
CEDAW	Convention on the Elimination of All Forms of Discrimination Against Women
CSO	Civil Society Organisation
DA	Disaster Assessment
DRM	Disaster Risk Management
DRR	Disaster Risk Reduction
EIA	Environmental Impact Assessment
EWS	Early Warning System
GHG	Greenhouse Gas
GIS	Geographic Information System
GWP	Global Water Partnership
IDP	Integrated Development Plan
IPCC	Intergovernmental Panel on Climate Change
ISO	International Organization for Standardization
IWRM	Integrated Water Resources Management
LDC	Least Developed Country
LED	Local Economic Development
MoU	Memorandum of Understanding
NGO	Non-Governmental Organisation
NSDRM	National Strategy for Disaster Risk Management
OECD	Organisation for Economic Co-operation and Development
PPP	Public–Private Partnership
SADC	Southern African Development Community
SDG	Sustainable Development Goal

SEA	Strategic Environmental Assessment
SLM	Sustainable Land Management
ToR	Terms of Reference
UN	United Nations
UNDRR	United Nations Office for Disaster Risk Reduction
UNFCCC	United Nations Framework Convention on Climate Change
UN-Habitat	United Nations Human Settlements Programme
USAID	United States Agency for International Development
WHO	World Health Organisation
WFP	World Food Programme
WSSD	World Summit on Sustainable Development
ZIMSTAT	Zimbabwe National Statistics Agency

List of Figures

List of Tables

CHAPTER 1

Introduction to Disaster Risk Reduction and Urban Planning in Southern Africa

1.1 Contextual Background: Urbanisation in Southern Africa

The urban landscape in Southern Africa is undergoing a profound transformation. Over the past few decades, cities in countries such as Zimbabwe, South Africa, Mozambique, Zambia, and Malawi have experienced accelerated urban growth, largely driven by demographic expansion, rural-to-urban migration, and shifting economic structures. This urbanisation trend is expected to continue, with projections indicating that by 2050, more than 60% of the region's population will reside in urban areas (UN-Habitat, 2022). However, this growth has often been unplanned, informal, and inadequately supported by infrastructure or policy frameworks, leading to a rise in systemic vulnerabilities and urban inequality.

Urbanisation in Southern Africa is occurring within a context of persistent poverty, political instability in some countries, and chronic underinvestment in public infrastructure. Unlike the planned, economically anchored urbanisation processes seen in some developed regions, urban growth in Southern Africa has frequently outpaced the capacity of local governments to provide basic services and regulate spatial development. The result has been a proliferation of informal settlements, unregulated construction in hazardous areas, overloaded transport networks, and

F. Mangara, N. Dorasamy, *Sustainable Urban Development in Southern Africa*, https://doi.org/10.1007/978-3-032-08286-2_1

critical infrastructure deficits in water, sanitation, and waste management (Parnell & Pieterse, 2014).

The implications of these trends are dire. The expansion of urban areas without corresponding investment in resilience-oriented infrastructure has led to the entrenchment of risk. In many cities, marginalised populations settle in environmentally hazardous locations—flood plains, unstable hillsides, or near industrial waste sites—exposing themselves to recurring disasters such as floods, landslides, fire outbreaks, and disease outbreaks. This condition, termed the "urban risk trap", reinforces cycles of vulnerability, poverty, and exclusion (Wisner et al., 2012).

Furthermore, the spatial patterns of urbanisation in the region reflect historical legacies of segregation, colonial planning, and economic exclusion. In cities such as Harare, Lusaka, and Durban, urban sprawl continues along lines of social and spatial inequality, reinforcing divisions in access to services, security, and opportunity. The governance systems in place often lack the institutional coherence and resources needed to manage these processes effectively (Harrison et al., 2008).

1.2 Climate Change and Urban Vulnerability

Climate change compounds the urban challenges already present in Southern Africa. Rising temperatures, erratic rainfall, prolonged droughts, and intensified storms now characterise the climate reality for many urban centres in the region (Niang et al., 2014). Cities such as Maputo, Beira, and Gweru have witnessed increasingly severe cyclones, coastal erosion, flooding, and public health emergencies linked to climate variability. The consequences of these hazards are felt most acutely by low-income and informal settlement dwellers, who often live in substandard housing with limited access to emergency services.

Southern African cities are particularly vulnerable to climate change impacts due to their geography, infrastructure deficits, and institutional weaknesses. For example, in Mozambique, Cyclones Idai (2019) and Freddy (2023) caused widespread destruction in urban centres, displacing hundreds of thousands of people and exposing deficiencies in planning and disaster preparedness. Similarly, water shortages in cities such as Windhoek and Harare have become chronic due to prolonged droughts, mismanagement, and poor investment in sustainable water systems (Ziervogel et al., 2016).

Urban areas act as both contributors to and victims of climate change. While greenhouse gas emissions in Southern Africa are relatively low compared to global standards, energy inefficiencies, reliance on fossil fuels, and unsustainable consumption patterns in urban areas contribute to environmental degradation. At the same time, the lack of climate-resilient urban infrastructure, limited early warning systems, and poor inter-sectoral coordination have hindered adaptation efforts (Dodman et al., 2017). Crucially, the climate crisis intersects with socio-economic inequality, further marginalising vulnerable populations. Women, the elderly, children, and persons with disabilities often face disproportionate risks during disasters, and post-disaster recovery is slow and uneven. These dynamics underscore the importance of integrating climate-sensitive planning within urban governance systems.

1.3 Infrastructure Gaps and Disaster Exposure

The infrastructure landscape in Southern African cities is defined by inequality, informality, and fragility. Roads, drainage systems, electricity networks, and public transport services are often inadequate, poorly maintained, or absent altogether. These deficits exacerbate vulnerability during times of crisis. For instance, the absence of stormwater drainage in many informal settlements leads to routine flooding during the rainy season, damaging property and spreading waterborne diseases such as cholera and typhoid (Van Niekerk, 2022).

Moreover, public infrastructure is frequently developed without consideration of hazard exposure or future climate scenarios. Infrastructural planning remains reactive rather than anticipatory, resulting in repeated damage to facilities that are not built to withstand extreme weather events. The cost of inaction is significant: disaster-related infrastructure damage places further strain on municipal budgets, which are already stretched by competing developmental priorities (World Bank, 2021).

The informality of urban development presents a major challenge to resilient infrastructure planning. In cities such as Blantyre, Maseru, and Bulawayo, informal construction practices dominate the housing and small-scale commercial sectors, often without adherence to safety standards or spatial plans. Infrastructure provision in these contexts is ad hoc and community-led, with limited support from government actors. While such self-organisation may reflect resilience and ingenuity, it is not a substitute for structured, risk-sensitive planning.

Transport systems, a critical component of urban resilience, are also insufficiently developed in many Southern African cities. Congested, unsafe, and inefficient public transport systems limit mobility during emergencies and reduce access to health services, schools, and markets. The failure to invest in inclusive and disaster-resilient transport systems undermines social and economic development, particularly in peripheral settlements where formal infrastructure is scarce.

1.4 Governance Challenges in Southern African Cities

Urban governance in Southern Africa is marked by fragmentation, weak institutional coordination, political instability in certain contexts, and chronic underfunding. The responsibilities for urban planning, land management, disaster risk reduction, and infrastructure development are often split across multiple departments and levels of government, with limited collaboration or integrated strategy. This siloed governance structure impedes efforts to implement coherent urban resilience policies (Pieterse & Parnell, 2014). Corruption, capacity shortages, and political interference further undermine urban governance. In several cases, local governments lack the autonomy or technical expertise needed to enforce zoning laws, conduct environmental impact assessments, or coordinate risk reduction activities. Furthermore, rapid political turnover and inconsistent funding streams disrupt long-term planning processes, leading to policy fragmentation and implementation paralysis (Smit & Musango, 2015).

Community participation in urban governance remains limited, particularly in informal and marginalised areas. While participatory planning frameworks exist on paper, in practice, they are often tokenistic or poorly resourced. This exclusion limits the effectiveness of DRR strategies, as communities are not consulted on the risks they face or the solutions they require. Without community buy-in, even the best-intentioned resilience interventions risk failure. Moreover, urban governance systems in Southern Africa have struggled to mainstream disaster risk reduction into broader development planning. DRR is often treated as a standalone sector managed by civil protection agencies or emergency services, rather than as a cross-cutting issue embedded within all aspects of urban planning. This institutional isolation perpetuates a reactive approach to disasters, with an emphasis on emergency response rather than prevention and preparedness (UNDRR, 2022).

1.5 Disaster Risk Reduction: Definitions, Frameworks, and Relevance

Disaster Risk Reduction (DRR) encompasses policies, strategies, and practices aimed at reducing the damages caused by natural hazards. The United Nations Office for Disaster Risk Reduction (UNDRR) defines DRR as “the concept and practice of reducing disaster risks through systematic efforts to analyse and reduce the causal factors of disasters”. These include reducing exposure to hazards, lessening vulnerability of people and property, and improving preparedness for adverse events. Globally, DRR has gained significant traction through the Sendai Framework for Disaster Risk Reduction 2015–2030, which calls for a paradigm shift from managing disasters to managing risk. The framework emphasises the importance of understanding risk, strengthening disaster governance, investing in resilience, and enhancing preparedness. It encourages member states to integrate DRR into development planning at national and local levels (UNDRR, 2015).

In the Southern African context, DRR is increasingly recognised as essential to sustainable development. The region is prone to a range of hazards, including floods, droughts, cyclones, wildfires, and epidemics. The economic and social costs of these disasters are high, particularly in urban areas with high population densities and poorly developed infrastructure. DRR offers a pathway to reduce these impacts through proactive planning, early warning systems, risk-sensitive land use, and community-based preparedness strategies. Importantly, DRR is not merely a technical exercise but also a governance and social justice concern. Disasters disproportionately affect poor and marginalised communities, reinforcing inequalities and undermining long-term development gains. Effective DRR requires inclusive processes that recognise local knowledge, build institutional capacity, and empower citizens to reduce their own risk (Lavell & Maskrey, 2014).

1.6 Urban Planning: Instruments, Institutions, and Implementation Gaps

Urban planning in Southern Africa is mandated to guide land use, spatial development, and the provision of infrastructure and services. However, its practical application has been hindered by outdated legislative frameworks, institutional fragmentation, and inadequate technical capacity. Many urban areas in the region still operate under inherited colonial planning statutes, which are poorly aligned with current socio-economic and environmental realities (Watson, 2009). Implementation gaps are particularly stark at the local government level, where municipalities frequently lack the resources, skilled personnel, and political autonomy required to enforce plans. Urban development often unfolds in an unregulated or semi-regulated fashion, with a proliferation of informal settlements and structures in hazard-prone areas (Harrison et al., 2008). In cities such as Harare, Maputo, and Lusaka, strategic urban development frameworks exist but are rarely implemented due to limited institutional coherence, weak enforcement, and inconsistent political support (UN-Habitat, 2020).

Furthermore, spatial planning instruments are not routinely updated to incorporate emerging risks such as climate change, flood exposure, or geotechnical hazards. This disconnection between risk knowledge and planning implementation exacerbates vulnerability and undermines efforts to build urban resilience (Van Niekerk, 2022). In many cases, urban planning functions as a bureaucratic tool rather than a transformative instrument for inclusive, safe, and resilient urban development.

1.7 The Intersection of DRR and Urban Planning

The intersection of disaster risk reduction (DRR) and urban planning is increasingly recognised as a critical site for integrated action. Both fields aim to safeguard lives, livelihoods, and assets, and both influence how risk is produced or mitigated in urban areas. Urban planning determines the spatial distribution of populations, infrastructure, and services, while DRR provides the tools and frameworks to assess hazards, reduce vulnerability, and enhance adaptive capacity (UNDRR, 2015).

Incorporating DRR into urban planning involves mainstreaming risk considerations into development control, zoning regulations, building codes, infrastructure design, and service delivery systems (Birkmann et al., 2011). It also entails cross-sectoral collaboration between urban planners, environmental managers, disaster managers, and local communities. In cities such as Durban, Cape Town, and Beira, attempts have been made to institutionalise such integration through climate resilience planning units and risk-informed urban strategies (Ziervogel et al., 2016).

However, the integration of DRR and urban planning remains fragmented across much of Southern Africa. National DRR policies often lack explicit linkages to urban development frameworks, while spatial planning policies may not adequately account for risk assessments or hazard maps (Adelekan et al., 2015). Bridging this gap requires structural reforms in institutional mandates, capacity development for planners, and a shift towards proactive, anticipatory governance.

1.8 The Rationale for Integrated Approaches

The rationale for integrating DRR and urban planning lies in the recognition that disasters are not merely the result of natural hazards but are deeply shaped by social, political, and spatial factors. Poor land-use planning, unregulated settlement expansion, and infrastructure deficits are central drivers of disaster risk in urban areas (Wisner et al., 2012). Hence, embedding risk-informed approaches within planning practice offers a powerful avenue to address underlying vulnerabilities and build more inclusive, resilient cities.

Integrated planning enables cities to transition from reactive disaster response to anticipatory risk management. It aligns development trajectories with risk profiles, ensures investments are safeguarded from hazard exposure, and helps avoid maladaptive practices such as building on flood plains or sealing urban wetlands (Satterthwaite et al., 2018). Moreover, it supports co-benefits such as climate adaptation, environmental conservation, and social equity.

International policy frameworks reinforce this rationale. The Sendai Framework for Disaster Risk Reduction (2015–2030) emphasises the importance of mainstreaming DRR across development sectors, including urban planning (UNDRR, 2015). The New Urban Agenda (2016) and Africa's Agenda 2063 similarly advocate for resilient urban development rooted in integrated planning, inclusive governance, and community engagement (African Union, 2015; UN-Habitat, 2016).

1.9 Key Challenges in Integrating DRR and Urban Planning

Despite growing awareness, several obstacles hinder the effective integration of DRR and urban planning in Southern Africa. One of the foremost challenges is institutional fragmentation. Urban governance responsibilities are often split across multiple sectors, including planning, housing, infrastructure, environment, and disaster management, resulting in misaligned mandates and poor inter-agency coordination (Pieterse & Parnell, 2014). Another critical barrier is the lack of updated and localised risk data. Many municipalities do not possess current hazard maps, vulnerability assessments, or exposure models, making it difficult to incorporate risk considerations into planning decisions (Lavell & Maskrey, 2014). Even when data is available, it is often stored in central government departments or academic institutions and is not easily accessible to planners at the local level.

Financial constraints further compound the challenge. DRR activities are frequently underfunded, and budget allocations for resilience are often not mainstreamed into development financing (World Bank, 2021). Additionally, planners may not have the legal authority to enforce risk-sensitive zoning or relocate communities from high-risk areas, especially in the face of political resistance or community opposition. Lastly, informality poses a major structural challenge. A large portion of urban development in the region occurs outside formal planning channels. Informal settlements are rarely covered by planning schemes or DRR strategies, yet they are among the most exposed and vulnerable urban areas (Roy, 2005). Integrating DRR into planning thus requires inclusive approaches that acknowledge and engage with the informal reality of urbanisation in Southern Africa.

1.10 Objectives of the Book

This book seeks to bridge the gap between disaster risk reduction (DRR) and urban planning in the Southern African context. It responds to the growing urgency for integrated and contextually grounded approaches to urban resilience, particularly as cities in the region face increasing pressures from climate change, rapid urbanisation, and infrastructural decay.

The specific objectives of the book are to:

1. Examine the drivers of urban vulnerability and risk in Southern African cities, with particular emphasis on informal settlements, institutional fragmentation, and socio-economic inequality.
2. Evaluate the extent to which DRR frameworks are embedded in urban planning policies and practices across the region.
3. Identify the barriers—legal, political, institutional, and financial—that constrain the integration of DRR into planning systems.
4. Present case studies of successful and innovative practices where urban resilience has been enhanced through integrated approaches.
5. Provide actionable recommendations for national and local governments, planners, and development partners to strengthen the resilience of Southern African cities through improved governance, planning reforms, and inclusive DRR strategies.

These objectives are aligned with international development frameworks such as the Sendai Framework, the Sustainable Development Goals (SDGs), and the New Urban Agenda, all of which call for inclusive, safe, and resilient urban environments (UNDRR, 2015; UN-Habitat, 2016).

1.11 Conclusion

This introductory chapter has set the foundation for understanding the rationale and structure of the book. It has situated the urbanisation process in Southern Africa within a broader context of risk, inequality, and institutional fragmentation. The chapter has also highlighted how disaster risk is not a natural phenomenon, but the outcome of poor planning, governance failures, and entrenched vulnerability. The case for integrating DRR and urban planning has been made clear. Without such integration, cities will continue to reproduce cycles of risk and exclusion, undermining long-term development gains. The rest of the book explores how integrated, inclusive, and proactive urban planning can reduce disaster risk and foster resilience in the face of a changing climate and growing urban complexity. By advancing both critical reflection and practical insights, this book aims to support the transformation of Southern Africa's cities into resilient, sustainable, and equitable spaces for all.

References

Adelekan, I. O., Johnson, C., Manda, M., Matyas, D., Mberu, B. U., Parnell, S., & Satterthwaite, D. (2015). Disaster risk and its reduction: An agenda for urban Africa. *International Development Planning Review, 37*(1), 33–43.

African Union. (2015). *Agenda 2063: The Africa we want.* African Union Commission.

Birkmann, J., Garschagen, M., Kraas, F., & Quang, N. (2011). Adaptive urban governance: New challenges for the second generation of urban adaptation strategies to climate change. *Sustainability Science, 5*(2), 185–206.

Dodman, D., Leck, H., Rusca, M., & Colenbrander, S. (2017). African urbanisation and urbanism: Implications for risk accumulation and reduction. *International Journal of Disaster Risk Reduction, 26*, 7–15.

Harrison, P., Todes, A., & Watson, V. (2008). *Planning and transformation: Learning from the post-apartheid experience.* Routledge.

Lavell, A., & Maskrey, A. (2014). The future of disaster risk management. *Environmental Hazards, 13*(4), 267–280.

Niang, I., Ruppel, O. C., Abdrabo, M. A., Essel, A., Lennard, C., Padgham, J., & Urquhart, P. (2014). Africa. In *Climate change 2014: Impacts, Adaptation, and vulnerability.* IPCC Working Group II. Cambridge University Press.

Parnell, S., & Pieterse, E. (2014). *Africa's urban revolution.* Zed Books.

Pieterse, E., & Parnell, S. (2014). Africa's urban revolution in context. In S. Parnell & E. Pieterse (Eds.), *Africa's urban revolution* (pp. 1–17). Zed Books.

Roy, A. (2005). Urban informality: Toward an epistemology of planning. *Journal of the American Planning Association, 71*(2), 147–158.

Satterthwaite, D., Archer, D., Colenbrander, S., Dodman, D., Hardoy, J., Mitlin, D., & Patel, S. (2018). Building resilience to climate change in informal settlements. *One Earth, 1*(4), 391–405.

Smit, S., & Musango, J. K. (2015). Exploring the connections between urban form and future energy consumption: A review. *Renewable and Sustainable Energy Reviews, 63*, 694–705.

UNDRR. (2015). *Sendai framework for disaster risk reduction 2015–2030.* United Nations Office for Disaster Risk Reduction.

UNDRR. (2022). *Global assessment report on disaster risk reduction.* United Nations Office for Disaster Risk Reduction.

UN-Habitat. (2016). *The new urban agenda.* United Nations.

UN-Habitat. (2020). *World Cities Report 2020: The value of sustainable urbanization.* UN-Habitat.

UN-Habitat. (2022). *The state of African cities 2022.* UN-Habitat.

Van Niekerk, D. (2022). Disaster risk governance in Africa: A review of progress and challenges. *International Journal of Disaster Risk Science, 13*(1), 1–12.

Watson, V. (2009). The planned city sweeps the poor away... Urban planning and 21st century urbanisation. *Progress in Planning, 72*(3), 151–193.

Wisner, B., Gaillard, J. C., & Kelman, I. (Eds.). (2012). *Handbook of hazards and disaster risk reduction*. Routledge.

World Bank. (2021). *Resilient infrastructure for a changing climate*. World Bank.

Ziervogel, G., Pelling, M., Cartwright, A., Chu, E., Deshpande, T., Harris, L., et al. (2016). Inserting rights and justice into urban resilience: A focus on everyday risk. *Environment and Urbanisation, 29*(1), 123–138.

CHAPTER 2

Theoretical Foundations of Urban Resilience and Sustainable Development

2.1 Introduction

The twenty-first century is being shaped by two interlinked megatrends: rapid urbanisation and escalating climate change. By 2050, over 70% of the world's population will reside in urban areas, with the fastest urban growth occurring in sub-Saharan Africa (UN-Habitat, 2020). At the same time, cities are increasingly recognised as frontline arenas in the fight against climate-related disasters, rising inequality, and unsustainable development (Dodman et al., 2012; IPCC, 2022). The notion of urban resilience, defined as the capacity of urban systems to absorb, adapt to, and recover from shocks, has thus gained prominence in both academic and policy circles (Meerow et al., 2016; Leichenko, 2011). Likewise, sustainable development has been elevated on global agendas through initiatives like the Sustainable Development Goals (SDGs), notably SDG 11, which calls for making cities inclusive, safe, resilient, and sustainable (United Nations, 2015). These twin concepts are deeply interlinked, as building resilient urban systems is vital for achieving long-term sustainability, and sustainable development measures can, in turn, reduce disaster risks.

Southern Africa represents a particularly important region for engaging with resilience and sustainability discourses. Its cities, including Maputo, Johannesburg, Durban, Harare, and Lusaka, are expanding rapidly, often in unplanned and informal ways, and simultaneously experiencing heightened

F. Mangara, N. Dorasamy, *Sustainable Urban Development in Southern Africa*, https://doi.org/10.1007/978-3-032-08286-2_2

exposure to hazards such as floods, cyclones, droughts, infrastructure failures, and governance breakdowns (Satterthwaite et al., 2020). Urban growth in the region has outpaced the provision of formal housing and infrastructure, leading to the proliferation of informal settlements that lack basic services. These urban centres consequently face a "double exposure" to environmental and socio-political stressors, as the impacts of climate change (for example, more frequent floods or droughts) intersect with entrenched socio-economic vulnerabilities (for example, poverty, inequality, and weak governance). Historical legacies of colonial planning and racial segregation have produced fragmented and unequal urban landscapes (Parnell & Robinson, 2012; Turok & Scheba, 2019), further exacerbating contemporary risks. Marginalised communities disproportionately bear the brunt of disasters, often inhabiting high-risk areas (like floodplains or unstable slopes) and lacking the assets or political voice to cope with shocks (IPCC, 2014; UN-Habitat, 2020).

Within this context, theoretical clarity is urgently needed to guide practice. Integrating DRR into urban planning has emerged as a critical strategy for building resilient and sustainable cities by proactively reducing hazard exposure and vulnerability through informed land-use and infrastructure decisions (UNISDR, 2015; World Bank, 2019). However, the successful implementation of such strategies requires a solid understanding of the underlying concepts and frameworks of resilience and sustainability, especially as they pertain to the complex realities of Southern African cities. This chapter, therefore, provides a foundational discussion of urban resilience and sustainable development, focusing on their application in disaster-prone, rapidly urbanising contexts. The goal is not only to introduce these concepts but also to critically evaluate how they are interpreted, operationalised, and contested, particularly in the Global South, where standard models often encounter distinctive challenges. By examining key theoretical foundations and their relevance to issues like informality, climate change, and governance, the chapter sets the stage for context-sensitive approaches to urban resilience that will be further explored in subsequent chapters of this book.

2.2 Conceptualising Urban Resilience

2.2.1 Definitional Evolution

The term "*resilience*" originates from the Latin *resilire*, meaning "to rebound" or "to spring back". Its use in scholarly discourse has evolved significantly over time. Early applications of resilience in the engineering sense emphasised the ability of a system to return to equilibrium after a disturbance effectively; to bounce back to its previous state. This concept was later expanded by ecologists like Holling (1963) into ecological resilience, highlighting systems' capacities not just to rebound but to undergo change and reorganisation in response to disturbance (Gunderson & Holling, 2002). By the 2000s, resilience thinking had further broadened. Scholars emphasised adaptive cycles and the potential for systems to learn and transform through disturbances, rather than simply resist them.

In contemporary urban studies, resilience is increasingly viewed as a dynamic process involving multiple scales, actors, and domains (Ahern, 2011; Meerow et al., 2016). This socio-ecological and socio-technical interpretation moves beyond the idea of maintaining or quickly restoring the status quo. Instead, *urban resilience* encompasses the capacity not only to withstand shocks like floods or pandemics but also to adapt and even transform urban systems in ways that reduce long-term risk and enhance well-being (Leichenko, 2011; Coaffee & Lee, 2016). Thus, modern definitions of urban resilience recognise that cities are complex, open systems composed of interacting physical, social, economic, and ecological components that must continually evolve in the face of changing conditions. This evolution in meaning reflects a shift from seeing resilience as a static property of systems to understanding it as a process and an outcome of deliberate planning, learning, and adaptation.

2.2.2 Dimensions of Urban Resilience

Cities are complex assemblages of people, infrastructure, ecosystems, and institutions; urban resilience is inherently multidimensional. Several core dimensions of resilience are typically highlighted in the literature, each interacting with the others to determine a city's overall resilience (Fig. 2.1):

- **Physical/Infrastructure Resilience:** This refers to the robustness and reliability of the built environment and critical services. It involves the capacity of physical structures—buildings, roads, bridges, water and energy systems, and communications networks—to withstand and function during disruptive events. For instance, the city of Durban has faced repeated infrastructure failures during severe storms, including collapsed drainage and power outages, leading to loss of life and economic damage (Roberts et al., 2012).

Fig. 2.1 The five interconnected dimensions of urban resilience—social, economic, physical, institutional, and environmental—form the basis for assessing the robustness and adaptability of urban systems. (Source: Authors 2025)

Strengthening physical resilience may involve building to hazard-resistant standards, upgrading informal housing, retrofitting ageing infrastructure, and incorporating redundancy so that failures in one component (for example, a pumping station) do not paralyse the entire system.

- **Social Resilience:** This dimension captures the ability of urban communities and social networks to withstand, cope with, and recover from adversities. Key factors include social cohesion, the strength of community organisations, access to education and information, and the extent of social safety nets (Aldrich & Meyer, 2015). High social resilience means that people help each other in crises, knowledge and resources are shared, and vulnerable groups are supported. In Johannesburg's informal settlement of Diepsloot, for example, strong community ties and grassroots initiatives have enabled residents to mobilise assistance and rebuild after fires or floods, illustrating how social capital supports recovery. Conversely, social fragmentation or exclusion can leave certain groups (such as the urban poor, migrants, or the elderly) isolated and less able to respond to shocks.

- **Economic Resilience:** Urban resilience has an important economic aspect. This refers to the capacity of the local economy to absorb impacts and keep functioning, or to rapidly restore functionality after a shock. This includes the diversification of economic activities, the financial health of households and businesses, and access to emergency funds or insurance. A resilient urban economy can buffer job losses or price spikes following a disaster and can also mobilise resources for reconstruction. For example, cities with diverse industries and strong small-business networks may better withstand an economic downturn or a climate disaster than mono-industrial towns (Adger et al., 2005; Dodman et al., 2012). In Southern Africa's many informal economies, economic resilience might involve community savings groups, alternative livelihoods, and social enterprises that provide income when formal systems falter.
- **Institutional/Governance Resilience:** This dimension concerns the capacity of urban governance systems, including municipal authorities, emergency services, and civic institutions, to effectively anticipate and respond to risks. It encompasses qualities such as leadership, transparency, coordination across agencies and government levels, and the flexibility to learn and adapt policies based on experience (Duit & Galaz, 2008; Aylett, 2015). Robust institutions can enforce land use plans, building codes, and environmental regulations that reduce risk, and they can mount timely, coordinated disaster responses. By contrast, weak or fragmented governance can severely undermine urban resilience. For instance, in Harare, fragile intergovernmental coordination and resource constraints have at times delayed disaster response and hindered risk-sensitive planning. Strengthening governance resilience often requires capacity-building within agencies, clearer mandates and communication channels, and inclusive decision-making that incorporates community inputs (Bulkeley et al., 2013).

- **Environmental/Ecosystem Resilience:** Cities are not closed systems; they depend on and affect natural ecosystems. Environmental resilience refers to the health and regenerative capacity of urban and peri-urban ecosystems (wetlands, rivers, forests, coasts) that provide vital services like flood regulation, temperature moderation, and water purification. When these ecosystems are degraded, cities become more vulnerable to hazards (for example, paving over wetlands removes natural flood buffers, thereby increasing flood risk). In Maputo, for example, widespread encroachment on wetlands through informal construction has reduced the city's ability to absorb heavy rainfall, contributing to more frequent and severe urban flooding (Brown et al., 2014). Conversely, protecting and restoring ecosystems can greatly enhance urban resilience. Durban's extensive investment in restoring mangroves and dune forests under its Municipal Climate Protection Programme has been shown to reduce flood and storm surge impacts while providing co-benefits like biodiversity and recreation (Roberts et al., 2012; Munang et al., 2013). Environmental resilience thus highlights the importance of integrating green infrastructure and ecosystem management into urban planning.

These dimensions are deeply interconnected, and weaknesses in any one can undermine resilience in the others. For instance, a breakdown in governance (institutional resilience) can lead to poor maintenance of drainage infrastructure (physical resilience) or inequitable disaster relief efforts that erode social trust (social resilience). A holistic approach to urban resilience, therefore, requires attention to all these facets. Comprehensive initiatives such as the City Resilience Index have been developed to measure multiple dimensions of resilience, including the robustness of infrastructure, the health of ecosystems, the preparedness of institutions, and the capacities of communities, thereby helping cities identify gaps and track progress (World Bank, 2019). In summary, conceptualising urban resilience in a multidimensional way provides a more complete picture of what makes a city resilient or vulnerable, and it underscores that building resilience is not the purview of any single sector but a shared and cross-cutting agenda.

2.3 Sustainable Development in the Urban Context

2.3.1 From Environmentalism to Sustainability

The concept of sustainable development entered the global discourse prominently in the 1980s with the release of the Brundtland Commission's report *Our Common Future* (Brundtland Commission, 1987). This report famously defined sustainable development as development that "meets the needs of the present without compromising the ability of future generations to meet their own needs". Initially, the sustainability agenda was driven largely by environmental concerns—for example, preventing resource depletion and pollution associated with rapid industrialisation. Over time, however, it evolved into a broader framework that balances three interdependent pillars: environmental integrity, social equity, and economic viability (often referred to as the triple bottom line). In an urban context, this means pursuing urban growth and modernisation in ways that protect ecosystems, advance social justice, and foster economic prosperity.

Within urban planning and policy, early sustainability efforts in the 1990s focused on limiting the environmental footprint of cities. Scholars and planners advocated for approaches like "sustainable urbanism" or "smart growth", emphasising compact city form, higher-density development, energy-efficient buildings, investment in public transit, and the preservation of green spaces (Beatley, 2000; Jabareen, 2006). For example, concepts such as the eco-city and new urbanism emerged, promoting walkable neighbourhoods, mixed land uses, and transit-oriented development as models that could reduce car dependency and greenhouse gas emissions while improving liveability. Many European and North American cities adopted these ideas, implementing green belts, bicycle infrastructure, and strict environmental regulations for new developments.

In the context of African and other developing-world cities, however, the application of these classical sustainability models faces challenges. Critics argue that imported models of sustainable urbanism often fail to account for the prevalence of informality and poverty in cities of the Global South (Watson, 2009). For instance, a blanket emphasis on compact, high-tech development might overlook the needs of large informal settlements or the realities of limited municipal budgets and capacities. If sustainability plans do not incorporate the vast informal housing and economic sectors where a large share of urban Africans live and work, they risk being ineffectual or even exclusionary. Spatial justice has thus become a key concern: ensuring that sustainability interventions (like creating green public spaces or upgrading transport) benefit low-income and marginalised residents, not just urban elites. There is an increasing recognition that sustainable development in the urban Global South must explicitly grapple with issues of land tenure, housing affordability, basic service provision, and social inclusion (Campbell, 1996; Watson, 2009). In Southern Africa, for example, policies must reconcile environmental objectives with pressing social needs like alleviating urban poverty and expanding access to water, sanitation, and electricity.

2.3.2 The Role of SDG 11 and the New Urban Agenda

The adoption of the United Nations Sustainable Development Goals (SDGs) in 2015 marked a significant shift in the international development discourse towards an integrated vision of sustainability that explicitly includes cities. SDG 11: "Make cities and human settlements inclusive, safe, resilient and sustainable" directly links urbanisation with both sustainability and resilience objectives, signalling global consensus that urban areas are central to achieving sustainable development (United Nations, 2015). SDG 11 and its targets encourage countries and cities to upgrade slums, expand public transport, engage in participatory planning, and strengthen capacity for disaster risk management, among other goals. Around the same time, the New Urban Agenda was adopted at the Habitat III conference, providing a roadmap for sustainable urban development. The New Urban Agenda emphasises principles such as the right to the city, inclusive governance, and integrated urban planning that aligns spatial, social, and environmental priorities (UN-Habitat, 2016). Together, these frameworks represent a normative benchmark for urban policymakers, outlining what needs to be done to achieve sustainable and resilient cities.

Translating these global frameworks into action, however, has proven challenging, especially in Southern African cities. Municipal governments often struggle with limited financial resources, technical expertise, and institutional capacity to implement comprehensive sustainability plans (Todes, 2011; Cirolia et al., 2016). There can be a significant gap between high-level planning ambitions and on-the-ground realities. For example, the city of Lusaka in Zambia developed an urban development plan that espoused resilience and sustainability principles, but enforcement of the plan's provisions has remained weak due to political contestation, fragmented authority, and resource constraints (Goodfellow, 2014). Similarly, many cities in the region have incorporated climate change adaptation or DRR goals into their strategic plans on paper, yet they struggle to prioritise and fund concrete projects like drainage improvements or affordable housing at scale.

Another challenge is ensuring that the pursuit of SDG 11 is aligned with local priorities. In practice, global goals must be "localised", adapted to each city's context. Southern African cities have unique socio-economic and environmental conditions. Thus, the pathways to achieving SDG 11 will not be identical to those in wealthier or more regulated cities. For instance, upgrading informal settlements (an SDG 11 target) in a city like Maputo requires community engagement and incremental housing strategies tailored to local cultural and economic practices, whereas in a European city, the focus might be on energy-efficient retrofits of buildings. A one-size-fits-all implementation of the New Urban Agenda is neither feasible nor desirable. Recognising this, networks such as United Cities and Local Governments (UCLG) and UN-Habitat have been working with African municipalities to develop context-specific indicators and share best practices for sustainable urban development.

Ultimately, frameworks like SDG 11 and the New Urban Agenda offer valuable guidance and motivation for cities to align their development trajectories with sustainability and resilience. They provide a common language and set of objectives that can rally stakeholders, from national governments and city officials to community groups and international donors, around urban improvements. The emphasis on participation, inclusivity, and risk-sensitive planning in these frameworks is particularly pertinent for Southern African cities, many of which are trying to overcome colonial histories of exclusionary planning. While implementation remains uneven, these global agendas have at least put issues of urban informality, equity, and resilience squarely on the policy map, creating pressure and opportunities for innovation in the region (UN-Habitat, 2020).

2.3.3 *Interlinkages Between Urban Resilience and Sustainable Development*

Urban resilience and sustainable development are not separate goals; in practice, they strongly reinforce one another in the context of city planning. A city cannot be truly *sustainable* in the long term if it is constantly set back by disasters and shocks; conversely, building *resilience* against shocks inherently contributes to the sustainability of urban development progress. This synergy, sometimes called the resilience-sustainability nexus, is increasingly highlighted in both research and policy.

On one hand, resilient cities, those capable of withstanding and adapting to hazards, ensure that development gains (economic growth, poverty reduction, infrastructure investments) are not easily wiped out by extreme events. For example, if a city invests in strengthening flood defences, improving emergency response, and diversifying its water supply sources, it is not only reducing disaster risk but also safeguarding the continuity of services and livelihoods. Such measures protect schools, hospitals, and businesses from disruption, thereby supporting sustained socio-economic development (Dodman et al., 2012). In this manner, resilience acts as a foundation upon which other aspects of sustainability (like economic viability and social welfare) can be built and maintained.

On the other hand, pursuing the tenets of sustainable development tends to reduce underlying vulnerabilities and thereby promote resilience. Strategies such as equitable access to urban services, poverty alleviation, and environmental conservation tackle some of the root causes of disaster risk. For instance, providing secure, affordable housing and basic infrastructure in informal settlements can greatly lessen those communities' exposure and sensitivity to hazards (by moving people away from high-risk zones and into safer structures with clean water and sanitation). Similarly, efforts to decarbonise and green the urban economy, for example, expanding public transit and green spaces, not only mitigate climate change but often have co-benefits for resilience, like improved air quality, reduced urban heat, and alternative mobility options when fuel supplies are disrupted. An integrated public transport system that reduces carbon emissions also enhances mobility for residents during crises and can stimulate economic resilience by connecting people to their jobs more efficiently (World Bank, 2019). As another example, green infrastructure (parks, wetlands, urban forests) is a classic win-win in the sense that it contributes to environmental sustainability and quality of life, while also acting as a natural buffer against floods and heatwaves, thereby enhancing resilience (UN-Habitat, 2020).

Because of these interlinkages, the agendas of urban resilience and sustainable development are increasingly pursued simultaneously. Notably, SDG 11's language ties resilience into the definition of sustainable cities. City development strategies in Southern Africa (and elsewhere) are gradually moving towards this integrated thinking. In practice, integrated projects might include, for example, upgrading a drainage canal in an informal settlement (a DRR measure) in tandem with creating a linear park and community garden along it (a sustainability and liveability measure). Such interventions improve environmental conditions and provide community amenities while reducing flood risk.

One key to leveraging the resilience-sustainability nexus is risk-informed urban planning that ensures that long-term city plans and investments explicitly account for hazard exposure and climate change. If a city's development plan identifies safe land for expansion, protects critical ecosystems, and mandates resilient construction practices, then every increment of growth is more likely to be sustainable and shock-resistant. Conversely, development that ignores risk—for instance, allowing construction in floodplains or failing to build redundancy into electricity grids—can undermine both resilience and sustainability by setting the stage for future losses. Therefore, aligning urban planning and governance with both resilience and sustainability principles is essential. As will be explored later in this chapter, concepts like integrated development planning, mainstreaming climate adaptation, and inclusive governance are central to operationalising this alignment in Southern African cities, where the needs are urgent, and resources are often limited.

2.4 Vulnerability and Adaptive Capacity

2.4.1 Understanding Vulnerability in Urban Contexts

In the fields of disaster risk reduction and climate change adaptation, *vulnerability* is a core concept referring to the propensity of people or systems to be harmed by hazards. Vulnerability is generally understood as a function of exposure to hazards, sensitivity to their impacts, and the lack of capacity to cope or adapt (IPCC, 2014; Cutter *et al.*, 2003). It is *not* determined solely by the presence of a hazard (such as a flood or earthquake), but by the social, economic, physical, and political conditions that make some urban populations more susceptible to harm than others. For example, two neighbourhoods in the same city might be equally exposed to a flood hazard, but if one has sturdy houses, effective drainage, and wealthy residents, while the other consists of makeshift shacks in an informal settlement, the latter is far more vulnerable to suffering losses in a flood.

Key factors driving urban vulnerability include:

- **Exposure:** The degree to which people and assets are in harm's way. This often relates to geographic location, for example, settlements on floodplains, low-lying coasts, steep hillsides, or near industrial sites (UN-Habitat, 2020). In many Southern African cities, the urban poor have been pushed to marginal lands; for instance, informal housing in flood-prone zones of Johannesburg or along the coastline of Dar es Salaam greatly increases those communities' exposure to floods and storms.
- **Sensitivity:** The degree to which an exposed individual or group is likely to suffer harm. Sensitivity is influenced by factors such as the quality of housing, health status, livelihood robustness, and social support. For example, a family living in a concrete house with savings and insurance is less sensitive to a flood (even if exposed) than a family in a flimsy shack that might be washed away, causing loss of home and income. Socio-economic inequalities often mean that marginalised populations (for example, low-income households, women, the elderly, people with disabilities) have higher sensitivity to shocks due to poorer health, fewer assets, or discrimination that limits their access to relief (Wisner et al., 2004; Bradshaw, 2013).
- **Adaptive or Coping Capacity:** The ability of those exposed to avoid harm or recover. This includes access to resources like early warning information, mobility to evacuate, savings or credit to rebuild, and support networks that provide help (Walker et al., 2004). High capacity can offset exposure and sensitivity to some extent. For example, an organised community with evacuation plans and strong social ties might fare better in a flood than a disorganised community, even if both are equally exposed and sensitive.

Urban vulnerability in Southern African cities is often extreme because multiple vulnerability drivers coincide. Cities such as Harare and Maputo vividly illustrate this: large portions of the urban population live in informal settlements that have grown on unsafe lands like wetlands, riverbanks, and steep slopes (Mususa, 2012; Brown et al., 2014). These areas typically lack durable housing, proper sanitation, or reliable infrastructure, making them highly sensitive to any hazard. When heavy rains come, such settlements are prone to flooding and mudslides, and because they often lack stormwater drainage or waste collection, floodwaters can spread diseases and cause structural collapse. The residents, often impoverished, have few buffers—savings, insurance, and political influence to help them recover, thus they have low coping capacity. The proliferation of informality is not merely a result of individual choices but tied to systemic issues: land and housing markets exclude the poor, formal urban planning has historically marginalised certain groups (for example, during apartheid in South Africa or colonial regimes elsewhere), and governance failures have led to backlogs in service delivery and affordable housing. These structural factors hard-wire vulnerability into the urban fabric (Adger, 2006; Huchzermeyer, 2011).

Furthermore, urban vulnerability is intersectional, meaning that it is compounded when individuals or groups embody multiple sources of disadvantage (Ziervogel et al., 2017). For example, consider a female-headed household in an informal settlement in Durban: this household may be more vulnerable than others, not just because of poverty and hazardous location, but also due to gender dynamics. Women often have less access to resources and decision-making power; they may face greater obstacles evacuating if they must care for children or elders, and they might receive less information if warning systems are not designed to reach those who are home-bound or not literate. Studies have shown that in some Durban townships, female-headed households were less likely to be warned before floods and more likely to struggle during recovery, due to limited access to credit and social networks dominated by male community leaders (Roberts et al., 2012; Ziervogel et al., 2017). Children, the elderly, and people with disabilities in cities also face heightened vulnerabilities, as they might be physically less able to escape danger or may have specific health needs that are disrupted by disasters (Birkmann, 2006). Thus, understanding urban vulnerability requires looking at how hazards intersect with issues of poverty, gender, age, health, and social marginalisation.

2.4.2 *The Concept of Adaptive Capacity*

Adaptive capacity is essentially the flip side of vulnerability. It refers to the ability of individuals, communities, institutions, or systems to adjust to potential hazards, to take advantage of opportunities, and to respond to consequences in ways that moderate harm or exploit beneficial changes (Smit & Wandel, 2006; Engle, 2011). In simpler terms, it is a measure of how well an urban system can learn, innovate, and transform in the face of climate change or other stresses. High adaptive capacity can reduce overall vulnerability, as it enables proactive adaptation rather than just reactive coping.

In urban areas, adaptive capacity manifests in various forms and at multiple levels:

- At the *household or community level*, it includes knowledge of risks (for example, understanding flood patterns or heatwave dangers), access to assets (financial savings, alternative livelihoods, social support networks), and the ability to organise collectively for mutual aid. For example, a neighbourhood that has a community disaster fund, a volunteer emergency response team, or locally designed flood defences (like sandbag walls) is demonstrating higher adaptive capacity than one that does not (Pelling & High, 2005; Archer et al., 2014). Informal settlement communities often exhibit ingenious adaptive strategies born of necessity, from elevating homes on stilts to forming rotating credit clubs that help rebuild after events.
- At the *city or institutional level*, adaptive capacity involves effective governance, forward-looking planning, access to technology and information (like climate projections), robust institutions that can coordinate and respond, and flexible policies that can be adjusted as conditions change (IPCC, 2014; Folke, 2006). A city with high adaptive capacity would, for instance, integrate climate adaptation into its development plans, invest in early warning systems, continuously update building codes based on new risk information, and have contingency funds for emergency response and recovery.

Unlike resilience, which is often evaluated by how a system actually performs under stress (typically after a shock has occurred), adaptive capacity is more about the potential to respond effectively to future shocks or gradual changes (Engle, 2011). It is inherently proactive and forward-looking. Enhancing adaptive capacity means building up the assets, skills, partnerships, and institutions that allow for timely adaptation measures to be implemented.

In Southern Africa, we see stark contrasts in adaptive capacity across different cities and communities. Cape Town in South Africa is frequently cited as a city with relatively higher adaptive capacity in the region, especially following its recent experiences with climate stress. Facing a severe multi-year drought in the late 2010s (the "Day Zero" water crisis), Cape Town invested in diversifying water sources (through desalination plants, groundwater development), implemented aggressive public awareness and water conservation campaigns, rolled out smart water metres, and created disaster plans for water rationing. These efforts, supported by a relatively well-resourced municipal government and an active civil society, exemplify adaptive capacity in action. The city was able to avert the worst-case scenario of completely running out of water, and it learned and adjusted policies for future drought resilience (Ziervogel, 2019).

In contrast, a city like Beira in Mozambique has historically struggled with lower adaptive capacity. Beira is highly exposed to cyclones and sea-level rise; yet, its local government has limited funds and technical expertise, and governance is often fragmented between municipal, provincial, and national authorities. After Cyclone Idai struck in 2019, causing massive damage, recovery was slow and heavily dependent on international aid (IFRC, 2019). Planning departments in Beira face challenges in enforcing building standards or land use plans due to underfunding and informal growth of the city. Access to climate information and early warnings for the population has been improving but remains incomplete. All these constraints (financial, institutional, and informational) reflect a limited capacity to adapt ahead of disasters, meaning that Beira often finds itself in a reactive mode of crisis response rather than proactive risk reduction (GFDRR, 2020). Strengthening adaptive capacity in such a context might involve securing more stable funding for DRR, training local officials in climate adaptation planning, investing in data and mapping for risk areas, and empowering communities through awareness and preparedness programs.

Importantly, adaptive capacity in cities is not solely top-down (government-driven) or bottom-up (community-driven); it usually involves a combination of both. A well-adapted city requires enabling institutions (like policies that encourage climate-smart investments) as well as empowered communities that can act on their own behalf. For instance, a city government might provide small grants or tools for community groups to implement local resilience projects (rainwater harvesting, urban agriculture, etc.), marrying top-down support with bottom-up initiative. Building adaptive capacity thus often means creating partnerships among governments, NGOs, academia, the private sector, and residents to share knowledge and resources for adaptation.

Adaptive capacity is a crucial component of resilience: it is what allows urban actors to anticipate change, minimise harm, and embrace innovation in the face of uncertainty. Enhancing adaptive capacity in Southern African cities might include measures such as strengthening urban planning departments with climate expertise, establishing city-to-city learning networks, investing in education and communication so that the public is aware of risks and options, and promoting social organisations (youths and women's groups) that can spearhead local adaptation actions. As these capacities improve, South African cities are better positioned not only to recover from disasters but to avoid the worst impacts in the first place.

2.4.3 Integrating Vulnerability and Adaptive Capacity into Urban Planning

Recognising patterns of vulnerability and building adaptive capacity are essential for devising inclusive and effective urban plans. Risk-informed urban planning means that city planners use data on vulnerability (who is most at risk and where) and existing adaptive capacities (what resources and strengths communities have) to guide decisions about land use, infrastructure, and services (UNISDR, 2015). In practice, integrating these concepts into planning and policy involves several approaches:

- **Conducting Vulnerability Assessments:** City authorities can systematically map and assess vulnerability across neighbourhoods, identifying zones that combine high hazard exposure with highly vulnerable populations (for example, informal settlements in flood zones, or dilapidated inner-city housing at risk of fire/earthquakes). Tools like participatory GIS mapping, household surveys, and community consultations are used to capture the nuanced factors of vulnerability. For instance, Cape Town has undertaken community-based risk assessments in its informal settlements to pinpoint which areas lack adequate drainage or access to emergency response, thereby prioritising those for upgrades and training (Ziervogel et al., 2017).

Such assessments ensure that plans are grounded in reality and that the most at-risk groups are made visible in decision-making processes.

- **Prioritising Investments for the Most Vulnerable:** An equitable, resilience-oriented urban plan will channel resources to reducing vulnerabilities in high-risk communities. This could mean upgrading slum infrastructure (for example, paving roads for emergency vehicle access, installing storm drains and sanitation), strengthening critical lifeline services (like clinics, water supply, and schools) in poor areas, or creating safe refuges and evacuation routes for low-income districts (UN-Habitat, 2020). For example, in the city of Durban, the municipality's climate adaptation strategy explicitly prioritises informal settlements for certain interventions, such as slope stabilisation projects and the provision of rainwater harvesting tanks, recognising that these communities have both high exposure and low coping capacity for storms and water shortages.
- **Building Local Adaptive Capacity:** Urban policy can support programs that enhance the adaptive capacities of residents and local institutions. This might include education and training (for example, community workshops on first aid, firefighting, or climate-smart agriculture), establishing community-based early warning systems (as have been piloted in flood-prone areas of Mozambique with help from the Red Cross), and creating platforms for residents to participate in planning (Archer et al., 2014). In Maputo, for instance, NGOs and local authorities have collaborated to implement neighbourhood-level disaster committees that develop response plans for cyclones—a grassroots effort to boost preparedness (UN-Habitat, 2020). Building adaptive capacity also extends to city officials and planners. Through continuous professional development on DRR and climate adaptation and creating units within city governments dedicated to resilience, forward-looking practices can be institutionalised.
- **Fostering Public–Private and Multi-stakeholder Partnerships:** Given resource constraints in many Southern African cities, partnerships are key to mobilising additional capacity for resilience. Private companies can be incentivised to invest in resilient infrastructure (for example, developers including flood protections in new housing projects, or telecom firms ensuring cell towers have backup power). Public–private partnerships might fund early warning systems or insurance schemes for low-income populations. Civil society organ-

isations and academia often bring expertise and grassroots reach. For example, universities might help develop risk models, while NGOs facilitate community engagement. City plans that encourage such collaboration (through policy directives or liaison forums) can extend the reach of vulnerability reduction initiatives. The participation of a broad range of stakeholders also helps to ensure that different perspectives (including those of women, youth, and marginalised groups) inform urban resilience actions (Fig. 2.2).

By embedding considerations of vulnerability and adaptive capacity into urban planning, South African cities can move towards inclusive resilience, ensuring that resilience-building is not just about protecting shiny downtown infrastructure but about reducing risk for those who need it most. In the Southern African context, this means planning with a pro-poor, pro-equity lens: upgrading informal settlements, improving infrastructure in townships, enforcing risk-appropriate land use (so that, for example, schools or clinics are not built in flood basins), and enabling at-risk communities to voice their needs and be active agents in building resilience. Over time, such integrated planning can transform urban development paths, making them not only safer but also fairer and more sustainable.

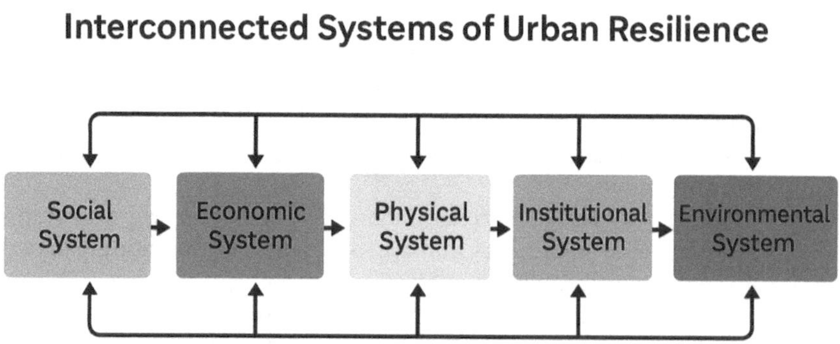

Fig. 2.2 Urban resilience is maintained through continuous interaction and feedback across five core systems; social, economic, physical, institutional, and environmental. (Source: Authors 2025)

2.5 Core Theoretical Frameworks for Urban Resilience and Sustainability

The challenges of building resilient and sustainable cities are complex, and they require robust theoretical lenses to guide analysis and action. Over the past few decades, several foundational frameworks have shaped academic and practical approaches to urban resilience. This section examines four such frameworks that are particularly relevant: (1) systems thinking and complexity theory, (2) social-ecological resilience, (3) sustainable urbanism, and (4) multi-level governance. Each provides a different perspective on how urban systems function, how they can fail, and how they might be steered towards greater resilience and sustainability.

2.5.1 *Systems Thinking and Complexity Theory*

Systems thinking conceptualises a city as a complex, interconnected web of subsystems spanning physical infrastructure, economic networks, social structures, and ecological processes (Meadows, 1999; Batty, 2007). Rather than viewing problems (or solutions) in isolation, a systems perspective emphasises relationships, feedback loops, and the dynamic behaviour that emerges from interactions. In the context of urban resilience, this is crucial because a shock in one part of the city can cascade through other parts in unexpected ways, a phenomenon known as systemic risk (Ahern, 2011). For example, a seemingly minor event like a localised flash flood can trigger far-reaching impacts: floodwaters might block a major road, causing city-wide traffic paralysis; contaminated water can lead to disease outbreaks; power supply might fail if a substation is affected, interrupting business operations across the metropolis. Such scenarios were observed in Johannesburg, where heavy rains in one area caused flooding that disrupted transportation networks and commerce city-wide. Systems thinking urges us to consider these interdependencies when planning for resilience—improving drainage isn't just about flood control; it is also about maintaining mobility, public health, and economic stability.

Complexity theory, closely related to systems thinking, further recognises that cities are complex adaptive systems (CAS) (Holling, 2001; Allen & Holling, 2010). This means cities are not only complicated (with many moving parts) but also adaptive; they change and learn over time as people respond to problems and as the urban system self-organises. A key insight from complexity theory is the existence of non-linearity, feedback loops, and tipping points in system behaviour. In urban contexts, positive feedback loops can amplify changes. For instance, urban sprawl can feed on itself: as people move to the periphery (perhaps to seek cheaper land), investment in roads and services follows them, which in turn makes even further areas attractive for settlement, thereby extending sprawl further (a self-reinforcing cycle that can increase car dependence and ecological footprint). Conversely, negative feedback loops can stabilise a system: for example, if increasing flood incidents prompt the city to enforce stricter land-use zoning (keeping people out of floodplains), that intervention can dampen the cycle of risk accumulation. Recognising feedback helps in identifying leverage points—places in the system where a small, focused action could have large effects (Meadows, 1999).

Complexity theory also highlights thresholds or tipping points. These are critical points at which the system's state changes qualitatively. In climate resilience, this might be the threshold beyond which an ecosystem that supports the city (say, a wetland) collapses and can no longer regenerate, or a social threshold beyond which distress leads to the breakdown of community cohesion or mass migration. Crossing a threshold can lead to irreversible or hard-to-reverse changes—a point of no return. For example, once groundwater in a city's aquifer is overdrawn to a certain point, saltwater intrusion might permanently ruin it; or if a city's average temperature increases beyond a certain level, heat-related mortality might spike dramatically. An infamous urban example of a tipping point is infrastructure failure cascades: if a city's power grid goes down for more than a few days, it may reach a point where water supply (pumps), transportation (fuel, signals), and communications (cell towers) start failing en masse, pushing the city into a humanitarian crisis. Complexity thinking in urban resilience seeks to identify such thresholds (Dodman et al., 2012) and ensure systems stay within safe operating limits (Folke et al., 2010).

Applying systems and complexity frameworks to Southern African cities underscores the importance of integrated approaches. For instance, the chronic flooding in parts of Lusaka, Zambia, cannot be solved just by engineering bigger drains alone; it requires understanding the system: how uncollected solid waste clogs drainage (a social/institutional failure), how informal settlement patterns put more houses in flood zones (a land-use issue linked to economic forces), and how deforestation upstream exacerbates runoff (an ecological feedback). A purely sectoral fix will likely be insufficient or create new problems. Instead, systems thinking would promote a multi-pronged intervention: improve waste management (social system), enforce land-use regulations or provide safer housing alternatives (planning system), and conserve wetlands to absorb runoff (ecological system).

Complexity theory also encourages adaptive management, since cities can't be fully controlled or predicted, planning should be iterative and flexible. Policies should be treated as experiments: monitor their outcomes, learn, and adjust course as needed (Holling, 2001). For example, rather than a rigid 30-year master plan that assumes a certain growth pattern, a city might adopt a scenario-based planning approach, regularly revisiting and revising plans as socio-economic trends and climate projections evolve. This ethos is particularly relevant in informal contexts where top-down data is sparse, and ground realities shift quickly (Watson, 2009). In many African cities, informal settlements can expand or change character within a few years due to migration or economic shifts, so resilience plans need to be updated frequently. Adopting a complexity perspective means planners accept uncertainty and change as givens and build cities that are safe-to-fail (able to absorb failures) rather than trying to be fail-safe in an impossible bid to prevent all failures (Ahern, 2011).

2.5.2 Social-Ecological Resilience

The concept of social-ecological resilience extends systems thinking by explicitly focusing on the coupled relationship between human societies and natural ecosystems (Folke, 2006; Folke et al., 2010). It rejects treating the urban environment and the natural environment as separate domains; instead, it views them as one integrated social-ecological system. In an urban setting, this perspective is a reminder that cities depend fundamentally on nature's services and that human actions, in turn, affect the health of the ecosystems around and within cities.

Key principles of social-ecological resilience include maintaining diversity (of species and livelihoods), managing connectivity, encouraging learning and participation, and promoting self-organisation and adaptive governance in resource management (Folke et al., 2010; Ostrom, 2009). In practical terms for cities, it means urban planning must consider ecological processes (like water flows, soil regeneration, and biodiversity) as integral to the urban system's resilience. One important aspect is the role of ecosystem services in urban resilience. Ecosystem services are typically categorised as follows:

- **Provisioning Services:** Supply of materials like food, fresh water, fuel, and fibre.
- **Regulating Services:** Natural regulation of climate, floods, diseases, water quality, and pollination.
- **Cultural Services:** Non-material benefits like recreation, aesthetic enjoyment, spiritual fulfilment, and cultural heritage that ecosystems provide.
- **Supporting Services:** Underlying processes such as nutrient cycling, soil formation, and primary production that make the other services possible.

Urban areas might seem removed from nature, but they rely on these services in many ways. For example, wetlands and vegetated areas (regulating services) can absorb excess rainfall and mitigate flood peaks, as noted earlier with Durban and Maputo's wetlands. Urban forests and green parks help regulate local temperatures and improve air quality (regulating services), while also offering recreational space (cultural service). Urban agriculture or community gardens can provide food and cooling (provisioning and regulating services). Even biodiversity in cities, such as pollinators like bees, contributes to urban food security and the health of urban ecosystems.

Social-ecological resilience emphasises that undermining these services can directly increase urban risk. For instance, if a city paves over its wetlands for development, it may experience much worse flooding because it has lost nature's buffering capacity (as happened in parts of Lagos, Nigeria, and similarly in some Southern African cities). If rivers are heavily polluted and degraded, they can't provide clean water or moderate floods, again heightening vulnerability. Conversely, investing in the restoration or conservation of ecosystems is a powerful resilience strategy. In Durban, a well-known example is the city's incorporation of ecosystem-based adaptation into its climate resilience planning. By restoring dune forests along the coast and rehabilitating river catchments, Durban has bolstered natural defences against storm surges and improved water management, while also creating jobs and protecting biodiversity (Roberts et al., 2012; Munang et al., 2013). This approach, often termed green infrastructure or nature-based solutions, is gaining traction because it can be cost-effective and yield multiple benefits.

Southern African cities often have a mix of formal and informal practices that affect social-ecological systems. In many peri-urban areas, for instance, residents rely on urban agriculture, harvesting of wild foods, or the use of natural herbs (provisioning services). Maintaining green open spaces and fertile soils in and around cities thus has direct human benefits. Additionally, many communities have indigenous knowledge about managing local ecosystems, such as traditional rainwater harvesting techniques, sacred groves that are protected from logging, or rotational grazing practices that maintain grasslands (Nyong et al., 2007). Social-ecological resilience calls for valuing and integrating such local knowledge into formal urban planning, rather than overriding it. In Zimbabwe, for example, some urban authorities have worked with local communities on wetland management, blending scientific hydrological assessments with community insights on where and when flooding occurs, leading to better co-management of those wetlands.

A challenge in applying social-ecological resilience thinking in cities is institutional silos, for example, city departments for parks/environment are often separate from those for housing/infrastructure. A resilience approach would have them work together, for example, planting trees along roads is not just the parks department's job for beautification; it is also a climate adaptation measure (shade reduces heat, roots absorb runoff) that the infrastructure department should co-own. Similarly, water utilities should coordinate with environmental agencies to protect the watersheds that supply city reservoirs (as Johannesburg's authorities have started doing by supporting conservation in the rural Drakensberg mountains, which feed its rivers).

Another component is considering the urban metabolism, the flows of resources like water, energy, and materials through the city and aiming to make that metabolism more circular and in tune with natural cycles (Andersson et al., 2014). Efforts like wastewater recycling, urban composting for agriculture, and solar energy adoption reduce the city's draw on distant ecosystems and make local systems more self-reliant, thereby increasing resilience in times of external supply shocks.

The social-ecological framework reminds us that cities need nature. The resilience of an urban area is partly a function of the resilience of its supporting ecosystems. Therefore, protecting and enhancing green and blue (water) infrastructure is not a luxury or purely an environmental objective, but a pragmatic strategy for risk reduction and sustainability. As climate change accelerates, the importance of ecosystem-based approaches is only growing. Coastal cities will need mangroves and reefs as sea storms intensify; inland cities will need watershed management as droughts alternate with intense rains. Social-ecological resilience in Southern African cities thus involves reorienting urban development to work with natural systems—preserving floodplains, planting trees, harvesting rainwater, fostering urban gardening, and ensuring that communities have a stake and voice in these environmental stewardship efforts.

2.5.3 *Sustainable Urbanism*

While social-ecological resilience focuses on human-nature linkages, *sustainable urbanism* is a framework that marries urban planning principles with sustainability goals. It seeks to create cities that are not only environmentally sustainable but also economically viable and socially equitable over the long term (Wheeler, 2013; Beatley, 2000). Sustainable urbanism provides a vision of what the form and function of a sustainable city should look like. Key principles commonly cited include:

- **Compact Urban Form:** Avoiding urban sprawl by promoting higher-density development within existing urban footprints. A compact city reduces land consumption (saving agricultural land and ecosystems) and makes public transport and local commerce more feasible.
- **Mixed Land Use:** integrating residential, commercial, and recreational spaces so that people can live, work, and play without needing long commutes. This reduces travel distances and fosters vibrant, safe neighbourhoods.
- **Sustainable Transport:** Prioritising public transit, walking, and cycling infrastructure over private car use. This reduces traffic congestion, lowers greenhouse gas emissions, and improves air quality and public health.
- **Green Building and Infrastructure:** Designing buildings for energy and water efficiency (through insulation, solar design, and rainwater harvesting), and incorporating features like green roofs or solar panels. Also, using green infrastructure like parks, permeable pavements, and urban trees to manage stormwater and heat.
- **Inclusive Public Spaces and Amenities:** Ensuring that all urban residents have access to clean, safe public spaces (parks, plazas) and services (schools, clinics), contributing to social cohesion and quality of life.

For cities in the Global North, these principles have been operationalised in models such as the 15-minute city (where all basic needs can be met within a 15-minute walk or bike ride) or transit-oriented development (clustering development around transit hubs). Many European cities (for example, Copenhagen, Freiburg) are often held up as exemplars of sustainable urbanism, with extensive bike lanes, mixed-use zoning, and renewable energy use.

In Southern African cities, the vision of sustainable urbanism holds great appeal but faces contextual hurdles. Historically, many cities in the region were designed (under colonialism or apartheid) in opposition to these principles, with segregated land uses, car-centric layouts, and spatial exclusion of the poor to peripheral townships or informal settlements (Turok, 2016). Reconfiguring such urban forms is a long-term challenge. However, there are initiatives moving in the right direction.

One notable example is Johannesburg's Corridors of Freedom project (Harrison et al., 2019; Turok & Scheba, 2019). Launched in the mid-2010s, this initiative aimed to reshape the apartheid spatial legacy by creating high-density, mixed-use development corridors along new bus rapid transit (BRT) routes. The idea was to link previously isolated townships with the economic core through efficient public transport and to stimulate affordable housing and businesses along these corridors, thereby promoting both mobility and inclusivity. Although the project encountered implementation challenges (budget constraints, political shifts), it demonstrated an innovative attempt at sustainable urbanism: integrating land use and transport planning to achieve social and environmental objectives. Residents along the Rea Vaya BRT corridors have seen improved access to jobs and services, and the city has concurrently invested in cycling lanes and pedestrian-friendly design in some areas.

Other Southern African cities are also adopting pieces of the sustainable urbanism agenda. Cape Town has invested in transit-oriented development around its MyCiTi BRT system and created dense mixed-use precincts in the central city to encourage inner-city living across income groups (though affordability remains an issue). Nairobi (Kenya, while not in Southern Africa, offers a regional reference) has seen a surge in interest in green building, with new commercial buildings meeting LEED standards, which is inspiring similar moves in places like Johannesburg and Pretoria for corporate offices. Windhoek in Namibia pioneered urban water recycling (a form of infrastructure sustainability) to deal with chronic water scarcity, an approach that has lessons for other cities facing climate-induced water stress.

Yet, sustainable urbanism in this region must adapt to local realities: high levels of informality and limited government capacity. A strict plan enforcing compact growth may not succeed if 60% of growth is informal and outside formal planning control. Thus, some scholars argue for a more incremental and participatory approach to sustainable urbanism in African cities (Watson, 2014). This could mean working with informal settlement communities to gradually upgrade and densify their neighbourhoods with better infrastructure (rather than trying to replace them with top-down planned housing) or designing transport solutions that include informal transit modes (minibus taxis in South Africa or *dala-dalas* in Tanzania) rather than focusing solely on formal buses or rail.

Another aspect is economic sustainability. Southern African cities need to create jobs and livelihoods for growing urban populations, so sustainability plans must be meshed with economic development. This might involve supporting the informal economy (which is often the green economy by necessity, for example, repair, recycling, urban farming) and steering it towards safer and more productive practices. For instance, helping informal waste pickers organise and integrate with municipal recycling schemes can improve both livelihoods and environmental outcomes.

Sustainable urbanism provides a comprehensive blueprint for future cities that are low-carbon, resource-efficient, and inclusive. While many Southern African cities are at early stages in this journey, elements of this vision are emerging. The key will be to localise sustainable urbanism, finding ways to use its principles in affordable housing projects, public space improvements in townships, the redevelopment of decaying CBDs, and the extension of services to new peripheral settlements. Each step that makes a neighbourhood more walkable, or saves energy, or mixes income groups, also tends to make the city more resilient to shocks (because diverse, well-connected communities can often respond better to disruptions than segregated, car-dependent ones). Therefore, sustainable urbanism and resilience planning go hand in hand: one builds the long-term foundation, the other prepares for the disturbances along the way.

2.5.4 *Multi-level Governance*

Urban resilience and sustainable development are not achieved by city governments alone; they require coordination across various levels of government and sectors of society. The multi-level governance framework looks at how different levels of decision-making—from local to provincial to national to global—interact in shaping outcomes on the ground (Betsill & Bulkeley, 2006). For urban resilience, multi-level governance is critical because policies and resources at one level (say, national disaster legislation or international climate finance) can enable or hinder actions at another level (like a municipal adaptation project or a community initiative).

In Southern Africa, as in many places, cities operate within a hierarchy of governance that often includes local/municipal authorities, regional or provincial authorities, national government ministries (for housing, environment), and international bodies or donors. Effective vertical integration means these layers communicate and align their objectives. For example, a national climate change policy might allocate funds or technical support for city-level resilience projects; conversely, cities may pilot innovative approaches that inform national policies (UN-Habitat, 2020). Horizontal coordination is equally important, across departments or sectors at the same level. Within a city, this means urban planners, emergency managers, public health officials, utility providers, and others working together rather than in silos.

A common governance challenge in Southern African cities is that mandates and resources are often fragmented. Many cities depend heavily on national governments for funding infrastructure and social services (World Bank, 2019). If national funding priorities do not include resilience, cities may struggle to finance DRR projects. For instance, a city might want to develop a comprehensive flood control system, but if the national government prioritises other infrastructure, or if intergovernmental fiscal transfers are limited, the city's plans may remain on paper (Goodfellow, 2014). In Mozambique, the response to Cyclone Idai revealed coordination problems. For instance, municipal authorities in Beira, provincial officials, national disaster agencies, and international NGOs were all active, but their efforts were not always synchronised, leading to overlaps in some areas and gaps in others (IFRC, 2019). This underscores the need for clearer governance frameworks for disaster response that delineate roles and improve communication before crises occur.

Multi-level governance theory also introduces the concept of polycentric governance (Ostrom, 2010), particularly relevant where formal governance is weak. Polycentric governance refers to a system where multiple centres of decision-making coexist and overlap, including non-governmental actors like community organisations, traditional leaders, or private sector coalitions. In cities marked by informality or limited state capacity, polycentric arrangements can fill voids. For example, in some informal settlements in Harare and Nairobi, residents have formed their own governance structures (for example, savings groups that finance community upgrades or street committees that handle security and basic services), which operate somewhat independently from the formal municipal government. These local structures often have legitimacy and detailed knowledge of local issues that distant bureaucracies lack (Cleaver, 2012). Ideally, a resilient governance system would *embrace these polycentric elements*, finding ways to partner and share responsibilities. This might mean the city council formally recognising and working with slum dweller federations on upgrading projects or delegating certain maintenance tasks to community committees with provided resources.

At the broader scale, multi-level governance in resilience involves linking city efforts to global frameworks. The Sendai Framework for Disaster Risk Reduction (2015–2030), for instance, urges all levels of government to integrate DRR into development planning and to cooperate regionally and internationally (UNISDR, 2015). Many Southern African countries have adopted the Sendai principles, but implementing them at the city level is still a work in progress. Similarly, commitments under the Paris Agreement on climate change and the SDGs trickle down to city action plans, often through national urban policies or climate strategies (United Nations, 2015). When international donors fund resilience projects (like the Rockefeller Foundation's 100 Resilient Cities initiative, which included cities like Durban), they often help establish multi-stakeholder platforms in cities that bring together officials, academics, and community voices around a resilience strategy.

One positive example of multi-level alignment can be seen in Cape Town's climate change efforts. The city has its own Climate Change Policy and Action Plan, which includes integrating DRR and climate adaptation into city planning. The provincial government of the Western Cape has supported this through its Green Economy agenda and disaster management programs, and nationally, South Africa's climate policy and funding mechanisms (such as the City Support Programme) have provided some technical and financial backing. Internationally, Cape Town engaged with C40 Cities and ICLEI networks, learning from other cities and attracting expertise. This synergy across levels helped Cape Town during its water crisis, where the national government provided drought relief funding and international peers shared water demand management strategies. However, it is worth noting that when governance fails, for example, if political conflict arises between city and national leaders from different parties, support can be withdrawn, illustrating the fragility of multi-level cooperation.

2.6 Intersecting Dynamics in Southern African Cities

The theoretical frameworks outlined above provide general tools and principles, but their expression in any given city is mediated by context. Southern African cities have particular historical, socio-economic, and environmental dynamics that shape how resilience and sustainability can be pursued. Three intersecting themes are especially prominent in this region: urbanisation and informality, climate risks and environmental pressures, and governance challenges. These factors often compound one another, creating a unique risk landscape and affecting the applicability of conventional solutions.

2.6.1 Urbanisation and Informality

Southern Africa is urbanising rapidly, but much of this growth is occurring outside formal planning and regulatory frameworks. In many cities, over half of the urban population lives in informal settlements or slums (UN-Habitat, 2020; Satterthwaite et al., 2020). For example, cities such as Harare, Lusaka, Maputo, and Luanda have seen the explosive expansion of peri-urban informal settlements. In Harare, an estimated 60% of new housing in recent decades has been informal, often on the urban periphery or in pockets within the city where vacant land or previously white-owned areas became available. Similarly, Maputo's metropolitan area is ringed by bairros (neighbourhoods) like Chamanculo and Maxaquene that originally grew informally and still lack full municipal services.

This prevalence of informality reflects a combination of factors: population growth outstripping the provision of affordable formal housing, rural-to-urban migration by people seeking livelihood opportunities, and "push" factors like conflicts or climate impacts displacing rural communities. It also stems from land and governance systems that have historically been exclusionary or inefficient. Under colonial rule, indigenous populations were often barred from settling in well-serviced urban zones; apartheid in South Africa forcibly segregated cities; post-independence planning regimes often continued to focus on servicing central business districts and affluent areas while neglecting poor newcomers. Additionally, formal land markets have tended to price out low-income households, forcing them to occupy land through informal or extra-legal means (Watson, 2009; Huchzermeyer, 2011). Bureaucratic procedures for obtaining land or building permits can be prohibitively slow and expensive, effectively nudging even those who might afford formal routes into informality due to necessity or frustration.

The result is a patchwork urban fabric where planned neighbourhoods with infrastructure and services exist alongside sprawling informal settlements that developed organically. Informality poses both challenges and potential for urban resilience:

On the one hand, informal settlements are often highly vulnerable. Their location is frequently determined by what land is available to the poor, which is often marginal land avoided by others—floodplains, steep hillsides prone to landslides, low-lying coastal zones, and polluted areas near dumps or industrial sites. These areas maximise exposure to hazards. Moreover, informal settlements typically suffer from inadequate infrastructure: little to no stormwater drainage (leading to frequent flooding and erosion), rudimentary or no sanitation (compounding health crises during floods or disease outbreaks), and overcrowded housing (raising fire risk and making evacuation or emergency access difficult). For example, in Lusaka, unplanned compounds like Kanyama experience annual floods because they are on flat, poorly drained terrain; houses and latrines are often inundated, creating sanitation disasters (Mususa, 2012). In Dar es Salaam's informal areas (to draw a parallel example), cholera outbreaks have been tied to floodwaters spreading human waste due to a lack of sewers. The physical layout of informal settlements, often with narrow, maze-like pathways, can hinder ambulances or fire trucks, delaying response when disasters strike.

Informal settlements also face social and economic stresses: residents usually have low incomes, precarious jobs (often informal themselves), and limited access to formal insurance or credit. Government presence (police and clinics) may be scant. These factors all reduce the capacity to prepare for, avoid, or bounce back from shocks. A heavy rain that might be a nuisance in a formal neighbourhood can turn into a life-threatening flood in an informal one due to these vulnerabilities.

On the other hand, informality can come with certain resilience assets. Communities in informal settlements often display strong social cohesion and innovation. Because they cannot rely on formal authorities, residents frequently self-organise to solve problems—a form of social resilience. For instance, savings groups run by women (as seen in many slums through networks like Slum Dwellers International) pool funds to improve homes or infrastructure, or to help members after disasters. Neighbours in informal areas tend to have dense social networks and may rapidly disseminate warnings by word of mouth or assist each other in evacuating belongings ahead of a flood (Archer et al., 2014). Informal communities also accumulate local knowledge about risks; they know which paths flood first, which roofs are most secure, which households have vulnerable persons, and they often adapt with DIY measures (raising floor levels and digging makeshift drains). This local knowledge and adaptive practice are important resources (Pelling & High, 2005). Moreover, informality sometimes enables flexibility. In formal urban environments, land use and building are rigid; in informal ones, people might relocate shelters from particularly dangerous spots after an event or retrofit dwellings incrementally as resources allow. There is a certain agility in how informal cities change that, if harnessed, could be oriented towards risk reduction.

From a governance perspective, informality is often seen as a problem to be solved. But resilient and sustainable urban development in Southern African cities will likely depend on working with informality rather than simply trying to eliminate it. Approaches like *in situ* upgrading (improving informal settlements where they are, by adding drainage, sanitation, and lighting), participatory planning where communities co-design interventions, and incremental formalisation (providing tenure security and basic services without forcing relocation) have shown promise. Examples include the Mukuru upgrading project in Nairobi or the community-led re-blocking of shack layouts in Cape Town's informal settlements to create firebreaks and access ways. These interventions reduce vulnerabilities while respecting the social fabric of informal areas.

Rapid urbanisation, coupled with informality, is the central backdrop for resilience efforts in the region. It means that any strategy must be inclusive of informal communities, tailoring solutions to be affordable, incremental, and co-produced with residents. It also challenges planners to address the structural causes: how to provide more affordable housing, how to reform land policy to allow low-income people access to safe land, and how to extend basic infrastructure networks in ways that keep pace with urban growth. Without tackling informality head-on, Southern African cities risk perpetuating a pattern of risk creation, as each year, more people settle in harm's way due to a lack of better options.

2.6.2 *Climate Risks and Environmental Pressures*

Southern African cities are on the frontline of climate change. The region has been experiencing rising average temperatures, changes in rainfall patterns, and more frequent and intense extreme weather events (IPCC, 2022). These changes compound existing urban stresses and introduce new challenges for resilience.

Increasing frequency and intensity of climate-related disasters are a major concern. Many cities have seen an uptick in severe floods. Intense rainfall events, sometimes associated with cyclones or tropical storms, have caused destructive urban flooding. The case of Cyclone Idai (2019) stands out: it struck Mozambique, Zimbabwe, and Malawi, devastating the city of Beira and causing flooding in inland cities like Chimanimani. Idai was one of the worst disasters in the region's recent history, illustrating the catastrophic potential of such events (World Bank, 2019). Coastal cities like Beira and Maputo face dual threats of heavier rainfall and storm surges amplified by rising sea levels, leading to more frequent inundation of low-lying urban districts. Inland, cities like Lusaka and Gaborone grapple with erratic rainfall, where heavy downpours lead to flash floods that infrastructure cannot handle, followed by longer dry spells.

At the opposite extreme, droughts are also hitting cities. Southern Africa has a cyclical drought pattern (influenced by phenomena like El Niño), but climate change is intensifying these. Cape Town's water crisis in 2017–2018, where reservoirs neared depletion, was a wake-up call. Gaborone and Harare have similarly faced severe water shortages in recent years, leading to rationing. Droughts not only threaten water supply but also food security in cities (urban consumers face price hikes as agriculture is impacted) and can drive rural-urban migration, swelling city populations unexpectedly.

Another creeping risk is heatwaves and rising urban heat. Many Southern African cities (for example, Maputo, Lusaka) have seen a higher incidence of extremely hot days. Urban heat islands, where built-up areas become significantly hotter than rural surroundings, exacerbate this, posing health risks, especially to the elderly and those without access to cooling or green spaces. High heat can also impair infrastructure (softening roads, straining power grids due to AC demand) and reduce labour productivity.

Environmental degradation further heightens vulnerabilities. As cities expand, they often encroach on natural buffers. Deforestation in catchment areas upstream of cities leads to more runoff and siltation downstream, worsening floods. Wetland encroachment is particularly problematic. Wetlands act like sponges, absorbing rainfall and releasing it slowly. When informal or even formal developments fill in wetlands (as has happened in Kampala's Lubigi swamp or Harare's wetlands), cities lose critical flood control and face waterlogging and water quality issues. The example of Lusaka is illustrative—the city sits on a flood-prone plain with underlying karstic limestone; rapid urban growth onto its wetlands has removed natural drainage and also threatened the aquifer recharge (Mususa, 2012). Consequently, even moderate rains now cause localised flooding and contamination of shallow wells.

Pollution and ecological stress also matter. Cities dealing with severe air pollution (like Harare from vehicles and industry) or water pollution (like the Msimbazi river in Dar es Salaam, choked with waste) find that these issues compound disaster impacts. Polluted drainage channels can lead to toxic floodwaters, and heat plus air pollution multiply health problems.

For Southern African cities, addressing climate and environmental pressures involves a two-pronged approach: mitigation (reducing greenhouse gas emissions to slow future climate change) and adaptation (coping with the changes already underway). While mitigation has global benefits, local co-benefits (like cleaner air from less traffic) are relevant; however, adaptation is the more urgent priority given the immediate threats.

Resilience strategies need to tackle both the symptoms and root causes of risk. On the symptom side, cities must invest in protective infrastructure: for example, storm surge barriers for coastal cities, expanded drainage and retention ponds for flood management, drought-proof water supply systems (diversifying sources, reducing leaks, recycling wastewater). For instance, Durban has implemented a mix of grey and green infrastructure, improving drains in flood hotspots but also restoring upstream wetlands in the Umlazi River catchment to reduce flood peaks. On the root cause side, measures include conserving remaining natural ecosystems (like riverine forests, mangroves, open green space) that shield cities, enforcing land-use regulations to prevent construction on high-risk sites (Anguelovski et al., 2016), and integrating climate considerations into all urban projects (for example, not building critical facilities in areas projected to be underwater in 30 years).

Cities are also increasingly focused on *early warning systems* and disaster preparedness for climate extremes. Installing river gauges, rainfall radar, and community alert networks (SMS or sirens) can save lives by giving people time to evacuate or protect assets. In some Southern African cities, partnerships with meteorological services and telecom companies have enabled warning messages to be sent to residents ahead of cyclones or heavy rains. However, reaching informal settlements with warnings remains challenging due to a lack of address systems and sometimes language or trust barriers; hence, the involvement of local leaders and NGOs is key.

Another vital aspect is the climate-sensitive design of urban infrastructure. For example, road designs now consider heavier rain loads; building codes in some places are being updated for wind resistance and heat; new housing schemes may incorporate water storage for drought periods. The concept of climate-proofing development is becoming part of the urban planning lexicon.

2.6.3 Governance and Institutional Fragmentation

Governance quality often determines whether good ideas and plans for resilience translate into action. Many Southern African cities operate in contexts of constrained governance capacity and sometimes fragmented authority structures. This has deep historical roots: colonial administrations were more focused on control and extraction than inclusive development; post-colonial states sometimes centralised power at the expense of local governance; and structural adjustment in the 1980s–90s weakened many public institutions. Additionally, political instability or patronage systems in some countries have led to frequent turnover in city leadership and variable commitment to long-term planning.

A prevalent issue is fragmentation whereby responsibilities for urban management are split among multiple institutions that may not coordinate well. For instance, a metropolitan area might be divided among several municipalities, each with its own budget and priorities, while key utilities (water, electricity) are run by national parastatals, and disaster management is handled by a national agency or the military. In such a scenario, no single entity is fully in charge of resilience. This can lead to gaps, for example, an informal settlement falls just outside the city boundary, so it does not receive services, and the adjacent local authority lacks resources or will to cover it, leaving a "no-man's land" of governance. Overlapping mandates can also cause confusion. For instance, in Maputo, the existence of both a city council and a metropolitan master plan authority, plus national ministries owning some infrastructure, has sometimes resulted in contradictory decisions or delayed actions (World Bank, 2019).

Weak institutional capacities are another challenge. City governments often have limited revenue bases. Many depend on property taxes and service fees, but in largely informal cities, these are hard to collect widely. Consequently, essential departments (like planning, engineering, emergency services) may be understaffed or under-skilled. Training and retaining technical staff are a challenge, leading to reliance on external consultants or donor-funded projects that may not be sustained. When a disaster strikes, these weaknesses become evident, for instance, disaster risk management units may not have detailed contingency plans or resources prepositioned, and recovery efforts can stall due to bureaucratic bottlenecks or corruption.

Political dynamics also play a role. In some cases, there is tension between different levels of government controlled by different political parties, which can slow down collaboration. Johannesburg's climate strategy, for example, experienced disruptions when city leadership changed hands politically, causing shifts in priorities and some loss of institutional memory (Harrison et al., 2019). In other instances, urban issues may be politicised, for example, upgrading informal settlements could be seen as legitimising them, which some politicians resist due to pressures from middle-class constituencies or landowners.

Against this background, improving governance resilience is as important as improving physical resilience. Key approaches include:

- **Institutional Reform and Capacity Building:** This might involve decentralising certain powers and funds to city governments (if overly centralised) so they can act more nimbly, or conversely, creating metropolitan authorities to coordinate across fragmented municipalities (as attempted in Johannesburg and Lagos). Civil service training programs, better salaries, and twinning arrangements with well-run cities can gradually enhance skills. The creation of dedicated units for resilience or climate change within city administrations (like Durban's Climate Protection Branch) helps mainstream these issues. Clarity of roles through city statutes or national urban policies is critical, so that, for example, everyone knows who is responsible for maintaining stormwater drains or leading community outreach for DRR.

- **Participatory Governance:** Including communities in decision-making can improve legitimacy and the execution of resilience projects. City governments are increasingly experimenting with participatory budgeting (allowing residents to decide some spending priorities) or involving resident committees in monitoring service delivery. This not only empowers communities (as mentioned in Sect. 2.8.1 on participatory planning) but can also extend the reach of government in contexts where trust is low. When residents see their input valued, they may be more likely to cooperate (for example, moving structures that block a drainage channel if they understand the risk). For instance, in the upgrading of informal settlements in Kisumu, Kenya (again outside Southern Africa but relevant), community groups were part of project implementation, hiring local labour, overseeing the construction of drains, which improved quality and acceptance. Durban's approach of engaging informal settlement dwellers in climate adaptation initiatives (like tree planting on slopes to prevent erosion) is a Southern African example that builds local ownership (Roberts et al., 2012).
- **Inter-sectoral and Inter-governmental Coordination Mechanisms:** Cities can establish resilience task forces or committees that bring together different departments (housing, infrastructure, health and environment) on a regular basis to discuss resilience objectives and progress (Bulkeley et al., 2013). Some have set up data-sharing platforms or joint operations centres that, especially during emergencies, ensure all relevant bodies are synchronised. On a larger scale, forums that connect city officials with national agencies (for disaster management, climate, and finance) help align efforts. In Botswana, for example, the National Disaster Management Office works with district and city disaster committees to conduct drills and preparedness workshops, albeit the capacity varies.
- **Accountability and Transparency:** Corruption or mismanagement can severely hinder resilience (for example, if building inspectors accept bribes to allow unsafe construction, or if emergency relief

supplies are diverted). Strengthening governance means enforcing accountability through audits, community watchdogs, and free media. When people trust their institutions, compliance with risk reduction measures (like evacuation orders or water restrictions during drought) is much higher.

2.7 Critiques and Limitations of Dominant Frameworks

The preceding sections have outlined mainstream concepts and frameworks for urban resilience and sustainability. While these provide invaluable guidance, it is crucial to critically examine them, especially when applied to Southern African cities or broader Global South contexts. Many dominant frameworks were developed based on experiences in the Global North or idealised conditions, and they may carry implicit assumptions that do not hold in low-income, informally urbanising cities (like Southern African cities). Without a critical lens, there is a risk of misapplying theories, overlooking local realities, or even doing harm under the banner of resilience.

2.7.1 Northern Bias in Resilience Theory

A common critique is that much resilience literature and policy have a Northern bias in terms of the conditions assumed and the solutions proposed (Vale, 2014; MacKinnon & Derickson, 2013). Programs championed by international organisations or donor agencies, such as the Rockefeller Foundation's 100 Resilient Cities, often started with models of governance and urban form found in wealthier cities. They tend to assume the presence of functional municipal institutions, formal land tenure systems, enforceable regulations, and a baseline of infrastructure conditions that, as we have seen, are frequently lacking in Southern contexts.

For example, a resilience strategy might suggest creating detailed risk maps and enforcing strict zoning to prevent construction in hazard-prone areas. However, in a city like Lusaka or Harare, where a large portion of construction is informal and happens outside official approval, and where planning authorities have limited reach, this approach might have limited impact unless accompanied by measures to address informality and provide alternatives (Coaffee & Lee, 2016). Simply importing a technical tool (like a fancy GIS-based risk model) will not build resilience if the local government cannot translate that knowledge into action on the ground due to capacity or legitimacy issues.

Similarly, many technocratic solutions promoted under the resilience banner, such as "smart city" technologies, big data, early warning systems, or large infrastructure projects like seawalls, often require substantial capital, technical know-how, and maintenance capabilities (Bahadur & Tanner, 2014). These can overshadow more community-scale or socially focused interventions, which might be more feasible and appropriate in resource-constrained settings. There is a danger that resilience can become a buzzword to attract funding for high-profile projects that do not necessarily tackle underlying vulnerabilities (this ties into the concept of "resilience-washing" discussed later).

Another bias is an implicit focus on shocks over stresses. Northern city discourse on resilience often emphasises acute disasters (hurricanes or terror attacks, for example), whereas in Southern cities, chronic stresses like daily water shortages, crime, or unemployment may be equally or more pressing but get less attention in resilience plans (Leichenko, 2011). A resilience plan that is all about climate-proof infrastructure but ignores, say, the stress of inadequate housing and services in informal settlements might miss the mark in terms of what really improves people's well-being and security day-to-day.

2.7.2 *Operational Challenges in Informal Contexts*

Many resilience frameworks presuppose data availability and formal governance structures that enable certain tools (Patel et al., 2015). For instance, applying standardised *resilience metrics* or indicators (like those in the City Resilience Index) requires collecting consistent data on infrastructure performance, service coverage, and socio-economic conditions, for example. In informal settlements, basic data such as population figures, maps of roads and drains, and building standards may be missing and/or outdated, or virtually unavailable. This makes it hard to even establish baseline resilience scores or monitor progress. Additionally, some indicators (like the percentage of buildings that comply with the code or the proportion of the population with insurance) are not very meaningful where most buildings are informal, and insurance is virtually absent. Thus, traditional benchmarking can underrepresent progress or capacities that do exist in informal settings (like community-led improvements) simply because they're not captured by formal datasets (Cirolia, 2017).

Another challenge is implementing interventions in informal contexts through conventional government channels. For example, a government might have funds to upgrade infrastructure for resilience (like paving roads or improving drainage), but in informal settlements, land ownership is often unclear, and residents may fear eviction if the government comes in. This can lead to resistance or mistrust, hindering projects. Upgrading an area might paradoxically raise land values and lead to poorer residents being pushed out (gentrification), which is counter to social resilience. So, there is often a catch-22 situation whereby the areas that most need investment (informal settlements) are hardest to intervene in due to legal and social complexities (Satterthwaite et al., 2020). This is not addressed well by generic frameworks that assume the presence of clear authority and property rights.

Donor-driven resilience projects can also falter in informal environments. A cited example is how slum upgrading programs in Maputo struggled to integrate formal resilience metrics, like the number of households with emergency plans, because such concepts were alien locally and data collection was problematic (Brown et al., 2014). In some cases, external frameworks imposed rigidly can lead to misallocation of effort. For instance, if a project is overly focused on achieving certain indicator targets (for example, number of workshops held on climate awareness), it might tick the boxes for the donor but not leave behind any lasting capacity if those workshops did not engage the right people or address the context-specific issues residents truly prioritise.

The fluidity and dynamism of informal settlements also challenge static planning. A resilience intervention might create a flood retention pond in an open area, only to find a few years later that the open area has been settled by new arrivals who were desperate for space, thus nullifying the intervention. Enforcement is difficult when people's immediate need for shelter and income overrides long-term risk considerations. In addition, informal economies and governance can conflict with formal systems. For instance, if a city tries to implement a rigid building code for resilience, it may inadvertently criminalise the ways people have built homes for decades. A sudden enforcement could render many people homeless or jobless. Thus, conventional regulatory approaches need adaptation, something like providing incremental, achievable building improvements instead of full compliance at once.

2.7.3 *The Risk of "Resilience-Washing"*

As resilience has become a buzzword, there is a concern that it can be co-opted to justify business-as-usual or even harmful policies under a veneer of progressiveness (Vale, 2014). This is analogous to "greenwashing", where companies market themselves as environmentally friendly without substantial action. In the urban context, "resilience-washing" refers to using the language of resilience to push agendas that may not truly reduce vulnerability or may sidestep difficult issues of inequality and justice.

One example might be real estate developments that brand themselves as resilient, perhaps because they include flood defences or solar power, but in doing so might privatise what should be public space or displace low-income communities from safe areas. A waterfront redevelopment project might claim to build a "resilient coast" with seawalls and luxury apartments, but if it simultaneously prices out fishermen or informal settlers who used to occupy that land (common in port cities), it is arguable whether this is a net gain for urban resilience or just profit-driven adaptation that benefits a few.

Similarly, in some cities, resilience has been interpreted in a narrow, security-focused way, leading to fortification or surveillance measures. For instance, citing the need to be resilient against terror or crime, authorities might increase policing or introduce technologies that encroach on civil liberties. If these measures disproportionately target certain groups, which can erode social cohesion, it may ironically undermining social resilience by fostering distrust.

There is also a tendency for sloganeering. That is, cities declare themselves "resilient cities" and create glossy resilience strategies, but without ensuring implementation. It becomes a checkbox exercise for international recognition (Pelling et al., 2018). While having a strategy is a good first step, the risk is that political leaders might then feel the job is done or use the existence of a strategy to deflect criticism ("we have a resilience plan, so we are prepared"). Meanwhile, actual investment in infrastructure or community programs may not materialise.

Another subtle issue is that resilience discourse sometimes places the onus on communities to be resilient without commensurate support, essentially shifting responsibility. Governments might celebrate how poor communities cope with floods year after year (as evidence of their resilience), instead of feeling urgency to improve conditions so they do not have to cope with such floods in the first place. In worst cases, this can slide into blaming victims. For instance, if a community does not bounce back quickly after a disaster, perhaps they were "not resilient enough", rather than examining structural failures or insufficient external aid. To guard against resilience-washing, critics argue that resilience must be coupled with principles of equity and transformation (Leichenko, 2011). It is not enough to maintain the status quo and bounce back to it if the status quo is one of unjust vulnerability distribution. True resilience-building should question and seek to change why certain people are at risk. This means grappling with politics: land rights, wealth distribution, and empowerment of marginalised groups.

In Southern African cities, characterised by deep inequalities, a resilience project that does not engage with issues of land ownership, informal settlement rights, or poverty alleviation might be superficial. For example, relocating a flood-prone informal community to safer ground sounds plausible, but if the new location is far from livelihoods and social networks, the community may end up worse off economically or just return to another informal site. A resilience lens that is only technocratic could miss these human factors.

These critiques do not dismiss the frameworks and strategies of resilience and sustainable development, but they call for caution and contextual adaptation. They highlight that applying models without critical thought may lead to ineffective or unjust outcomes. Recognising these limitations pushes practitioners to adjust frameworks: to incorporate local knowledge, to be humble about what standardised tools can achieve, to invest in social processes, not just physical ones, and to always ask "resilient for whom?" in evaluating policies. By addressing these critiques, acknowledging biases, adapting to informality, and insisting on genuine transformative action, the pursuit of urban resilience in Southern African cities can avoid pitfalls and become more truly inclusive, effective, efficient, and economic.

2.8 Pathways Towards Contextualised Urban Resilience

Given the limitations discussed above, there is a growing consensus that one-size-fits-all solutions will not suffice for building urban resilience in diverse contexts. Instead, there is a need for context-sensitive, inclusive, and transformative strategies that directly engage with local realities

(Bulkeley et al., 2013; Parnell & Pieterse, 2010). Southern African cities require approaches that empower local communities, bridge formal and informal systems, and blend global knowledge with indigenous practices. This section highlights several promising pathways for advancing urban resilience in a more grounded way, specifically tailored to the challenges and opportunities of cities in this region.

2.8.1 Risk-Informed Planning and Infrastructure Resilience

Integrating resilience thinking into the core of urban planning and infrastructure development is critical. Rather than treating resilience as an add-on, it should be mainstreamed into how cities expand and upgrade. Risk-informed urban planning means that decisions on land use, zoning, and development controls are guided by an understanding of hazard exposure and vulnerability patterns (UNISDR, 2015). This could involve designating high-risk zones (floodplains, unstable slopes, coastal erosion zones) as non-residential or low-density land uses, effectively creating buffer zones that limit the concentration of people and assets in harm's way. For example, Durban's city planners have delineated certain floodplain areas as public open space or parkland, preventing new informal settlements from taking root there and preserving those lands as natural flood buffers. While relocating existing communities is politically and ethically fraught, ensuring new development steers clear of known hazard zones is a straightforward risk-informed practice.

In tandem, resilient infrastructure design is about building systems that can withstand shocks or at least fail safely. Key principles include robustness (strong materials and design standards to handle extreme conditions), redundancy (backup systems or multiple pathways so that if one part fails, the system still works), and flexibility (systems that can be adjusted or upgraded as risks evolve). In practical terms, this might mean elevating roads and bridges in flood-prone areas, constructing buildings to higher wind-load and seismic standards, creating loops in water and power networks so there are alternative routes if one segment is broken, and decentralising some services (like having multiple smaller electric substations instead of one big one, to avoid single points of failure).

Southern African cities, confronting infrastructure deficits, have an opportunity to "build back better" as they extend services. When a city like Beira rebuilds after a cyclone, incorporating improved engineering (for example, cyclone-resistant roofing, raised public facilities) ensures that reconstruction is not just replacing risk but reducing it. Simple measures like securing roofs with hurricane clips, elevating boreholes above flood height, or using flood-resistant materials in ground-floor construction can significantly reduce damage in future events (Dodman et al., 2012). The challenge is often cost, but in many cases, the incremental cost of resilience measures is small relative to the damages avoided.

Another aspect is green and blue infrastructure as part of resilient design. Recognising that hard infrastructure alone is insufficient, cities are combining grey and green solutions. For instance, rainwater harvesting and infiltration measures (like bioswales or porous pavements) help manage stormwater and replenish groundwater while reducing the burden on sewers. Green belts and urban forests can act as windbreaks and cooling areas, mitigating heatwaves and storm winds. The city of Walvis Bay in Namibia, for example, has maintained a belt of dunes and wetlands between the town and the ocean that provides protection against storm surges, opting not to develop right to the shoreline.

Innovations around renewable energy and resource efficiency also bolster resilience. Decentralised solar power systems, like the micro-grids being piloted in some Maputo neighbourhoods, keep lights on when the main grid fails and reduce dependence on a single power source. Efficient water use and recycling (as seen in Windhoek's pioneering waste-to-potable water plant) ensure cities can endure droughts with less disruption. While these innovations are primarily about sustainability, they have clear resilience dividends: a city that can generate its own power or has multiple water sources is less likely to be crippled by a single failure (IPCC, 2014).

In practice, pushing this pathway means updating building codes and standards (and finding ways to enforce them incrementally even in informal construction, such as promoting resilient yet affordable building techniques), training engineers and planners in climate adaptation, and securing financing for infrastructure that explicitly accounts for resilience (often, multilateral development banks offer such financing with the rationale of long-term savings). It also means engaging communities in co-designing infrastructure—for example, involving residents in mapping drainage paths and identifying where culverts or dikes are needed, which can lead to more appropriate and maintained solutions.

2.8.2 *Participatory and Community-Led Planning*

Top-down planning has historically dominated many cities, but a shift is underway towards participatory and community-driven approaches as a means to more equitable and effective resilience building. The rationale is simple: residents, especially in informal settlements and other marginalised areas, have intimate knowledge of their environment and needs, and they are the first responders in any disaster. Engaging them in planning yields solutions that are better tailored to local realities and enjoy greater buy-in (Pelling & High, 2005; Mitlin, 2008).

One proven tool is participatory risk mapping. This involves community members creating maps of their neighbourhood, marking risk spots (flood-prone low points, locations of past fires, unsafe footpaths, etc.), critical resources (wells, clinics, community centres), and vulnerable households (elderly or disabled residents). Such exercises, often facilitated by NGOs or local officials, not only produce valuable data for planners but also raise awareness among residents and catalyse discussions on how to address the identified risks. In Cape Town's informal settlement of Sweet Home Farm, for example, a participatory mapping project led to the community lobbying for and collaborating in the installation of wider access lanes, which now serve as firebreaks after a string of devastating shack fires (Ziervogel et al., 2017).

Community-based early warning systems are another participatory measure. In some flood-prone townships of Durban, residents have organised simple watch networks: when heavy rains are forecast, volunteers monitor upstream water levels and use whistles or text messages to alert neighbours if flooding seems imminent (Ziervogel et al., 2017). They also identify which families need help to evacuate. Authorities can support such initiatives by providing training, equipment (like boots, torches, and two-way radios), and linking them with official meteorological alerts.

Neighbourhood action plans developed by residents can complement citywide plans. These might outline, for instance, how a community would respond in the first 48 hours after an earthquake when external help might not yet have arrived—designating safe gathering points, first aid volunteers, and temporary shelter locations. Having these micro-level plans ensures a more organised and faster response, reducing panic and ensuring that vulnerable members are looked after. Cities like Bulawayo, Zimbabwe, have engaged ward-level committees to prepare disaster response plans, which have not only improved readiness but also fostered trust between citizens and local government.

Crucially, participatory approaches build social capital, which is a key determinant of resilience (Aldrich & Meyer, 2015). As people collaborate on mapping or drills, they strengthen relationships and learn to work collectively. This social cohesion often translates into mutual aid during crises, neighbours will check on each other, share resources, and coordinate spontaneously. For participatory planning to be meaningful, authorities must be willing to share power and information. This can involve acknowledging community organisations as legitimate partners, devolving some decision-making, or providing small grants for communities to implement their own resilience projects (like clearing garbage from drains or reinforcing footbridges). It also means ensuring inclusive participation, bringing women, youth, and other often excluded voices to the table. In many instances, women's groups have been at the forefront of community resilience, as they manage water, food, and childcare daily and have a strong stake in safety. Their involvement can lead to identifying different priorities (for example, lighting in public spaces to improve safety at night, which is both a security and a resilience issue).

Participatory planning helps surface indigenous knowledge that might be overlooked. Elders might recall historical flood patterns or drought coping strategies that modern planners are not aware of. For example, rural-urban migrants might bring traditional methods of rainwater harvesting or building techniques that could be applied in new contexts if given recognition and support.

2.8.3 *Hybrid and Adaptive Governance Models*

When formal governance capacity is limited or where communities operate largely outside the formal system, hybrid governance arrangements can play a crucial role in building resilience. These involve collaborations between government actors, civil society (NGOs, community-based organisations, faith groups), the private sector, and sometimes traditional authorities or academic institutions (Cleaver, 2012; Watson, 2014). By pooling the strengths of different actors, hybrid models can compensate for any single actor's weakness and provide more agile responses to complex problems.

In Southern Africa, one area where hybrid governance has shown value is in water management during droughts. For instance, in Gaborone,

Botswana, faced with recurring droughts, a partnership emerged between government water agencies, the University of Botswana, and local NGOs to implement water conservation initiatives. They worked together on public awareness campaigns (NGOs going door-to-door educating about saving water), technical solutions (the university piloting low-cost greywater reuse systems for households), and policy input (advising the government on tiered tariffs to discourage excessive use). The involvement of civil society and academia lent credibility and community connection to what could otherwise be seen as top-down rationing measures, leading to broader public acceptance and participation in water-saving (Schreiner & Baleta, 2015).

Another example is slum upgrading and disaster preparedness in informal settlements. Purely state-driven efforts often falter in these areas, so successful projects have involved NGOs and community networks. In Namibia's informal settlements, a program called the Community Land Information Program (CLIP) facilitated partnerships where communities gathered their own data and plans for upgrading, and NGOs helped translate that into proposals that the government could fund. When it came time to, say, install drains or improve roads, local youth groups carried out the work with oversight from city engineers. This hybrid implementation built local skills and ensured the infrastructure was culturally appropriate (Mitlin, 2008).

Hybrid governance also extends to emergency response. After Cyclone Idai, the response in Mozambique saw the government working alongside international NGOs, the Red Cross, local church groups, and even private companies (which provided trucks and helicopters for relief). While coordination had issues, there were instances where local knowledge from community groups guided rescuers to neighbourhoods initially overlooked by formal maps, thus saving lives. Institutionalising such cooperation (for example, through pre-disaster agreements or platforms that link city disaster management units with civil society organisations) can lead to swifter, more inclusive responses in future events.

Adaptive governance is closely related and emphasises learning and flexibility. In a rapidly changing climate, governance systems must adapt based on feedback. A good practice is setting up multi-stakeholder resilience committees in cities that meet regularly to review progress on resilience actions, share new information (like updated climate projections or a recent near-miss incident), and adjust strategies accordingly. By including non-state actors in these committees, cities ensure a flow of information from the ground level and keep plans realistic. In Johannesburg, for example, the city's Resilience Strategy (developed under the 100 Resilient Cities initiative) led to the formation of a Resilience Office that convenes various departments and external advisors. Though still evolving, this sort of platform can help break down silos and allow experimental approaches to be tested and scaled up if they work.

Hybrid governance does come with challenges such as aligning different agendas, sustaining collaboration once initial enthusiasm or funding fades, and ensuring accountability (because diffused responsibility can lead to finger-pointing if things go wrong). However, when well-managed, it offers a pragmatic path in places where no single entity has all the answers or resources. It acknowledges that resilience is a collective effort involving governments to create enabling environments, communities to drive local action, NGOs to mediate and build capacity, and businesses to contribute innovation and investment. Especially in cities where trust in government is low, these hybrid models can slowly rebuild trust as people see results delivered through partnership.

2.8.4 Integrating Indigenous and Local Knowledge

Modern scientific approaches to resilience are powerful, but they should not overshadow the wealth of indigenous and local knowledge that communities have developed over generations to cope with climate variability, environmental hazards, and resource management (Nyong et al., 2007). In many African contexts, traditional practices and culturally embedded knowledge systems remain highly relevant and can be harnessed for resilience-building (Mavhura et al., 2013). Integrating these knowledge systems means validating, learning from them, and finding ways to incorporate them into contemporary planning and DRR efforts.

One area of indigenous knowledge is in climate forecasting and adaptation. Rural communities in Southern Africa have long observed natural indicators such as the flowering of certain plants, behaviour of animals, or patterns of winds to predict seasonal changes or extreme weather. Some of these communities have brought that knowledge with them into urban and peri-urban areas. For instance, older residents on the outskirts of Harare might recall signs of an impending drought or heavy rain season and could provide early warning that complements meteorological forecasts. Engaging with traditional leaders or elders in discussions about climate trends may reveal such indicators (for example, "if the marula trees fruit early, expect heavy rains"). While not infallible, this information can be combined with scientific data for a more robust early warning system.

Indigenous building techniques also offer lessons. Many vernacular architectures were well-adapted to local climates. For instance, the thick mud walls and thatched roofs in hot, arid regions that provide insulation, or raised homes on stilts in floodplains. In modern cities, people often abandon these in favour of concrete blocks and zinc sheets, which can be less suited (zinc roofs are notorious for making informal houses unbearably hot and are easily blown off in storms). Some architects and communities are revisiting traditional materials (adobe or bamboo) for more sustainable and resilient housing. For example, in northern Namibia, there is renewed interest in using traditional compaction of earth (improved with modern stabilisers) to build flood-resistant and thermally comfortable homes, as opposed to import-dependent cement blocks.

Traditional approaches to water management, such as rainwater harvesting from rooftops or communal ponds, can also be revitalised in cities to increase water security (UN-Habitat, 2020). In parts of Botswana and Zimbabwe, techniques like digging infiltration pits (to recharge groundwater) or using stone lines to slow runoff have been used in agriculture; adapted versions of these could help urban parks or gardens act as sponges to mitigate floods.

Cultural values and social norms play a role in resilience, too. Many Southern African cultures have practices of communal labour (for example, "*zunde raMambo*" in Shona culture, where community members collectively farm a field for the chief's granary to be used in times of need, or *"letsema"* in Tswana communities, collective work parties). These principles of mutual aid and preparation for lean times resonate with modern concepts of resilience. Urban community gardens, savings clubs (*"stokvels"* in South Africa), and burial societies are contemporary manifestations of such traditions that strengthen social safety nets. Integrating these knowledge systems means planners and scientists must engage with humility and openness. This could be done through workshops that bring together meteorologists and traditional rainmakers, or architects and local builders, for mutual learning (Parnell & Pieterse, 2010). It also means documenting practices before they disappear, involving universities or local researchers in capturing oral histories of how past disasters were dealt with and what coping strategies were employed.

There are some encouraging examples. For instance, in Maputo, an NGO worked with local healers and community leaders to revive the practice of planting certain trees believed to ward off strong winds around settlements; whether through spiritual belief or practical windbreak effect, the communities felt better protected and took pride in preserving those trees. In Zimbabwe, traditional leaders have been included in climate adaptation projects to leverage their authority in mobilising people for ecosystem restoration, framing riverbank protection as not only a scientific imperative but also a return to respecting the land as ancestors did.

However, integrating indigenous knowledge requires careful navigation to avoid romanticising all traditional practices (some may not be effective or appropriate in current conditions) or inadvertently reinforcing power imbalances (for example, not all community members may agree with a chief's perspective). The goal is not to replace modern science with traditional knowledge, but to use all available knowledge in pragmatic ways. Indigenous insights can inspire nature-based solutions, community engagement strategies, and culturally resonant messaging for resilience.

2.9 Conclusion

This chapter has established a comprehensive theoretical foundation for analysing urban resilience and sustainable development within the distinctive context of Southern Africa, specifically concerning Disaster Risk Reduction (DRR) and climate adaptation. It traced the conceptual evolution of resilience from its origins in engineering paradigms, emphasising stability and bounce-back recovery, towards more dynamic, adaptive, and transformative interpretations. These contemporary perspectives conceptualise resilience as an ongoing process of learning, systemic adjustment, and fundamental change—a necessary shift reflecting the inadequacy of rigid planning models when confronted with the profound social, environmental, and economic complexities inherent in Southern Africa's rapidly urbanising landscapes. Sustainable development was similarly examined beyond its initial environmental emphasis, evolving to encompass critical dimensions of social equity, inclusivity, and urban well-being, as enshrined in global frameworks like SDG 11 (Sustainable Cities and Communities) and the New Urban Agenda. These frameworks explicitly link sustainability with resilience, demanding that cities be capable of responding effectively to both chronic stresses and acute shocks while fostering long-term human and ecological prosperity.

Core analytical concepts, vulnerability, and adaptive capacity were explored to operationalise resilience within urban settings. Vulnerability was presented not merely as exposure to hazards, but as deeply conditioned by structural inequalities, pervasive informality, and systemic marginalisation. Consequently, effective resilience strategies must be inherently inclusive and equity-driven. Conversely, adaptive capacity highlights the critical resources, tools, and institutional frameworks that empower communities and urban systems to anticipate and respond proactively to change. Case insights from Cape Town and Beira starkly illustrated the uneven distribution of this capacity, underscoring the pivotal roles of governance structures, strategic planning, and community agency in determining urban outcomes. The chapter introduced and synthesised key theoretical frameworks: systems thinking, complexity theory, social-ecological resilience, and sustainable urbanism, providing essential lenses to comprehend the interconnectedness and inherent unpredictability of urban challenges. Crucially, the application of these frameworks necessitates significant adaptation to Southern African realities, where widespread informality and institutional constraints often impede the implementation of externally derived models. Adopting a critical perspective, the chapter identified limitations in mainstream resilience discourse when applied without contextual sensitivity. It advocated strongly for participatory governance models, hybrid planning approaches that integrate formal and informal systems, and the incorporation of indigenous and local knowledge as indispensable components of effective urban resilience strategies.

Achieving genuine resilience and sustainability in Southern African cities transcends technical solutions. It demands transformative approaches that are fundamentally inclusive, contextually grounded, and committed to systemic change. The theoretical insights consolidated in this chapter provide a vital blueprint for reimagining urban futures that are not only more secure and adaptable in the face of disaster and climate risk but are also characterised by greater social justice and community empowerment. This foundation sets the stage for subsequent empirical investigation into translating these principles into actionable, context-specific practice.

References

Adger, W. N. (2006). Vulnerability. *Global Environmental Change, 16*(3), 268–281.

Adger, W. N., Hughes, T. P., Folke, C., Carpenter, S. R., & Rockström, J. (2005). Social-ecological resilience to coastal disasters. *Science, 309*(5737), 1036–1039.

Ahern, J. (2011). From fail-safe to safe-to-fail: Sustainability and resilience in the new urban world. *Landscape and Urban Planning, 100*(4), 341–343.

Aldrich, D. P., & Meyer, M. A. (2015). Social capital and community resilience. *American Behavioral Scientist, 59*(2), 254–269.

Allen, C. R., & Holling, C. S. (2010). Novelty, adaptive capacity, and resilience. *Ecology and Society, 15*(3), 24.

Andersson, E., Barthel, S., Borgström, S., Colding, J., Elmqvist, T., Folke, C., & Gren, Å. (2014). Reconnecting cities to the biosphere: Stewardship of green infrastructure and urban ecosystem services. *Ambio, 43*, 445–453.

Anguelovski, I., Chu, E., & Carmin, J. (2016). Varieties of urban climate adaptation: Assessing transformative potential. *Journal of Planning Education and Research, 36*(3), 33–348.

Archer, D., Luansang, C., & Boonmahathanakorn, S. (2014). Knowing your city: Community profiling and the right to the city. *Environment and Urbanization, 26*(1), 235–250.

Aylett, A. (2015). Institutionalizing the urban governance of climate change adaptation: Results of an international survey. *Urban Climate, 14*, 4–16.

Bahadur, A. V., & Tanner, T. (2014). Policy climates and climate policies: Analysing the politics ofbuilding urban climate change resilience. *Urban Climate, 7*, 20–32.

Batty, M. (2007). *Cities and complexity: Understanding cities with cellular automata, agent-based models, and fractals*. MIT Press.

Beatley, T. (2000). *Green urbanism: Learning from European cities*. Island Press.

Betsill, M., & Bulkeley, H. (2006). Cities and the multilevel governance of global climate change. *Global Governance, 12*(2), 141–159.

Birkmann, J. (2006). Measuring vulnerability to promote disaster-resilient societies: Conceptual frameworks and definitions. *Measuring vulnerability to natural hazards: Towards disaster resilient societies, 1*(9), 3–7.

Bradshaw, S. (2013). *Gender, development and disasters*. Edward Elgar Publishing.

Brown, D., McGranahan, G., & Dodman, D. (2014). *Urban informality and building a more inclusive, resilient and green economy*. IIED Working Paper. IIED.

Bulkeley, H., Castán Broto, V., & Maassen, A. (2013). Low-carbon transitions and the reconfiguration of urban infrastructure. *Urban Studies, 51*(7), 1471–1486.

Campbell, S. (1996). Green cities, growing cities, just cities?: Urban planning and the contradictions of sustainable development. *Journal of the American Planning Association, 62*(3), 296–312.

Cirolia, L. (2017). Fractured fiscal authority and fragmented infrastructures: Financing sustainable urban development in Cape Town. *Urban Forum, 28*(3), 243–267.

Cirolia, L., Görgens, T., van Donk, M., Smit, W., & Drimie, S. (2016). *Urban infrastructure in sub-Saharan Africa—Harnessing land values, housing and transport*. African Centre for Cities.

Cleaver, F. (2012). *Development through bricolage: Rethinking institutions for natural resource management*. Routledge.

Coaffee, J., & Lee, P. (2016). *Urban resilience: Planning for risk, crisis and uncertainty*. Palgrave Macmillan.

Cutter, S. L., Boruff, B. J., & Shirley, W. L. (2003). Social vulnerability to environmental hazards. *Social Science Quarterly, 84*(2), 242–261.

Dodman, D., Bicknell, J., & Satterthwaite, D. (Eds.). (2012). *Adapting cities to climate change: Understanding and addressing the development challenges*. Routledge.

Duit, A., & Galaz, V. (2008). Governance and complexity—Emerging issues for governance theory. *Governance, 21*(3), 311–335.

Engle, N. L. (2011). Adaptive capacity and its assessment. *Global Environmental Change, 21*(2), 647–656.

Folke, C. (2006). Resilience: The emergence of a perspective for social–ecological systems analyses. *Global Environmental Change, 16*(3), 253–267.

Folke, C., Carpenter, S. R., Walker, B., Scheffer, M., Chapin, T., & Rockström, J. (2010). Resilience thinking: Integrating resilience, adaptability and transformability. *Ecology and Society, 15*, 20. https://doi.org/10.5751/ES-03610-150420

GFDRR (Global Facility for Disaster Reduction and Recovery). (2020). *Mozambique Cyclone Idai post disaster needs assessment*. World Bank Group.

Goodfellow, T. (2014). The institutionalisation of "noise" and "silence" in urban politics: Riots and compliance in Uganda and Rwanda. *Cities, 36*, 248–255.

Gunderson, L. H., & Holling, C. S. (2002). *Panarchy: Understanding transformations in human and natural systems*. Island Press.

Harrison, P., Gotz, G., Todes, A., & Wray, C. (2019). Materialities, subjectivities and spatial transformation in Johannesburg's inner city. *Urban Studies, 56*(3), 567–583.

Holling, C. S. (1973). Resilience and stability of ecological systems. *Annual Review of Ecology and Systematics, 4*(1), 1–23.

Holling, C. S. (2001). Understanding the complexity of economic, ecological, and social systems. *Ecosystems, 4*(5), 390–405.

Huchzermeyer, M. (2011). *Cities with 'slums': From informal settlement eradication to a right to the city in Africa*. UCT Press.

IFRC (International Federation of Red Cross and Red Crescent Societies). (2019). *Mozambique: Cyclone Idai emergency appeal operations update*. IFRC.

IPCC. (2014). *Climate change 2014: Impacts, adaptation, and vulnerability* (Contribution of Working Group II to the Fifth Assessment Report). Cambridge University Press.

IPCC. (2022). *Climate change 2022: Impacts, adaptation and vulnerability* (Contribution of Working Group II to the Sixth Assessment Report). Cambridge University Press.

Jabareen, Y. (2006). Sustainable urban forms: Their typologies, models, and concepts. *Journal of Planning Education and Research, 26*(1), 38–52.
Leichenko, R. (2011). Climate change and urban resilience. *Current Opinion in Environmental Sustainability, 3*(3), 164–168.
MacKinnon, D., & Derickson, K. D. (2013). From resilience to resourcefulness: A critique of resilience policy and activism. *Progress in Human Geography, 37*(2), 253–270.
Mavhura, E., Manyena, S. B., & Collins, A. E. (2013). Indigenous knowledge, coping strategies and resilience to floods in Muzarabani, Zimbabwe. *International Journal of Disaster Risk Reduction, 5*, 38–48.
Meadows, D. H. (1999). *Thinking in systems: A primer.* Chelsea Green Publishing.
Meerow, S., Newell, J. P., & Stults, M. (2016). Defining urban resilience: A review. *Landscape and Urban Planning, 147*, 38–49.
Mitlin, D. (2008). With and beyond the state—Co-production as a route to transformation. *Environment and Urbanization, 20*(2), 339–360.
Munang, R., Thiaw, I., Alverson, K., Liu, J., & Han, Z. (2013). The role of ecosystem services in climate change adaptation and disaster risk reduction. *Current Opinion in Environmental Sustainability, 5*(1), 47–52.
Mususa, P. (2012). Contested urbanism in Lusaka: Politics in the history of Zambia's urban development. *Urban Forum, 23*(1), 61–79.
Nyong, A., Adesina, F., & Osman Elasha, B. (2007). The value of indigenous knowledge in climate change mitigation and adaptation strategies in Africa. *Mitigation and Adaptation Strategies for Global Change, 12*(5), 787–797.
Ostrom, E. (2009). A general framework for analyzing sustainability of social-ecological systems. *Science, 325*(5939), 419–422.
Ostrom, E. (2010). Polycentric systems for coping with collective action and global environmental change. *Global Environmental Change, 20*(4), 550–557.
Parnell, S., & Pieterse, E. (2010). The 'right to the city': Institutional imperatives of a developmental state. *International Journal of Urban and Regional Research, 34*(1), 146–162.
Parnell, S., & Robinson, J. (2012). (Re)theorizing cities from the Global South: Looking beyond neoliberalism. *Urban Geography, 33*(4), 593–617.
Patel, S., Grey, C., & Levine, S. (2015). *Urban resilience: Lessons from Kampala, Entebbe and Jinja* (Working Paper). Overseas Development Institute.
Pelling, M., & High, C. (2005). Understanding adaptation: What can social capital offer assessments of adaptive capacity? *Global Environmental Change, 15*(4), 308–319.
Pelling, M., O'Brien, K., & Matyas, D. (2018). Adaptation and transformation. *Climate Change, 20*(4), 667–677.
Roberts, D., Boon, R., Diederichs, N., Douwes, E., Govender, N., Mcinnes, A., Mclean, C., O'Donoghue, S., & Spires, M. (2012). Exploring ecosystem-based

adaptation in Durban, South Africa: "Learning-by-doing" at the local government coal face. *Environment and Urbanization, 24*(1), 167–195.

Satterthwaite, D., Archer, D., Colenbrander, S., Dodman, D., Hardoy, J., Mitlin, D., & Patel, S. (2020). Building resilience to climate change in informal settlements. *One Earth, 2*(2), 143–156.

Schreiner, B., & Baleta, H. (2015). Broadening water governance: Water resources management in South Africa. *Water Policy, 17*(6), 1122–1139.

Smit, B., & Wandel, J. (2006). Adaptation, adaptive capacity and vulnerability. *Global Environmental Change, 16*(3), 282–292.

Todes, A. (2011). Reinventing planning: Critical reflections. *Urban Forum, 22*(2), 115–133.

Turok, I. (2016). South Africa's new urban agenda: Transformation or compensation? *Local Economy, 31*(1–2), 9–27.

Turok, I., & Scheba, A. (2019). The 'Corridors of Freedom' and the future of urbanization in Johannesburg. *Urban Forum, 30*(1), 1–17.

UN-Habitat. (2016). *New Urban Agenda* (Habitat III). United Nations.

UN-Habitat. (2020). *World cities report 2020: The value of sustainable urbanization.* United Nations Human Settlements Programme.

UNISDR (United Nations International Strategy for Disaster Reduction). (2015). *Sendai framework for disaster risk reduction 2015–2030.* United Nations.

United Nations. (2015). *Transforming our world: The 2030 agenda for sustainable development.* UN General Assembly Resolution 70/1. United Nations.

Vale, L. J. (2014). The politics of resilient cities: Whose resilience and whose city? *Building Research & Information, 42*(2), 191–201.

Walker, B., Holling, C. S., Carpenter, S. R., & Kinzig, A. (2004). Resilience, adaptability and transformability in social–ecological systems. *Ecology and Society, 9*(2), 5.

Watson, V. (2009). The planned city sweeps the poor away: Urban planning and 21st century urbanisation. *Progress in Planning, 72*(3), 151–193.

Watson, V. (2014). Co-production and collaboration in planning—The difference. *Planning Theory & Practice, 15*(1), 62–76.

Wisner, B., Blaikie, P., Cannon, T., & Davis, I. (2004). *At risk: Natural hazards, people's vulnerability and disasters* (2nd ed.). Routledge.

World Bank. (2019). *Resilient cities project: Resilience frameworks and tools for urban development.* World Bank Group.

Ziervogel, G. (2019). Building transformative capacity for adaptation planning and implementation that works for the urban poor: Insights from South Africa. *Ambio, 48*(5), 494–506.

Ziervogel, G., Waddell, J., Smit, W., & Taylor, A. (2017). Flooding in Cape Town's informal settlements: Barriers to collaborative urban risk governance. *South African Geographical Journal, 99*(2), 153–173.

CHAPTER 3

Historical Context: Urban Growth and Disaster Risks in Southern Africa

3.1 Introduction

To understand the contemporary challenges of sustainable urban development and disaster risk in Southern Africa, it is essential to analyse the historical trajectories that have shaped its cities. The region's urban form and vulnerability patterns are not accidental; they are the result of centuries of socio-political engineering, spatial exclusion, and governance transitions. From pre-colonial trade settlements to colonial segregationist policies and post-independence urban growth, each period has contributed to the complexity of risk, infrastructure disparity, and resilience outcomes observed in the present.

Urban development in Southern Africa has historically evolved under the pressures of conquest, capital accumulation, and racial stratification (Parnell & Pieterse, 2010). The colonial legacy of "dual cities", characterised by stark divides between privileged and marginalised urban populations, continues to influence urban expansion, service delivery, and exposure to hazards (Huchzermeyer, 2011). Post-colonial reforms, while politically transformative, often inherited bureaucratic systems ill-equipped to address informal growth, environmental degradation, and the intensifying impacts of climate change (Turok, 2016). Moreover, the disaster risks faced by Southern African cities, ranging from cyclones in coastal Mozambique to floods in Lusaka and heatwaves in Johannesburg, are

F. Mangara, N. Dorasamy, *Sustainable Urban Development in Southern Africa*, https://doi.org/10.1007/978-3-032-08286-2_3

deeply intertwined with historical urban development patterns. Settlements that were marginalised during colonial rule now constitute some of the most vulnerable zones due to poor drainage, substandard housing, and weak infrastructure.

Therefore, this chapter explores how urban growth trajectories, institutional legacies, and spatial configurations across different historical periods have contributed to disaster risk profiles and the uneven capacities for resilience in the region. By examining the colonial and post-colonial context of urbanisation and governance, we can understand the root causes of present-day vulnerabilities. Each section of this chapter highlights a specific historical phase or theme—from indigenous urban practices to apartheid city planning and contemporary informal expansion—and links it to current disaster risk challenges. In doing so, the chapter provides a foundation for integrating disaster risk reduction (DRR) into urban planning by learning from the past and addressing its lingering effects.

3.2 Pre-colonial Urbanisation in Southern Africa

Before colonial intervention, urbanisation in Southern Africa was shaped by indigenous governance systems, trade networks, and ecological adaptation. Contrary to colonial-era narratives that depicted Africa as exclusively rural or "undeveloped", pre-colonial Southern Africa featured complex settlement patterns and vibrant urban centres linked to long-distance trade and regional political authority (Hall, 1987; Freund, 2007). Cities such as Great Zimbabwe (which thrived between the eleventh and fifteenth centuries) and Mapungubwe (flourishing in the thirteenth century) were sophisticated in their socio-political organisation and economic functions. Great Zimbabwe, in particular, functioned as a hub of regional trade in gold and ivory, with far-reaching ties to Swahili city-states along the Indian Ocean coast. These early urban centres demonstrated principles of sustainable settlement, including strategic proximity to water sources, integration with the natural landscape, and decentralised spatial layouts that reduced congestion and environmental degradation.

Pre-colonial cities also employed traditional land use practices and indigenous ecological knowledge systems to manage resources and mitigate hazards. Sacred groves, rotational farming, and rainwater harvesting were integral to urban–environment interactions (Tshiguvho, 2008). In many communities, disaster risk was mitigated through social cohesion and collective action: strong community networks, spiritual leadership, and customary laws governing land use helped buffer against environmental shocks such as droughts or floods. While the overall scale of urbanisation was modest compared to modern standards, these early cities exhibited a form of resilience rooted in communal governance, adaptability, and low environmental impact. Importantly, the disruption of these systems through colonisation later laid the foundation for institutional disempowerment and spatial marginalisation. The imposition of foreign planning ideals often erased or delegitimised indigenous urban governance and land management practices, contributing to the historical discontinuities in risk governance observed today (Myers, 2011). In sum, Southern Africa's pre-colonial urban heritage shows that urban resilience is not a new concept—it was embedded in traditional practices that balanced human settlements with the environment and collective risk management.

3.3 Colonial Urban Planning and Its Legacy

3.3.1 Segregated Cities and Spatial Inequality

Colonialism fundamentally altered the trajectory of urban development in Southern Africa. From the late nineteenth century onward, cities became sites of extraction, administrative control, and, above all, racial segregation. Colonial urban planning was explicitly exclusionary, designed to entrench white settler dominance while relegating Black African populations to peripheral townships or so-called "native reserves" (Home, 1997; Mabin & Smit, 1997). In South Africa, for example, the 1913 Natives Land Act and the 1923 Native (Urban Areas) Act institutionalised racial spatial planning, leading to the emergence of dual cities: well-serviced urban cores reserved for Europeans and overcrowded, under-resourced peripheries for Africans (Christopher, 1994; Parnell, 1992). Similar spatial patterns emerged in Harare (then Salisbury), Lusaka, and Windhoek under British and German colonial rule (Freund, 2007; Myers, 2003). These colonial cities were not only segregated by race but also functionally zoned to serve the interests of extractive industries and colonial administration, with minimal regard for ecological balance or the long-term sustainability of the urban form.

Colonial authorities implemented urban planning schemes rooted in European notions of modernity, such as rigid zoning laws, gridiron street layouts, and centralised sanitation models. However, these imported frameworks were often misaligned with local ecological conditions and indigenous social dynamics (Watson, 2009). For instance, inflexible zoning practices failed to accommodate the mixed-use livelihoods common in African communities, and urban boundaries were deliberately drawn to limit African settlement near economic hubs. This dissonance created cities ill-suited to their environments and peoples. Crucially, the legacy of segregation had lasting implications for disaster vulnerability. African residential areas were frequently located on marginal lands deemed undesirable by the colonial authorities, such as floodplains, steep slopes, or poorly drained low-lying zones (Simone, 2004). Lacking formal infrastructure or services, these locations became hotspots of urban risk. Many of today's informal settlements in cities like Maputo, Harare, and Durban can trace their origins to these colonial-era exclusions, which forced Black communities into hazard-prone peripheries (Huchzermeyer, 2011; UN-Habitat, 2020). Furthermore, the colonial state's emphasis on controlling "urban natives" through influx control policies and pass laws stifled the development of African urban agency and planning capacity (Parnell, 1992; Mamdani, 1996). Africans in urban areas were viewed by colonial regimes as transient labourers rather than legitimate urban citizens, excluding them from meaningful participation in shaping city growth. This institutional disempowerment and exclusion of the majority population contributed to the enduring weakness of inclusive urban governance and disaster risk management in the post-colonial era. In effect, colonial urban policies not only created divided cities but also planted the seeds of socio-spatial inequalities that continue to exacerbate urban vulnerability to this day.

3.3.2 *Colonial Infrastructures and Environmental Disruption*

While colonial regimes did invest in urban infrastructure such as railways, roads, and port facilities, these investments were overwhelmingly designed to facilitate resource extraction, commerce, and settler convenience rather than inclusive or ecologically sound urban development (Freund, 2007; Mamdani, 1996). Infrastructure and public services were typically concentrated in European settler zones, with peripheral African areas left severely under-serviced, reinforcing a spatial inequality that persists today (Parnell & Robinson, 2012). The environmental consequences of colonial infrastructure development were significant. The drive to exploit minerals and agricultural commodities led to deforestation, soil erosion, and pollution of major water bodies. For example, railroad and mining corridors across

Southern Africa often disregarded environmental stewardship, resulting in *imperial gullies* and land degradation (Showers, 2005). Urban road systems were constructed without adequate drainage in many towns, leading to increased surface runoff and flooding in adjacent low-income neighbourhoods (Douglas et al., 2008). In Lusaka, for instance, colonial-era plans made little provision for stormwater management in the crowded African "compounds", contributing to recurring flash floods in those areas during Zambia's post-independence years (Mususa, 2012).

Colonial infrastructure policies also had a discriminatory character in the provision of basic services. Sewerage and water networks were extended to European suburbs while bypassing African townships. In Johannesburg, early twentieth-century sewer systems deliberately excluded townships like Alexandra and Soweto, leading to chronic sanitation problems and disease outbreaks in those communities (Beall et al., 2002). These uneven infrastructure investments have had long-term implications. Decades later, areas once denied proper sanitation still struggle with heightened public health risks, which are now amplified by climate-induced flooding and water scarcity. Environmental modifications made for colonial economic gain often heightened disaster risks for the future. In coastal cities such as Beira and Maputo, for example, colonial port expansions and harbour dredging disrupted natural coastal processes, reducing the buffering capacity of mangroves and wetlands against storm surges and sea-level rise (Brown et al., 2014). These engineered landscapes, though beneficial to colonial trade, left behind degraded ecosystems that modern city planners must now grapple with in an era of intensifying climate hazards. In summary, colonial urban planning bequeathed Southern Africa not only segregated social geographies but also distorted urban ecosystems. The combination of racially biased service provision and environmentally insensitive infrastructure development under colonial rule created urban landscapes where risk is unevenly distributed, a legacy that post-colonial governments would find challenging to reverse.

3.4 Post-colonial Urban Growth and Informality

The transition to independence in the mid-twentieth century brought political liberation to most Southern African countries, but it did not immediately transform urban spatial structures or development logics. Colonial institutions such as municipal authorities, land titling systems, and zoning laws were largely retained after independence, limiting the scope for structural reform in how cities were managed (Watson, 2009; Parnell & Pieterse, 2010). New governments faced immense pressures: rapid rural-to-urban migration, limited financial resources, and high public expectations for improved service delivery and housing. In many cases, cities began to grow faster than the state's capacity to plan or provide, leading to an explosion of informal settlements on the urban periphery (Turok, 2016; Satterthwaite et al., 2020). Indeed, urban population growth rates in Southern Africa have consistently exceeded 4% per year since the 1970s, with much of this growth occurring in informal or peri-urban areas (UN-Habitat, 2020).

The post-independence decades saw a dramatic expansion of unplanned urban neighbourhoods. In Harare, Zimbabwe, during the 1980s and 1990s, for example, efforts to keep up with housing demand, through site-and-service schemes and public housing projects fell short of the need. This gap resulted in a proliferation of informal housing areas on the city's periphery (Kamete, 2006). Similarly, in Maputo, Mozambique, population pressure combined with weak urban land management led to the expansion of bairros (informal neighbourhoods) in low-lying zones that are vulnerable to flooding and lack proper waste disposal (Jenkins, 2013). Across the region, cities like Lusaka, Gaborone, and Windhoek also experienced rapid informal growth as low-income migrants settled wherever land was available, often without secure tenure or infrastructure.

Informality is often misunderstood as a "failure" of planning, but it is better viewed as a *consequence* of rigid planning systems, exclusionary land markets, and governance shortfalls (Roy, 2005; Huchzermeyer, 2011). The reality is that the majority of the urban poor in Southern Africa cannot afford formal housing or navigate bureaucratic land titling processes. As a result, they have little choice but to occupy unregulated areas where basic services are absent or unreliable. Critically, these informal settlements tend to be located in environmentally hazardous areas like floodplains, unstable hillsides, or deforested urban fringes, resulting in elevated disaster risk for their residents (Douglas et al., 2008; Smit & Parnell, 2012). While such locations often offer proximity to jobs in the city, their marginalisation from infrastructure networks (like storm drains, roads, and electricity grids) and from early warning systems means communities are highly exposed to climate-related hazards. Post-colonial governments, struggling with limited resources and sometimes fragmented institutional authority, have often been unable to systematically improve conditions in informal settlements. This has cemented a pattern where urban informality and vulnerability go hand in hand—a direct legacy of the unmet urban planning and equity challenges carried over from the colonial era. The growth of these settlements underscores the urgent need for more inclusive urban planning approaches that can accommodate population growth without perpetuating risk (Table 3.1).

3.5 Urban Disaster Risk in Historical Perspective

The evolution of disaster risk in Southern African cities is inextricably linked to historical patterns of urbanisation, governance, and inequality. Urban vulnerability to hazards is a product of these socio-economic and institutional factors, not just of natural event frequency (Adger, 2006). Historically, disasters have not only been natural phenomena but also socially constructed events; their impacts are shaped by who and what is exposed, the fragility of infrastructure, and the capacity (or lack thereof) of urban institutions to respond effectively (Wisner et al., 2004; Pelling, 2003). In the colonial era, urban disasters were often viewed through a racialised lens. For example, flooding in African townships might be dismissed by colonial authorities as a "hygiene" or discipline problem rather than recognised as a failure of infrastructure planning. This led to punitive responses, such as forced evictions of affected communities, rather than structural investments to reduce risk (Parnell, 1992). The colonial state's selective concern for white-settler areas meant that disaster preparedness and resilient infrastructure were concentrated in elite zones, reinforcing patterns of exclusion (Beall et al., 2002).

In the late apartheid period and early post-independence era, disasters continued to expose these urban inequalities. The 1987 floods in Durban displaced thousands of people living in informal settlements along the

Table 3.1 A comparison between colonial-era urban planning models and post-independence urban development in Southern African cities, highlighting persistent structural inequalities

Colonial Era	*Post-Independence*
Racial Segregation	Unregulated Growth
Infrastructure for Elites	Informal settlements
Planned Spatial inequality	Governance challenges

Source: Authors (2025)

Umgeni River; yet instead of relocating these communities to safer areas, authorities allowed many to rebuild in the same flood-prone locations, perpetuating a cycle of vulnerability (Maharaj, 1997). During the 2000s, major events underscored the region's risk disparities. In 2000, for instance, the Limpopo River floods displaced over 100,000 people across Mozambique, Zimbabwe, and South Africa, most of them from informal settlements with inadequate protective infrastructure (Kellett & Caravani, 2013).

More recently, Cyclone Idai in March 2019 became one of the worst disasters on record in Southern Africa, vividly illustrating the compounding effects of hazard exposure and urban vulnerability. Idai made landfall near the Mozambican city of Beira and ravaged parts of Mozambique, Zimbabwe, and Malawi, killing over 1,000 people and affecting an estimated 3 million others (IFRC, 2019). The cyclone's intense winds and heavy rains caused catastrophic flooding, breaching informal levees, and obliterating poorly constructed homes. Entire neighbourhoods in Beira, many of them informal or low-income areas on low-lying land, were destroyed or submerged. The humanitarian crisis that followed, including disease outbreaks, highlighted how cities with weak infrastructure and social safety nets suffer disproportionately in extreme events.

In addition to weather-related calamities, public health crises have also underscored urban risk patterns. In Harare, Zimbabwe, recurring cholera outbreaks (notably in 2008–2009 and again in the 2010s) were linked to the failure of water supply and sanitation systems in the city's high-density townships. These outbreaks, which caused thousands of cases and numerous fatalities, reflect both infrastructural decay and the long-standing neglect of peripheral, impoverished neighbourhoods (Chigudu, 2020). Such health disasters reveal that "slow" or chronic stresses in cities, like inadequate water infrastructure, can swiftly turn into acute crises, especially where governance is weak.

The historical neglect of risk-sensitive planning is compounded by persistently weak land-use regulation and disaster governance in many Southern African cities. Building codes and environmental zoning laws are often outdated or poorly enforced. For instance, despite the existence of formal urban planning frameworks in cities like Lusaka and Maputo, informal (and unsafe) construction continues unabated in high-risk zones due to factors such as bureaucratic inertia, political patronage, or corruption (Goodfellow, 2014; Jenkins, 2013). Past experiences of state-led evictions and forced removals have also created deep mistrust between many urban communities and government authorities. This mistrust can hamper disaster risk reduction efforts: residents may be reluctant to evacuate during storms or to participate in risk assessments, fearing that authorities might use these as pretexts for demolition or relocation (Archer et al., 2014; Huchzermeyer, 2011). Furthermore, when disasters do occur, the *recovery trajectories* are often unequal. In cities like Johannesburg and Durban, access to insurance or financial resources means that middle and upper-income neighbourhoods can recover relatively quickly, whereas poorer informal settlements may languish for long periods without full reconstruction (Roberts et al., 2012; Ziervogel, 2019). This uneven resilience in the aftermath of disasters serves to further entrench historical inequalities. Overall, the historical perspective reveals that urban "natural" disasters in Southern Africa are deeply conditioned by human decisions: where people live, how cities are built, and who has the resources to cope. Reducing risk, therefore, requires addressing these underlying socio-spatial and governance factors that have been woven into the fabric of cities over time.

3.6 Governance Transitions and Disaster Risk Management

Governance, the structures, processes, and institutions through which decisions are made and implemented, plays a central role in shaping urban resilience and disaster risk reduction. In Southern Africa, the transitions in governance since independence have varied across countries, yet they share common challenges of institutional fragmentation, limited fiscal capacity, and uneven decentralisation (Pieterse & Parnell, 2014; UN-Habitat, 2020). In the immediate post-independence period, many states retained centralised control over urban planning and service delivery. While this model sometimes provided policy coherence from the top, it often stifled local innovation and accountability. For example, Zimbabwe's Urban Councils Act of 1973 remained largely unchanged after independence in 1980, which meant that the powers of city authorities like Harare City Council were still tightly circumscribed by the central government, entrenching bureaucratic inertia and slow responses to new urban challenges (Kamete, 2006). Similarly, in Mozambique, municipal governments historically lacked the autonomy and resources to implement integrated DRR strategies, relying heavily on directives (and financial support) from national ministries and international donors (Jenkins, 2013; IFRC, 2019).

Decentralisation reforms introduced in the 1990s and 2000s aimed to empower local governments across the region. In theory, devolving authority would enable cities to take the lead in development planning and disaster response, tailoring solutions to local needs. However, in practice, decentralisation has often been uneven and sometimes superficial. In cities like *Lusaka* and *Gaborone*, for instance, local councils still lack control over critical urban functions such as land allocation, waste management, and housing approvals. These powers remain vested in national ministries or parastatal agencies (Goodfellow, 2014; Cirolia, 2017). As a result, local governments can be hamstrung in addressing the very issues, such as informal settlement upgrading or land-use enforcement, that are key to reduce disaster risks. Furthermore, the institutional architecture for DRR in many Southern African cities is fragmented across multiple departments and sectors, with little coordination. Emergency services, environmental management units, public health departments, and infrastructure agencies may operate in silos, resulting in duplicated efforts or even conflicting mandates. This lack of integrated urban risk governance can lead to delays or gaps during crises. For example, in Harare, the absence of a unified disaster management platform among city departments contributed to an ineffectual response to recurrent urban flooding and cholera outbreaks (Chigudu, 2020).

Governance capacity at the municipal level is also undermined by resource constraints. Many city governments operate with inadequate budgets, limited access to climate finance, and shortages of skilled personnel. These limitations severely restrict their ability to invest in risk-reducing infrastructure (like drainage or reinforced housing), to enforce building regulations in fast-growing informal areas, or to conduct community outreach and preparedness programs (Satterthwaite et al., 2020; Roberts et al., 2012). The result is often a reliance on reactive disaster responses (frequently with help from national agencies or international NGOs) rather than proactive risk mitigation, planned and led by the city.

Despite these challenges, there are promising signs of governance innovation in the region. Some cities have begun to break down silos and adopt more collaborative approaches. Durban (eThekwini Municipality in South Africa), for example, developed a cross-sectoral climate adaptation program in the 2000s that explicitly integrates DRR into urban development planning, bringing together departments of housing, drainage, and environmental management (Roberts & Diederichs, 2002). Cape Town has invested in partnerships for knowledge co-production with universities and civil society to improve climate risk data and planning capacity, which has informed its resilience strategies (Ziervogel, 2019). These examples demonstrate that, even within constrained institutional settings, leadership and inclusive planning processes can enhance resilience outcomes. Scaling up such initiatives across Southern African cities will require deeper reforms in urban governance: strengthened mandates and resources for local governments, clearer vertical coordination between municipal, provincial, and national levels, and better mobilisation of both domestic revenue and international support for urban risk reduction. In essence, the governance transition story in Southern Africa's cities is one of slow progress with pockets of innovation. Overcoming the historical legacy of centralised, exclusionary, and fragmented governance is crucial for enabling more effective and equitable disaster risk management in the future.

3.7 Continuities and Transformations in Urban Vulnerability

Urban vulnerability in Southern Africa today reflects a mix of historical continuities and emerging dynamics. On the one hand, colonial and apartheid-era spatial configurations remain deeply entrenched in the urban landscape; on the other, new processes such as climate change, worsening inequality, and global economic shifts are introducing additional layers of complexity to urban risk profiles.

3.7.1 Historical Continuities

As discussed earlier, the geography of vulnerability in most Southern African cities still mirrors the inequitable spatial arrangements laid down during the colonial and apartheid periods. Informal settlements and low-income townships continue to occupy environmentally marginal areas—floodplains, steep slopes, and reclaimed wetlands—while more affluent (often formerly white) suburbs enjoy better infrastructure, services, and institutional support (Watson, 2009; Satterthwaite et al., 2020). In Johannesburg, for example, the spatial legacy of apartheid is visible in the persistence of peripheral townships such as Soweto and Alexandra, which remain relatively disconnected from the city's economic hubs and major transport networks (Turok & Scheba, 2019). These areas, originally established under segregation, still struggle with inadequate services and higher exposure to hazards like flooding and fire.

Land tenure insecurity also remains a significant source of vulnerability. In cities like Harare and Maputo, residents of informal settlements live with the constant threat of eviction or relocation. This insecurity discourages them from investing in home improvements or community infrastructure that could reduce disaster risk (Huchzermeyer, 2011; Jenkins, 2013). A shack dweller is unlikely to build a robust house or install proper drainage if they fear the settlement may be demolished. Lack of formal recognition by authorities often excludes these communities from official municipal planning and emergency response systems. They may be literally off the map when it comes to early warning or infrastructure upgrade plans.

Moreover, institutional mistrust, rooted in histories of forced removals, service neglect, and authoritarian governance, continues to undermine efforts to build urban resilience. In many cities, there is wariness and scepticism among marginalised communities towards government initiatives. Residents who have experienced or learned of past injustices may suspect ulterior motives if asked to relocate from a dangerous site or to participate in a new planning project. As noted, communities are sometimes reluctant to evacuate during disasters or to cooperate with officials due to fear that temporary evacuations could become permanent displacements (Mitlin, 2008; Archer et al., 2014). This distrust is a major barrier to inclusive DRR and climate adaptation strategies. Overcoming it requires long-term confidence-building and genuine power-sharing with local residents in decision-making.

Many vulnerabilities in Southern African cities today are path-dependent—they follow the tracks laid by history. The social and spatial marginalisation engineered in the past has proven stubbornly persistent. Any serious attempt to reduce urban disaster risk must therefore grapple with these historical continuities: the entrenched poverty in certain locations, the enduring service deficits, and the fraught state–society relations that complicate interventions.

3.7.2 Emerging Urban Risks

While the historical roots of vulnerability remain significant, new and intensifying risks have emerged in recent decades. Chief among these is climate change, which is amplifying the frequency and severity of natural hazards affecting cities. Southern Africa is experiencing rising average temperatures, more erratic rainfall patterns, and a greater incidence of extreme weather events—trends documented by climate scientists and already observable on the ground (IPCC, 2022; Ziervogel et al., 2017). These changes exacerbate existing challenges such as water scarcity, infrastructure stress, and vector-borne diseases in urban areas. Coastal cities face higher risks of storm surges and flooding due to sea-level rise, while interior cities see increased heatwaves and sudden heavy downpours that their drainage systems were never designed to handle. For example, Lusaka's rainy seasons have become more unpredictable; the mushrooming of informal settlements along the city's natural drainage channels in recent years has worsened flood impacts, as intense rains overwhelm an outdated sewer and drainage system (Mususa, 2012). In Windhoek, recurring droughts and rising temperatures compound water shortages, which are made worse by the city's sprawling low-density development and limited investment in alternative water sources (Schreiner & Baleta, 2015).

Urbanisation itself, in its current form, is becoming a risk factor. The uncontrolled expansion of peri-urban areas without proper planning oversight or infrastructure provision is creating entirely new zones of vulnerability at the metropolitan fringe. These are places that perhaps were rural or open land 20 years ago but are now densely populated informal suburbs with little stormwater infrastructure or health services. Such areas can become flashpoints for disaster when a cyclone strikes or a disease spreads, as they lack the buffers that more established urban neighbourhoods might have. Socio-economic inequality has also, in many cases, deepened or at least remained stark in African cities since the 1990s. Issues like high youth unemployment, the growth of informal employment, and underinvestment in public services are contributing to urban unrest and eroding social cohesion (Pieterse & Parnell, 2014). These conditions create a "risk accumulation" process, where multiple economic, social, and environmental vulnerabilities interact and intensify over time (Birkmann et al., 2013). For instance, a community that is economically marginalised, politically excluded, and living in an ecologically sensitive location faces compounded risks, that is more than the sum of its parts.

At the same time, technological shifts are offering new tools for risk reduction—but not uniformly so. Advances in digital technology, such as remote sensing, GIS mapping, and mobile phone networks, have made it possible to map risks and communicate warnings in real time like never before. Cities can potentially leverage satellite data to identify flood-prone zones or use SMS networks to alert citizens of impending hazards. However, the *digital divide* in Southern Africa means these technologies are often least accessible to those who need them most. The poorest residents may not have smartphones or reliable Internet, and data about informal areas may be scarce. If not deliberately made inclusive, high-tech approaches to DRR can inadvertently reinforce existing inequalities (Brown et al., 2014; UN-Habitat, 2020). An early warning app, for example, is of little use to a settlement with no electricity or network coverage. Thus, bridging information and technology gaps is itself an emerging challenge to ensure that modern methods benefit all segments of urban society.

The COVID-19 pandemic of 2020 exposed and exacerbated urban vulnerabilities in new ways. Pandemic lockdowns and economic disruptions hit informal workers and the urban poor especially hard since they lack savings and social protection. High-density informal settlements struggled with implementing public health measures like social distancing or frequent handwashing, due to overcrowded housing and inadequate water supply. The limited healthcare infrastructure in many city townships meant that outbreaks were harder to control, and trust issues sometimes led communities to be wary of government health interventions. The pandemic has reignited debates around the importance of social safety nets, housing quality, and universal basic services in building urban resilience (Satterthwaite et al., 2020). It underscored that resilience is multidimensional; a city must be able to withstand not only environmental shocks but also health crises and economic downturns. This has brought renewed attention to integrated risk governance that addresses both chronic stresses and acute shocks in tandem.

3.8 Implications for Disaster Risk Reduction and Sustainable Urban Planning Today

The historical evolution of urbanisation and disaster vulnerability in Southern Africa presents both lessons and imperatives for present and future urban planning. As cities across the region continue to grow, often in precarious, unplanned ways, disaster risk reduction (DRR) cannot remain an afterthought. It must be embedded as a core function of urban planning, governance, and development finance. The following implications and strategies emerge from the historical context and case studies discussed:

3.8.1 *Integrating DRR into Urban Planning Systems*

A critical implication is the need for proactive integration of DRR into statutory urban planning frameworks. Urban planners should incorporate multi-hazard risk assessments into city development plans from the outset, rather than reacting to disasters after they occur. This involves updating zoning regulations, building codes, and master plans to account for the known spectrum of risks—floods, cyclones, droughts, landslides, fires—and for future climate variability and ecosystem changes (UN-Habitat, 2016; Roberts et al., 2012). In practice, risk-informed planning could mean designating high-risk zones (for example, floodplains, unstable slopes) as no-build or limited development areas, or mandating that any structures built there have special reinforcements and mitigation features. It also means investing in nature-based solutions, for example, preserving wetlands within and around cities to serve as natural sponges for floodwaters, or maintaining green belts that can reduce the urban heat island effect and absorb runoff. Infrastructure design standards should be revisited with resilience in mind, ensuring that roads, bridges, drainage, and public facilities can withstand the kinds of extreme events that are increasingly likely.

However, integration on paper is not enough without robust implementation on the ground. A recurring theme in Southern Africa is the gap between plans and enforcement. Many municipalities lack the resources, technical skills, or political backing to enforce DRR-sensitive regulations, especially in informal or low-income areas where the need is greatest. Therefore, national governments and development partners must invest in *institutional strengthening* and capacity-building for local authorities (Goodfellow, 2014; Satterthwaite et al., 2020). This could include training city planners and engineers in climate adaptation and DRR, increasing budget allocations for enforcement operations, and creating mechanisms for community monitoring of land-use changes. Decentralising financial resources to municipalities (fiscal devolution) is also crucial so that cities can fund small-scale mitigation projects like drainage improvements or slope stabilisation in vulnerable neighbourhoods. Without empowered and well-equipped city governments, even the most progressive policies will remain unfulfilled aspirations. Integrating DRR into urban planning must therefore be coupled with empowering local institutions to carry it out.

3.8.2 *Prioritising Informality and Equity*

Given that the majority of urban growth in Southern Africa is occurring in informal settlements, DRR strategies must be designed with informality at the centre, not as an adjunct. This requires rethinking planning tools and engagement models to suit the fluid, complex environments of informal neighbourhoods, where formal data is often lacking and land tenure is insecure (Watson, 2009; Patel et al., 2015). One implication is that cities should shift from viewing informal settlements solely as problems to be eradicated, and instead work with these communities as partners in building resilience. Innovative, flexible approaches can significantly reduce risk while also building trust between residents and the government. For example, community-led risk mapping exercises can help identify local hazard hotspots (blocked drainage channels, eroded embankments) that outsiders might overlook. Incremental upgrading initiatives, improving pathways, adding flood defences or retaining walls bit by bit, can make a tangible difference in reducing everyday risks. Co-production of infrastructure, where communities contribute labour or local knowledge and authorities provide technical support or materials, has shown success in some instances (Archer et al., 2014; Ziervogel et al., 2017). These approaches not only reduce risk but also empower residents and incorporate their priorities. They should be supported by policies like tenure regularisation (to give residents more security and incentive to invest in safer construction), targeted public investment in informal areas, and legal protections against forced eviction. Preventing evictions is important because displacing communities without adequate alternatives often just shifts and exacerbates vulnerability, as historical evidence shows.

Urban risk governance must also prioritise social equity and inclusion across various dimensions. As history has demonstrated, women, children, the elderly, people with disabilities, and other marginalised groups often face disproportionate risks and barriers in disasters. Any resilience-building program should ensure these groups have a voice and receive targeted support. For instance, early warning systems need to reach everyone, including those who might not be literate or who may not have access to smartphones, possibly through multiple communication channels like radio, community volunteers, and visual signals. Disaster response plans should account for the needs of those who cannot easily evacuate without assistance (the elderly or disabled). Including women and youth in community disaster committees can improve the responsiveness of plans, as they bring different perspectives and knowledge of community dynamics. Studies have shown that gender and social inclusion are central to effective DRR: women's empowerment in particular correlates with improved community resilience and quicker recovery (Bradshaw, 2013). Thus, building resilience is not just about physical infrastructure but also about social infrastructure—the networks and capacities of diverse community members to act collectively. Programs that enhance literacy, provide leadership training, or support savings groups in informal settlements can indirectly bolster resilience by strengthening the community's ability to organise and respond. In summary, making equity a cornerstone of DRR means that reducing the risks of the most vulnerable populations is treated as a top priority, not an afterthought. By addressing historical inequities—whether they be spatial (slums vs. suburbs) or social (marginalised groups)—cities will be safer and more resilient for everyone.

3.8.3 Leveraging Data and Technology

Rapid advances in technology offer new opportunities to strengthen urban DRR, but these tools must be harnessed thoughtfully and inclusively. Geospatial analytics, satellite imagery, and AI-driven modelling can greatly improve urban risk assessment and planning. For example, high-resolution satellite data and drone imagery can help map floodplains and informal settlements to a degree of detail not possible before, identifying where exactly interventions are needed. Early warning systems for floods or cyclones can now rely on sophisticated weather forecasting models and broad networks of sensors, potentially providing more lead time and precise information. City planners can use GIS-based simulations to test how different development scenarios might impact runoff or heat distribution. However, to ensure that these technologies benefit the most vulnerable, they should be integrated with participatory methods and made accessible through open data platforms and inclusive communication channels (Brown et al., 2014). An open-source risk map that community members can view and update, for instance, can empower local groups to advocate for action in high-risk areas. Likewise, if a city deploys an SMS alert system for disasters, it should be in local languages and consider the literacy levels of the recipients.

Crowd-sourced data and community science are also valuable resources for DRR. Residents equipped with simple tools (even just mobile phones) can collect information on rainfall, blocked drains, or building damages, which, when aggregated, provide real-time situational awareness to authorities. Such approaches have been used in some cities to complement official data, especially in informal settlements where official monitoring may be absent. Investments in digital literacy and community training are essential alongside the hardware and software. If a flood warning app is rolled out, communities need to be trained on how to interpret and act on the warnings. If digital platforms are used for reporting issues, people need to trust that their input will be heard and used. Bridging the digital divide might involve creating physical "resilience hubs" in informal settlements equipped with Internet access, where community members can receive training, access early warnings, and coordinate responses. It also involves ensuring data is used ethically and transparently, for instance, that mapping informal areas doesn't lead to punitive actions against those communities, but rather to support.

Overall, leveraging data and technology can greatly enhance the precision and timeliness of urban DRR, a significant upgrade from the historical situation where cities often had to react blindly or based on anecdotal information. However, technology is a means, not an end. Its success will depend on effective governance (as discussed) and on empowering people to make use of information. When modern tools are combined with local knowledge and buy-in, they can help cities anticipate and manage risks far better than in the past. The key is to make sure these innovations are applied in the service of reducing vulnerability, not just producing elegant data that sits on a shelf.

3.8.4 *Planning for Transformation, Not Just Risk Reduction*

Finally, it is important to frame disaster risk reduction not only as a technical effort to manage hazards, but as part of a broader transformative agenda for Southern African cities. The ultimate goal is not merely to prevent losses from disasters, but to build cities that are more equitable, inclusive, and environmentally sustainable. This requires linking DRR with broader movements and frameworks such as climate change adaptation, *just transitions* (shifting to sustainable economies in a way that is fair and inclusive), and the "right to the city", which emphasises social justice in urban development (Parnell & Pieterse, 2010; Bulkeley, 2013). In practical terms, this means DRR strategies should simultaneously aim to tackle the structural drivers of risk that we have identified in this chapter: inequality, exclusion, weak governance, and ecological decline. For instance, relocating a flood-prone informal settlement to safer ground should also be seen as an opportunity to provide better housing and services to that community, thereby addressing social rights as well as physical safety. Upgrading drainage infrastructure can be labour-intensive. Cities could design such projects to create local jobs and build skills, contributing to poverty reduction. Restoring an urban wetland for flood mitigation also creates green space that can improve the quality of life and biodiversity.

Urban resilience-building efforts must go beyond reactive emergency response and incremental fixes. They should be integrated into a vision of urban transformation that challenges the legacy of spatial injustice. This might involve, for example, rethinking public transportation and land use together so that low-income communities are no longer isolated and can access opportunities, which in turn boosts their resilience. It also means pursuing climate justice, ensuring that the burdens of climate change and the benefits of resilience investments are shared fairly, given that those who pollute least (the urban poor) often suffer the most from climate impacts. Cities need to mobilise financing mechanisms that support pro-poor adaptation, such as community climate funds or subsidised insurance schemes for vulnerable groups. In academia and policy, concepts like *transformative adaptation* are gaining traction, recognising that incremental changes will not be sufficient if climate extremes continue to intensify (Pelling, 2011; Leichenko, 2011). For Southern African cities, transformation could mean redesigning urban layouts to undo apartheid spatial patterns (for example, creating affordable housing in well-located areas), aggressively pursuing renewable energy and decentralised services to make infrastructure more resilient and accessible, and institutionalising participatory governance so that communities drive the changes that affect them.

Effective DRR in the region should be seen as a catalyst for positive urban change. Rather than a narrow field concerned only with hazards, it overlaps with and supports goals of sustainable development, economic resilience, and social justice. The history we have examined shows that the cost of not taking this integrated view, past urban planning that ignored risk and equity, led to the problems we face now. Thus, planning for the future must internalise those lessons and aim for transformation. Only by addressing the root causes of vulnerability can Southern African cities break the cycle of disaster–rebuild–disaster and instead move towards a more resilient and prosperous trajectory.

3.9 Conclusion

The trajectory of urban development in Southern Africa is deeply shaped by a legacy of spatial injustice, systemic inequality, and institutional fragility. From pre-colonial settlements rooted in environmental harmony, through colonial regimes marked by racial and spatial exclusion, to post-independence urbanisation defined by informality and rapid, unregulated growth, each era has profoundly influenced the production, distribution, and management of disaster risk. These historical patterns have entrenched vulnerabilities, particularly among marginalised urban populations who continue to bear the brunt of hazards due to inadequate infrastructure, weak governance, and spatial segregation. Contemporary challenges such as climate change, demographic pressures, and evolving political landscapes further compound this complexity. These emerging dynamics test the capacity of current urban systems and demand a shift from reactive to anticipatory approaches in disaster risk reduction (DRR) and sustainable urban planning. Addressing these intertwined issues calls for a paradigm shift in how cities are conceived, governed, and financed. Planners and policymakers must move beyond technocratic responses, embracing historically informed, inclusive strategies that actively dismantle the root causes of risk.

Central to this transformation is the empowerment of vulnerable communities. Their lived experiences, local knowledge, and engagement are vital for designing contextually relevant, socially just, and adaptive solutions. Urban resilience, therefore, must be anchored in both equity and participation. As this chapter has illustrated, history is not simply a backdrop to urban risk; it is a dynamic force that continues to shape contemporary vulnerabilities and governance responses. Acknowledging and learning from this history is imperative for Southern African cities to break persistent cycles of exclusion and risk. Moving forward, bridging the gap between policy intent and practical implementation will be key to ensuring that resilience and development are not competing goals, but mutually reinforcing imperatives in the pursuit of safer, more just urban futures.

References

Adger, W. N. (2006). Vulnerability. *Global Environmental Change, 16*(3), 268–281.

Archer, D., Davilla, J., & Peel, C. (2014). Knowing your city: Community profiling and the right to the city. *Environment and Urbanization, 26*(1), 235–250.

Beall, J., Crankshaw, O., & Parnell, S. (2002). *Uniting a divided city: Governance and social exclusion in Johannesburg*. Earthscan.

Birkmann, J., Cardona, O. D., Carreño, M. L., Barbat, A. H., Pelling, M., Schneiderbauer, S., Kienberger, S., Keiler, M., Alexander, D., Zeil, P., & Welle, T. (2013). Framing vulnerability, risk and societal responses: the MOVE framework. *Natural Hazards, 67*, 193–211.

Bradshaw, S. (2013). *Gender, development and disasters*. Edward Elgar Publishing.

Brown, D., McGranahan, G., & Dodman, D. (2014). *Urban informality and building a more inclusive, resilient and green economy*. IIED Working Paper. IIED.

Bulkeley, H. (2013). Climate change and urban governance: A new politics? In *Routledge international handbook of social and environmental change*. Routledge.

Chigudu, S. (2020). *The political life of an epidemic: Cholera, crisis and citizenship in Zimbabwe*. Cambridge University Press.

Christopher, A. J. (1994). *The atlas of apartheid*. Routledge.

Cirolia, L. R. (2017). Fractured fiscal authority and fragmented infrastructures: Financing urban development in Cape Town. *Urban Forum, 28*(3), 291–307.

Douglas, I., Alam, K., Maghenda, M., McDonnell, Y., McLean, L., & Campbell, J. (2008). Unjust waters: Climate change, flooding and the urban poor in Africa. *Environment and Urbanization, 20*(1), 187–205.

Freund, B. (2007). *The African city: A history*. Cambridge University Press.

Goodfellow, T. (2014). The institutionalisation of "noise" and "silence" in urban politics: Development booms in Kampala and Kigali. *Cities, 36*, 248–255.

Hall, M. (1987). *The changing past: Farmers, kings and traders in Southern Africa 200–1860*. David Philip.

Home, R. (1997). Of planting and planning: The making of British colonial Durban. *Journal of Southern African Studies, 23*(3), 457–470.

Huchzermeyer, M. (2011). *Cities with 'Slums': From informal settlement eradication to a right to the city in Africa*. UCT Press.

IFRC. (2019). *Mozambique: Cyclone Idai emergency appeal, operational update*. International Federation of Red Cross and Red Crescent Societies. IFRC.

IPCC. (2022). *Climate change 2022: Impacts, adaptation and vulnerability*. Contribution of Working Group II to the Sixth Assessment Report. Cambridge University Press.

Jenkins, P. (2013). *Urbanization, urbanism, and urbanity in an African City: Home spaces and house cultures*. Palgrave Macmillan.

Kamete, A. Y. (2006). The return of the jekemu: Governance and unofficial urban development in Harare, Zimbabwe. *Habitat International, 30*(4), 101–111.

Kellett, J., & Caravani, A. (2013). *Financing disaster risk reduction: A 20 year story of international aid*. ODI.

Leichenko, R. (2011). Climate change and urban resilience. *Current Opinion in Environmental Sustainability, 3*(3), 164–168.

Mabin, A., & Smit, D. (1997). Reconstructing South Africa's cities? The making of urban planning 1900–2000. *Urban Studies, 34*(8), 1431–1453.

Maharaj, B. (1997). Apartheid, urban segregation, and the local state: Durban and the Group Areas Act. *Urban Studies, 34*(3), 385–406.

Mamdani, M. (1996). *Citizen and subject: Contemporary Africa and the legacy of late colonialism*. Princeton University Press.

Mitlin, D. (2008). With and beyond the state: Co-production as a route to political influence, power and transformation for grassroots organizations. *Environment and Urbanization, 20*(2), 339–360.

Mususa, P. (2012). Contested urbanism in Lusaka: Community, political identity and housing. *Urban Forum, 23*(1), 33–47.

Myers, G. (2003). *Verandahs of power: Colonialism and space in urban Africa*. Syracuse University Press.

Myers, G. (2011). *African cities: Alternative visions of urban theory and practice*. Zed Books.

Parnell, S. (1992). Johannesburg's sanitization: The racial basis of municipal health policy in the 1920s. *Journal of Southern African Studies, 18*(3), 591–602.

Parnell, S., & Pieterse, E. (2010). The "right to the city": Institutional imperatives of a developmental state. *Urban Forum, 21*(3), 253–268.

Parnell, S., & Robinson, J. (2012). (Re)theorizing cities from the Global South: Looking beyond neoliberalism. *Urban Geography, 33*(4), 593–617.

Patel, S., Baptist, C., & D'Cruz, C. (2015). Knowledge is power—Informal communities assert their right to the city through SDI and community-led enumerations. *Environment and Urbanization, 27*(2), 271–291.

Pelling, M. (2003). *The vulnerability of cities: Natural disasters and social resilience*. Earthscan.

Pelling, M. (2011). *Adaptation to climate change: From resilience to transformation*. Routledge.

Pieterse, E., & Parnell, S. (2014). *Africa's urban revolution*. Zed Books.

Roberts, D., & Diederichs, N. (2002). Durban's climate protection programme: Tackling climate change in a South African city. *Environment and Urbanization, 14*(1), 175–184.

Roberts, D., Boon, R., Diederichs, N., Douwes, E., Govender, N., Mcinnes, A., Mclean, C., O'Donoghue, S., & Spires, M. (2012). Exploring ecosystem-based adaptation in Durban, South Africa: "Learning-by-doing" at the local government coal face. *Environment and Urbanization, 24*(1), 167–195.

Roy, A. (2005). Urban informality: Toward an epistemology of planning. *Journal of the American Planning Association, 71*(2), 147–158.

Satterthwaite, D., Archer, D., Colenbrander, S., Dodman, D., Hardoy, J., Mitlin, D., & Patel, S. (2020). Building resilience to climate change in informal settlements. *One Earth, 2*(2), 143–156.

Schreiner, B., & Baleta, H. (2015). Broadening water security in South Africa. *Water Policy, 17*(6), 1405–1424.

Showers, K. B. (2005). *Imperial Gullies: Soil erosion and conservation in Lesotho*. Ohio University Press.

Simone, A. (2004). *For the city yet to come: Changing African life in four cities*. Duke University Press.

Smit, W., & Parnell, S. (2012). Urban sustainability and human health: An African perspective. *Current Opinion in Environmental Sustainability, 4*(4), 443–450.

Tshiguvho, T. (2008). Indigenous knowledge systems: Weather and climate. In R. Davis (Ed.), *Climate risk and vulnerability: A handbook for Southern Africa*. Cape Town.

Turok, I. (2016). South Africa's new urban agenda: Transformation or compensation? *Local Economy, 31*(1–2), 9–27.

Turok, I., & Scheba, A. (2019). "Corridors of freedom" and the transformation of Johannesburg. *Urban Forum, 30*(2), 191–214.

UN-Habitat. (2016). *New Urban Agenda* (Habitat III outcome document). United Nations.

UN-Habitat. (2020). *World Cities Report 2020: The value of sustainable urbanization*. United Nations.

Watson, V. (2009). The planned city sweeps the poor away: Urban planning and 21st century urbanization. *Development Southern Africa, 26*(1), 151–167.

Wisner, B., Blaikie, P., Cannon, T., & Davis, I. (2004). *At risk: Natural hazards, people's vulnerability and disasters* (2nd ed.). Routledge.

Ziervogel, G. (2019). Building transformative capacity for adaptation: Community hubs and public works in Cape Town, South Africa. *Ambio, 48*(5), 529–539.

Ziervogel, G., Pelling, M., Cartwright, A., Chu, E., Deshpande, T., Harris, L., et al. (2017). Inserting rights and justice into urban resilience: A focus on everyday risk. *Environment and Urbanization, 29*(1), 123–138.

CHAPTER 4

Disaster Risk Reduction in Urban Planning: Global Practices and Southern African Applications

4.1 Introduction

In an era of increasing climate variability, urbanisation, and socio-economic inequality, disaster risk reduction (DRR) has become a critical component of sustainable urban development. As urban centres expand, often into hazard-prone areas, so does the exposure of populations, infrastructure, and ecosystems to climate-related and anthropogenic hazards. Integrating DRR into urban planning offers a proactive pathway to mitigate the impacts of such hazards, protect livelihoods, and build resilience. Globally, there is growing recognition that risk is socially constructed, shaped not only by exposure to hazards but also by underlying vulnerabilities related to governance, land use, infrastructure, and social exclusion (. Effective DRR strategies must therefore be holistic, participatory, and embedded within urban development policies and practices. They must move beyond emergency response to encompass long-term risk-sensitive planning, inclusive infrastructure design, and institutional coordination (Pelling et al., 2018; Satterthwaite et al., 2020).

While Southern Africa faces distinct developmental and ecological challenges, valuable lessons can be drawn from global frameworks and best practices. This chapter reviews key international DRR strategies, highlights successful case studies, and identifies common principles that could inform locally appropriate models in the Southern African context. In

F. Mangara, N. Dorasamy, *Sustainable Urban Development in Southern Africa*, https://doi.org/10.1007/978-3-032-08286-2_4

doing so, it provides a foundation for policymakers, urban planners, and civil society to design integrated and transformative approaches to urban risk governance.

4.2 Global Frameworks for DRR and Urban Planning

Through several key international agreements and institutional mechanisms, disaster risk reduction has gained prominence in global development and urban policy. These frameworks have defined norms and goals and influenced national legislation, urban planning standards, and financing mechanisms.

4.2.1 The Hyogo and Sendai Frameworks

The Hyogo Framework for Action (2005–2015) was a pivotal global initiative that shifted DRR from a reactive model to a proactive, resilience-building agenda. Its major priorities include institutional strengthening, knowledge management, and providing a structured approach to mainstreaming risk reduction (UNISDR, 2005). While widely adopted, the Hyogo Framework was critiqued for its limited attention to urban risk and its lack of enforcement mechanisms (Twigg, 2015).

The Sendai Framework for Disaster Risk Reduction (2015–2030) succeeded Hyogo and remains the most comprehensive global policy on DRR. It emphasises four key priorities: (1) understanding disaster risk, (2) strengthening disaster governance, (3) investing in DRR for resilience, and (4) enhancing disaster preparedness for effective response and recovery (UNDRR, 2015). Importantly, Sendai aligns DRR with sustainable development and climate adaptation, recognising that rapid urbanisation is a key risk driver. The Sendai Framework encourages integration across policy domains, including land-use planning, housing, and infrastructure investment. For example, Sendai's Priority 3 urges countries to promote risk-sensitive investments in critical infrastructure, housing, and services. This shift towards integrated resilience reflects a growing awareness that disasters are not merely "natural" events but also failures of governance, planning, and investment (Lavell & Maskrey, 2014; Leichenko, 2011).

4.2.2 *The Sustainable Development Goals (SDGs)*

The 2030 Agenda for Sustainable Development positions DRR at the heart of global development. Several Sustainable Development Goals, especially SDG 11 (Sustainable Cities and Communities), explicitly call for risk reduction and resilience-building. Target 11.5, for instance, aims to significantly reduce the number of deaths and the economic losses caused by disasters, focusing on protecting the poor and vulnerable (United Nations, 2015). SDG 13 (Climate Action) complements these efforts by promoting climate adaptation and risk-informed development. The SDGs and the Sendai Framework create a synergistic global agenda for integrating DRR into urban policy and practice. Many countries have responded by incorporating DRR into their national development plans, climate adaptation strategies, and urban resilience frameworks (Carabine, 2015; Satterthwaite et al., 2020).

However, implementation on the ground remains a challenge. Many low- and middle-income countries lack the institutional capacity, financial resources, and technical expertise to translate global commitments into actionable urban strategies. Moreover, data limitations and fragmented governance often hinder risk assessments and the formulation of risk-sensitive land use plans (Dodman et al., 2013; Roberts et al., 2012). These gaps highlight the importance of capacity-building and international support to achieve the DRR-related targets of the SDGs in urban areas.

4.2.3 *The New Urban Agenda*

Adopted at the United Nations Conference on Housing and Sustainable Urban Development (Habitat III) in 2016, the New Urban Agenda (NUA) reinforces the principles of inclusive, safe, resilient, and sustainable cities. It acknowledges that resilience must be integrated across sectors and scales, from infrastructure planning to participatory governance (UN-Habitat, 2016). The NUA specifically calls for "urban and territorial planning that incorporates disaster risk reduction and climate change considerations", and it advocates the adoption of spatial development strategies that prioritise social justice and ecological sustainability. In line with this mandate, many global cities have revised their planning codes and urban development policies to include hazard mapping, early warning systems, and nature-based solutions (Anguelovski et al., 2016; Elmqvist et al., 2013).

For instance, cities such as Medellín, Bangkok, and Rotterdam have operationalised the NUA's principles by embedding resilience into urban mobility initiatives, flood control programs, and housing policy. These cases demonstrate the potential for DRR to catalyse transformative urban planning provided that institutional capacity, stakeholder inclusion, and local adaptation are prioritised (Carmin et al., 2012; Revi et al., 2014).

4.2.4 *Other Global Instruments and Initiatives*

In addition to formal frameworks, various global platforms and initiatives have emerged to support urban resilience and DRR mainstreaming. Notable examples include the 100 Resilient Cities program (now the Global Resilient Cities Network), the United Nations Office for Disaster Risk Reduction's Making Cities Resilient campaign, and the Resilient Cities congress series hosted by ICLEI. These initiatives provide technical support, policy advocacy, and peer learning opportunities for municipalities seeking to integrate DRR into their development agendas (Arup, 2014; da Silva et al., 2012).

Furthermore, international financial mechanisms have increasingly prioritised urban DRR and climate resilience. Funds such as the Green Climate Fund, the Global Facility for Disaster Reduction and Recovery (GFDRR), and the Adaptation Fund now allocate significant resources to city-level resilience projects, although access to these funds remains skewed in favour of well-resourced municipalities in middle-income countries (Khan et al., 2024; Roberts & O'Donoghue, 2013). The proliferation of frameworks and funding opportunities suggests that the primary challenge is not the absence of guidance or resources, but rather the contextualisation and localisation of global principles. In practice, this means adapting international frameworks to address the realities of African urbanism, characterised by widespread informality, fragmented governance, and chronic infrastructure deficits (Watson, 2009; Parnell & Pieterse, 2010).

4.3 Case Studies of Global Best Practices

The operationalisation of global DRR frameworks often varies significantly across regions. While Southern African cities present unique socio-ecological challenges, there are important lessons to draw from cities that have successfully embedded DRR in their planning systems. This section presents a selection of case studies from diverse urban contexts, ranging from middle-income countries to advanced economies, to illustrate how different governance models, planning cultures, and financing architectures can promote urban resilience.

4.3.1 *Medellín, Colombia: From Violent City to Resilient City*

Medellín, once notorious as one of the most violent cities in the world, has transformed over the last two decades into a symbol of inclusive and innovative urban governance. Central to this transformation has been the integration of DRR into urban renewal and social development strategies (Brand & Dávila, 2011). The city's resilience strategy emerged from a deliberate effort to address environmental and socio-economic risks. Through a combination of top-down political commitment and bottom-up community participation, Medellín developed a series of spatial interventions, such as the *Metrocable* aerial cable car system, integrated transit corridors, and hillside public parks that linked informal settlements on steep slopes to the formal city infrastructure (Dávila, 2013). These projects reduced residents' exposure to landslides and flash floods and improved livelihoods by enhancing access to jobs, schools, and services in previously isolated neighbourhoods.

Crucially, Medellín institutionalised risk assessment within its urban planning processes. The municipal government established a georeferenced information system to map hazard-prone zones and to guide land-use decisions accordingly. Public investments were directed towards ecological restoration and slope stabilisation, and in high-risk areas, the city facilitated the relocation of vulnerable households through community consultation and compensation mechanisms (UN-Habitat, 2016).

Medellín's experience illustrates the importance of political vision, data-driven planning, and participatory governance in addressing complex urban risks. These elements are highly transferable to rapidly growing cities in Southern Africa, where similar challenges of informal expansion and topographical risk (for example, development on floodplains or unstable slopes) demand integrated solutions.

4.3.2 *Rotterdam, Netherlands: Climate-Proofing a Delta City*

As a low-lying delta city, Rotterdam faces chronic flood risks from rising sea levels and river surges. Rather than relying solely on defensive infrastructure like dikes and barriers, Rotterdam pioneered a climate-adaptive approach that integrates DRR into every aspect of urban design and policy (Aerts et al., 2014). One hallmark initiative is the city's "Room for the River" programme, which reclaims portions of the river's floodplain for water storage and uses green infrastructure, such as rain gardens, permeable pavements, and innovative water plazas, to manage stormwater in densely built neighbourhoods (Mees et al., 2016). These measures are designed to provide multiple co-benefits, including public recreational space, urban cooling, biodiversity enhancement, and flood mitigation.

Rotterdam has also institutionalised climate adaptation through a dedicated municipal program (the Rotterdam Climate Initiative) that coordinates action across sectors and actively engages residents in co-designing interventions. Advanced risk communication is central to this effort: the city operates real-time flood forecasting systems linked to emergency management services and routine urban operations. While Rotterdam enjoys high technical and financial capacity, its emphasis on innovation, multifunctionality, and cross-departmental mainstreaming offers valuable lessons for African cities facing growing hydro-meteorological threats. The Rotterdam example shows that even resource-constrained cities can begin with no-regret measures (like green infrastructure) and governance reforms that integrate DRR into everyday urban management.

4.3.3 *Bangkok, Thailand: Urban Flood Management in a Megacity*

Bangkok has long struggled with severe urban flooding, a problem exacerbated by rapid land conversion, land subsidence, and inadequate drainage infrastructure. The devastating 2011 Chao Phraya River floods, which inundated large parts of the city, served as a wake-up call and prompted a shift towards more integrated flood risk management (Marks & Lebel, 2016).

In response, the Bangkok Metropolitan Administration introduced a comprehensive flood control master plan that combines structural and non-structural measures. This includes large-scale engineering works, elevated roadways that double as flood barriers, an extensive network of canals and pumping stations, and designated flood-retention areas often referred to as "monkey cheeks"—and the restoration of urban wetlands to retain stormwater. Importantly, the city has also invested in community-based flood management, supporting local committees in at-risk districts to map hazards, maintain drainage channels, and coordinate emergency responses (Lebel et al., 2011).

Bangkok's evolving approach demonstrates the value of hybrid strategies that blend grey and green infrastructure, centralised planning with local action, and engineering solutions with governance innovation. Despite ongoing challenges, particularly related to inter-agency coordination and land tenure disputes, Bangkok's flood management system has improved in technical sophistication and social inclusion over the past decade. This experience is pertinent to Southern African coastal cities such as Maputo, which face recurrent flooding and drainage challenges; Bangkok's mix of infrastructural upgrades and community engagement provides a useful model for integrated urban flood risk management.

4.3.4 *Kigali, Rwanda: Integrated Urban Planning for Risk Reduction*

As one of Africa's fastest-growing cities, Kigali offers an important intra-continental example of proactive DRR integration into urban planning. Rwanda's post-genocide recovery agenda strongly emphasised planning and governance reform, and Kigali's 2013 city master plan included explicit DRR components such as slope protection, erosion control, and stormwater management (UN-Habitat, 2015).

The city has adopted a phased approach to upgrading informal settlements, incorporating basic risk-reducing infrastructure into the urban fabric. New access roads, drainage channels, and solid waste management systems have been introduced in partnership with local communities and international donor agencies (Uwayezu & de Vries, 2019). Unlike in many cities where informality is treated punitively, Kigali has taken steps to *regularise* and service its high-density informal neighbourhoods. By doing so, the city has reduced residents' exposure to floods and landslides while improving living conditions.

Kigali's experience underscores the potential for African cities to develop risk-sensitive planning practices through strong political leadership, clear land policies, and early engagement with risk considerations in the urbanisation process. It also illustrates how legal frameworks and fiscal tools can be aligned to support risk-informed development for example, Kigali's enforcement of land-use regulations and investment in public infrastructure have been calibrated to mitigate identified risks, demonstrating a model of urban growth that is both resilient and inclusive.

4.3.5 Durban, South Africa: Nature-Based Solutions in Climate Adaptation

Durban (eThekwini Municipality) stands out as one of the leading cities in Africa in terms of ecosystem-based approaches to climate resilience. The city's Municipal Climate Protection Programme, launched in the early 2000s, explicitly integrates biodiversity conservation with infrastructure planning to mitigate climate and disaster risks (Roberts & Diederichs, 2002; Roberts et al., 2012). This long-running program helped make Durban an early adopter of the idea that healthy ecosystems can form a first line of defence against urban hazards.

One key intervention has been the protection and restoration of the uMngeni River catchment, which reduces downstream flooding risk and helps ensure water quality for the metropolitan area. Durban has also employed forward-looking spatial planning tools to avoid development in high-risk areas (such as low-lying floodplains and unstable slopes), guided by an environmental planning framework and climate change strategy (Taylor et al., 2016). By maintaining green belts and buffers, the city not only mitigates hazard exposure but also creates recreational spaces and conservation areas, illustrating the multi-functional benefits of nature-based solutions.

Durban's governance model emphasises interdepartmental coordination, partnerships with academic institutions, and community-based adaptation pilot projects. These arrangements have improved the flow of climate risk information between city departments and promoted innovative projects (for example, community ecosystem restoration) at the neighbourhood level. Collectively, Durban's efforts reflect a shift away from reactive disaster response towards proactive, ecosystem-centred resilience-building. The city's successes in leveraging nature for urban risk reduction offer an instructive example for other Southern African cities grappling with resource constraints and high exposure to climate extremes (Table 4.1).

4.4 Key Themes and Cross-Cutting Insights from Global Practice

Across the global case studies reviewed, several recurring themes and strategic principles emerge. These are foundational to effective DRR within urban planning and can inform adaptive strategies for Southern African cities moving forward.

Table 4.1 Comparative governance structures for urban resilience in selected Southern African countries, highlighting institutional roles, integration mechanisms, and policy frameworks

Country	*DRR policy*	*Local government role*	*Institutional coordination*	*Urban planning integration*	*Civil society involvement*
South Africa	Yes	Strong	Integrated	Partial	High
Zimbabwe	Yes	Moderate	Fragmented	Weak	Low
Mozambique	Yes	Limited	Developing	Moderate	Moderate
Zambia	Partial	Emerging	Weak	Partial	Moderate
Botswana	Yes	Strong	Coordinated	Strong	High

Source: Authors (2025)

4.4.1 Risk-Sensitive Land Use and Spatial Planning

A consistent feature of successful DRR interventions is the incorporation of hazard and vulnerability assessments into land-use planning and zoning. In cities like Medellín and Kigali, for example, spatial plans are informed by detailed risk maps, and development in hazard-prone areas is either restricted or accompanied by protective infrastructure (Dávila, 2013; Uwayezu & de Vries, 2019). This stands in contrast to many Southern African cities, where risk information is often fragmented or not fully integrated into planning, and enforcement of land-use regulations remains weak (Watson, 2009).

To build resilience, urban planning must become dynamic, risk-informed, and supported by robust regulatory frameworks. This includes regularly updating hazard maps, conducting rigorous environmental impact assessments, and aligning urban growth boundaries with ecological carrying capacity and hazard thresholds (Leichenko, 2011). Incorporating risk considerations into master plans and development control not only reduces exposure but also guides safer patterns of urban expansion.

4.4.2 Infrastructure for Resilience and Co-Benefits

Another key theme is the emphasis on infrastructure that serves dual or multiple functions. In Rotterdam, for instance, "water squares" and other engineered public spaces manage stormwater while also providing recreational amenities (Aerts et al., 2014). Similarly, green belts in Durban both protect critical ecosystems and mitigate flood risks, while offering cooling effects in hot weather (Roberts et al., 2012). Designing multi-functional infrastructure helps ensure cost-effectiveness and can enhance public acceptance of DRR investments. Such approaches are especially relevant in resource-constrained settings, where funding for standalone risk reduction projects may be limited. By embedding resilience into everyday infrastructure—for example, designing parks that also act as flood retention basins—cities can achieve co-benefits for public health, biodiversity, and urban liveability alongside risk mitigation (Elmqvist et al., 2013). In sum, infrastructure planned with resilience and co-benefits in mind can catalyse broader sustainability outcomes and optimise the use of scarce resources.

4.4.3 Community Participation and Co-Production

Effective DRR strategies are often deeply participatory. In both Bangkok and Medellín, community members are actively involved in identifying risks, maintaining local infrastructure (such as drains), and preparing for disaster response (Marks & Lebel, 2016). Such participation ensures that interventions are grounded in local knowledge and social realities. It also builds a sense of ownership among residents, which can be crucial for the long-term maintenance of DRR measures (for example, keeping drainage canals free of debris).

The co-production of resilience, whereby residents, local governments, NGOs, and technical experts jointly design and implement DRR solutions, allows for blending scientific expertise with local insights. Co-production helps overcome barriers related to trust, language, and the informal status of many settlements. It can also empower marginalised groups by valuing their input in decision-making. Ultimately, inclusive processes build social capital, a critical asset for recovery and collective action during crises (Aldrich & Meyer, 2015). Cities that institutionalise community engagement in DRR find that their interventions are more equitable, legitimate, and sustainable.

4.4.4 Institutional Integration and Governance Innovation

Global experiences underline the importance of breaking down institutional silos in city governance. In cities such as Rotterdam and Durban, climate adaptation and DRR are not treated as isolated functions but are embedded across multiple departments, from transportation planning to housing, water, and public works (Roberts & Diederichs, 2002). This horizontal integration ensures that different arms of city government work towards a common resilience goal and that policies in one sector (for example, land use) do not inadvertently increase risk in another.

Innovative governance arrangements have proven effective in mainstreaming DRR within city administrations. Examples include interdepartmental climate resilience task forces, the creation of Chief Resilience Officer positions or dedicated resilience units, and formal partnerships between cities and universities for climate research and policy support. Such models facilitate knowledge exchange, align priorities across sectors, and improve accountability for risk reduction (Bulkeley et al., 2013). Importantly, they also create institutional homes for DRR, helping to sustain political commitment beyond electoral cycles and individual champions.

4.4.5 *Financing Resilience*

The lack of dedicated funding for DRR and resilience initiatives is a persistent constraint across the Global South. However, several cities have shown creativity in leveraging diverse funding streams to support their programs. These streams include municipal bonds for infrastructure upgrades, international donor grants and climate funds, and public–private partnerships to share costs and expertise (da Silva et al., 2012). In Medellín, for instance, participatory budgeting processes have been used to direct resources to community-driven risk mitigation projects, ensuring that local priorities are funded. In Kigali, a phased approach to upgrading informal settlements has enabled cost-sharing between government budgets and community contributions, easing the financial burden on any single actor (Brand & Dávila, 2011; UN-Habitat, 2015).

Resilience financing strategies must be context-sensitive and equitable, supported by long-term planning. Blended finance models that combine public, private, and community resources can build financial resilience, but they require strong governance to ensure transparency and fairness. Ultimately, building the financial capacity of municipalities through improved revenue collection, creditworthiness, and access to external funds is essential for ensuring the continuity and sustainability of urban risk reduction efforts.

4.5 Lessons for Southern Africa

Southern African cities face complex, interlocking challenges: rapid urbanisation, deep-rooted inequality, weak institutions, and rising climate hazards. These factors have contributed to high levels of vulnerability, especially in informal settlements and marginalised communities. Nonetheless, the insights drawn from global practice offer a roadmap for contextually grounded, transformative change in the region's urban areas.

Notwithstanding the challenges, some cities in Southern Africa have begun integrating DRR into urban planning innovatively. For example, Durban's Municipal Climate Protection Programme is widely regarded as a pioneering model of ecosystem-based urban resilience (Roberts & Diederichs, 2002; Roberts et al., 2012). Johannesburg has also developed a Resilience Strategy under the 100 Resilient Cities initiative, aiming to address its shocks and stresses through a holistic approach to sustainability and risk management. With international support in Mozambique, Maputo's authorities have invested in upgrading stormwater drainage infrastructure and relocating at-risk communities to mitigate chronic flooding in the city's low-lying neighbourhoods (GFDRR, 2024). These efforts remain nascent and uneven in scale, but they demonstrate that global best practices can be adapted to local contexts. Building on such initiatives and on the principles distilled from worldwide experience, the following strategic priorities are suggested for Southern African cities.

4.5.1 Prioritise Risk-Informed Urban Planning

Southern African cities must elevate disaster risk considerations in core planning decisions. This requires improving the quality and accessibility of risk data (for example, flood maps, seismic zoning), integrating such data into urban development plans, and enforcing land-use zoning that protects ecological buffers and limits development in high-risk areas (Cirolia et al., 2016). Strategic spatial planning and clear and secure land tenure systems can reduce exposure while enabling more equitable urban expansion. For example, establishing urban growth boundaries or no-build zones in floodplains and wetlands can direct new housing and infrastructure to safer areas. Mainstreaming DRR into city master plans and regulatory instruments ensures that risk reduction is not an afterthought but a fundamental criterion in guiding urban growth.

4.5.2 *Institutionalise Resilience Across Governance Levels*

Mainstreaming DRR into municipal operations involves deliberate institutional innovation. City governments may need to create dedicated resilience or disaster risk management units, form intersectoral working groups that bring together departments like planning, water, and emergency services, and incorporate climate and risk metrics into budgeting and project appraisal processes (Pelling & Holloway, 2006). Local governments also need the legal authority and resources to implement and enforce the risk-sensitive policies that plans and regulations call for. In many countries, however, fragmented mandates and fiscal authority between national and local governments have led to gaps in urban service provision and under-investment in resilience (Cirolia, 2017). Clarifying roles and aligning incentives across governance levels is, therefore, critical.

Crucially, governance must be inclusive if it is to be effective. Building trust between the state and informal communities is essential for DRR in Southern African cities, where many of the population live in informal settlements. Participatory planning and community-based risk management should be scaled up, with civil society organisations often serving as intermediaries and capacity builders (Mitlin, 2008). Empowering community groups to participate in decision-making, for instance, through settlement-level resilience committees or public forums, can improve the relevance and uptake of DRR initiatives. It also helps ensure that emergency response plans, early warning systems, and redevelopment schemes adequately address the needs of the most vulnerable residents.

4.5.3 *Invest in Resilient and Inclusive Infrastructure*

Infrastructure in Southern Africa remains highly uneven, with significant deficits in informal and peri-urban areas. Resilience-building must focus on upgrading basic services, drainage, sanitation, water supply, and all-weather access roads using design principles that enhance adaptive capacity (Satterthwaite et al., 2020). So-called informal settlements in cities like Johannesburg suffer from inadequate stormwater drainage and substandard housing, making them hotspots of disaster vulnerability; targeted upgrading in these areas yields risk reduction and social and economic co-benefits (Brown et al., 2014). Infrastructure projects at all scales should be designed to maximise co-benefits, such as water conservation, urban cooling, and local employment creation, thereby aligning disaster risk objectives with broader development priorities.

Nature-based solutions, including wetland restoration, urban agriculture, reforestation, and the conservation of mangroves or dunes in coastal cities, should also be prioritised given their cost-effectiveness and ecological benefits. These approaches align with indigenous knowledge systems and can generate long-term social and environmental dividends (Munang et al., 2013; Ziervogel et al., 2017). For example, restoring wetlands around a city can provide natural flood storage and water filtration. At the same time, community-run urban agriculture on safe vacant land can improve food security and stabilise soils. By integrating grey infrastructure with green infrastructure, Southern African cities can synergistically address multiple challenges (flooding, heatwaves, food supply, etc.).

4.5.4 Expand Access to Resilience Finance

Many Southern African municipalities struggle to access global climate finance and DRR funding due to limited technical capacity, stringent data requirements, and administrative burdens. National governments and international donors have a role to support cities, for instance, through technical assistance for proposal writing, project preparation facilities, and simplified funding application processes. Building local capacity in financial management and project design will help cities tap into funds like the Green Climate Fund or the Adaptation Fund, which may be out of reach.

At the same time, innovative financing mechanisms should be explored to expand the resource base for urban resilience. Options include pooled regional resilience funds, municipal resilience bonds, and insurance schemes that transfer risk. Diaspora communities could also be engaged for contributions to resilience projects, given their interest in hometown development. On the community side, savings groups and co-financing models (where residents contribute a portion of project costs in cash or labour) have successfully bridged small-scale infrastructure gaps, as long as measures are in place to ensure equity and affordability (Patel et al., 2015). Ultimately, diversifying and localising the sources of resilience finance will make Southern African cities less dependent on unpredictable external grants and more capable of sustaining DRR efforts over the long term.

4.6 Conclusion

Disaster risk reduction (DRR) has become a critical foundation for sustainable urban development in the twenty-first century. As climate-induced hazards intensify and urbanisation accelerates, particularly in informal and underserved areas, the integration of DRR into urban planning has never been more urgent. This chapter has examined global frameworks, innovative practices, and guiding principles that underpin effective urban DRR, illustrating how cities can better anticipate, manage, and mitigate risk. Case studies from Medellín, Rotterdam, Bangkok, and Kigali illustrate that DRR is most effective when embedded within broader urban development processes. These examples reveal that success hinges not only on smart technologies and resilient infrastructure but equally on inclusive governance, institutional coherence, and long-term political commitment.

For Southern Africa, these insights are both timely and essential. Urban vulnerability in the region is shaped by historical marginalisation, governance gaps, and the systemic neglect of informal settlements. Yet, the region also holds significant potential—decentralisation trends, active civil society engagement, and enduring community resilience can be harnessed to drive transformative change. To achieve this, Southern African cities must transition from reactive disaster responses to proactive, inclusive, and evidence-based planning. This requires strengthening municipal institutions, upgrading informal settlements, expanding nature-based solutions, and ensuring that the voices of vulnerable communities shape policy and practice. Ultimately, DRR must be viewed not as a separate goal, but as integral to achieving equitable access to services, safe housing, and sustainable livelihoods. Building resilient urban futures demands addressing the social, spatial, and institutional roots of risk, guided by both global knowledge and local action.

References

Aerts, J. C. J. H., Botzen, W. J. W., Emanuel, K., Lin, N., de Moel, H., & Michel-Kerjan, E. O. (2014). Evaluating Flood Resilience Strategies for Coastal Megacities. *Science, 344*(6183), 473–475. https://doi.org/10.1126/science.1248222

Aldrich, D. P., & Meyer, M. A. (2015). Social capital and community resilience. *The American Behavioral Scientist, 59*(2), 254–269.

Anguelovski, I., Shi, L., Chu, E., Gallagher, D., Goh, K., Lamb, Z., Reeve, K., & Teicher, H. (2016). Equity impacts of urban land use planning for climate adaptation: Critical perspectives from the global north and south. *Journal of Planning Education and Research, 36*(3), 333–348.

Arup. (2014). *City resilience framework.* The Rockefeller Foundation & Arup Group.

Brand, P., & Dávila, J. D. (2011). Mobility innovation at the urban margins: Medellín's metrocables. *City, 15*(6), 647–661.

Brown, D., McGranahan, G., & Dodman, D. (2014). *Urban informality and building a more inclusive, resilient and green economy.* International Institute for Environment and Development.

Bulkeley, H., Castán Broto, V., & Maassen, A. (2013). Low-carbon transitions and the reconfiguration of urban infrastructure. *Urban Studies, 51*(7), 1471–1486.

Carabine, E. (2015). *The politics of the Sendai Framework for Disaster Risk Reduction: Lessons for the SDGs.* ODI working paper, Overseas Development Institute.

Carmin, J., Anguelovski, I., & Roberts, D. (2012). Urban climate adaptation in the global south: Planning in an emerging policy domain. *Journal of Planning Education and Research, 32*(1), 18–32.

Cirolia, L. (2017). Fractured fiscal authority and fragmented infrastructures: Financing urban development in Sub-Saharan Africa. *Urban Forum, 28*(3), 291–307.

Cirolia, L., Görgens, T., van Donk, M., Smit, W., & Drimie, S. (2016). *Urban infrastructure in Sub-Saharan Africa – Harnessing land values, housing and transport.* African Centre for Cities.

da Silva, J., Kernaghan, S., & Luque, A. (2012). A systems approach to meeting the challenges of urban climate change. *International Journal of Urban Sustainable Development, 4*(2), 125–145.

Dávila, J. D. (2013). Urban mobility and poverty: Lessons from Medellín and Soacha, Colombia. *DPU working paper 163.* UCL Development Planning Unit.

Dodman, D., et al. (2013). Understanding the nature and scale of urban risk in low- and middle-income countries. In *UNISDR global assessment report 2013 – Background paper.* UNISDR.

Elmqvist, T., Fragkias, M., Goodness, J., Güneralp, B., Marcotullio, P. J., McDonald, R. I., Parnell, S., Schewenius, M., Sendstad, M., Seto, K. C., & Wilkinson, C. (2013). *Urbanization, biodiversity and ecosystem services: Challenges and opportunities: A global assessment.* Springer Nature.

GFDRR. (2024, January). *Supporting resilient recovery in Mozambique.* Global Facility for Disaster Reduction and Recovery – Feature Story.

Khan, I., Ali, A, Ullah, W., Jan, M. A., Ullah, S., Laker, F. A., & Khan. (2024). Mainstreaming disaster risk reduction (DRR) into development: effectiveness of DRR investment in Khyber Pakhtunkhwa, Pakistan. *Frontiers in Environmental Science, 12,* 1474344. https://doi.org/10.3389/fenvs.2024.1474344

Lavell, A., & Maskrey, A. (2014). The future of disaster risk management. *Environmental Hazards, 13*(4), 267–280.

Lebel, L., Manuta, J. B., & Garden, P. (2011). Institutional traps and vulnerability to changes in climate and flood regimes in Thailand. *Regional Environmental Change, 11*, 45–58.

Leichenko, R. (2011). Climate change and urban resilience. *Current Opinion in Environmental Sustainability, 3*(3), 164–168.

Marks, D., & Lebel, L. (2016). Disaster governance and the scalar politics of incomplete decentralisation: Case studies from Asia. *Disasters, 40*(4), 491–511.

Mees, H., Crabbé, A., Alexander, M., Kaufmann, M., Bruzzone, S., Lévy, L., & Lewandowski, J. (2016). Coproducing flood risk management through citizen involvement: Insights from cross-country comparison in Europe. *Ecology and Society, 21*(3).

Mitlin, D. (2008). With and beyond the state: Co-production as a route to political influence, power and transformation for grassroots organizations. *Environment and Urbanization, 20*(2), 339–360.

Munang, R., Thiaw, I., Alverson, K., Liu, J., & Han, Z. (2013). The role of ecosystem services in climate change adaptation and disaster risk reduction. *Current Opinion in Environmental Sustainability, 5*(1), 47–52.

Parnell, S., & Pieterse, E. (2010). The 'right to the city' and the New Urban Agenda: Learning from the South. *Urban Forum, 21*(3), 253–268.

Patel, S., Grey, C., & Levine, S. (2015). *Urban resilience: Lessons from Kampala, Entebbe and Jinja*. Working paper, Overseas Development Institute.

Pelling, M., & Holloway, A. (2006). Legislation for mainstreaming disaster risk reduction. In *UNISDR, towards a culture of prevention (Africa regional dialogue)*. Africa Regional Dialogue.

Pelling, M., O'Brien, K., & Matyas, D. (2018). Adaptation and transformation. *Climate Change, 20*(4), 667–677.

Revi, A., Satterthwaite, D., Aragón-Durand, F., Corfee-Morlot, J., Kiunsi, R. B., Pelling, M., Roberts, D., Solecki, W., Gajjar, S. P., & Sverdlik, A. (2014). Towards transformative adaptation in cities: The IPCC's fifth assessment. *Environment and Urbanization, 26*(1), 11–28.

Roberts, D., Boon, R., Diederichs, N., Douwes, E., Govender, N., Mcinnes, A., Mclean, C., O'Donoghue, S., & Spires, M. (2012). Exploring ecosystem-based adaptation in Durban, South Africa: "Learning-by-doing" at the local government coal face. *Environment and Urbanization, 24*(1), 167–195.

Roberts, D., & Diederichs, N. (2002). Durban's climate protection programme: Bridging the gap between science and practice. *Environment and Urbanization, 14*(1), 159–168.

Roberts, D., & O'Donoghue, S. (2013). Urban environmental challenges and climate change action in Durban, South Africa. *Environment and Urbanization, 25*(1), 299–319.

Satterthwaite, D., Archer, D., Colenbrander, S., Dodman, D., Hardoy, J., Mitlin, D., & Patel, S. (2020). Building resilience to climate change in informal settlements. *One Earth, 2*(2), 143–156.

Taylor, A., Cartwright, A., & Sutherland, C. (2016). Institutional pathways for local climate adaptation: A comparison of three South African municipalities. *Environmental Science & Policy, 66*, 86–94.

Twigg, J. (2015). Disaster risk reduction. *Good Practice Review, 9*.

UNDRR. (2015). *Sendai framework for disaster risk reduction 2015–2030*. United Nations Office for Disaster Risk Reduction.

UN-Habitat. (2015). *Kigali City master plan (revised 2013)*. United Nations Human Settlements Programme.

UN-Habitat. (2016). New urban agenda. In *United Nations conference on housing and sustainable urban development (Habitat III)*.

UNISDR. (2005). *Hyogo framework for action 2005–2015: Building the resilience of nations and communities to disasters*. United Nations International Strategy for Disaster Reduction.

United Nations. (2015). *Transforming Our World: The 2030 Agenda for Sustainable Development*. New York: United Nations.

Uwayezu, E., & de Vries, W. (2019). Expropriation of urban land for public purpose in Rwanda: Governance challenges and ways forward. *Land, 8*(6), 91.

Watson, V. (2009). 'The planned city sweeps the poor away…': Urban planning and 21st century urbanisation. *Progress in Planning, 72*(3), 151–193.

Ziervogel, G., Waddell, J., Smit, W., & Taylor, A. (2017). Flooding in Cape Town's informal settlements: Barriers to collaborative urban risk governance. *South African Geographical Journal, 99*(2), 153–173.

CHAPTER 5

Land Use Management and Disaster Risk Reduction in Southern African Cities

5.1 Introduction

Urbanisation is a defining characteristic of the twenty-first century, with global urban populations expected to reach 68% by 2050 (United Nations, 2018). In Southern Africa, urban growth has been both rapid and unstructured, often resulting in sprawling informal settlements, land degradation, and increased vulnerability to climate-related hazards such as floods, cyclones, and droughts (UN-Habitat, 2020; Dodman et al., 2013). The uneven expansion of cities like Johannesburg, Durban, and Maputo highlights the pressing need for a more coherent and risk-informed approach to land-use planning. Land use management is one of the most influential instruments available to policymakers and urban planners for shaping urban resilience. It determines the allocation of land for housing, infrastructure, green space, industry, and agriculture. When executed effectively, it can mitigate disaster risks, promote sustainable development, and ensure social equity (UNISDR, 2015). Conversely, poor land use practices can exacerbate vulnerabilities, particularly in informal settlements located in hazard-prone areas (Satterthwaite et al., 2020).

This chapter focuses on the intersection of land use management and disaster risk reduction (DRR), exploring how spatial planning, zoning regulations, ecosystem-based approaches, and community engagement can be leveraged to reduce urban vulnerabilities. Drawing on both global

F. Mangara, N. Dorasamy, *Sustainable Urban Development in Southern Africa*, https://doi.org/10.1007/978-3-032-08286-2_5

best practices and empirical evidence from Southern African cities, the chapter offers a comprehensive assessment of challenges, innovations, and pathways for integrating DRR into land governance.

5.2 Theoretical Foundations of Land Use Management and DRR

Understanding the theoretical underpinnings of land use management and DRR is critical for effective urban resilience strategies. This section explores the concepts of risk-informed planning, green infrastructure, and participatory governance in the context of urban development and climate risk.

5.2.1 *Risk-Informed Land-Use Planning*

Risk-informed land-use planning integrates hazard assessments, exposure mapping, and vulnerability analyses into spatial development strategies (UNISDR, 2015). It aims to prevent the construction of settlements and infrastructure in high-risk zones, reduce environmental degradation, and allocate land for climate-adaptive uses such as buffer zones and floodways. Central to this approach is hazard mapping. Accurate, up-to-date maps help local authorities identify floodplains, landslide-prone slopes, and areas exposed to sea-level rise (World Bank, 2019). For instance, Bangkok has integrated flood modelling into its urban master plan, ensuring that drainage infrastructure and building codes align with hydrological forecasts (Marks & Lebel, 2016). Similarly, in Cape Town, the local government developed a floodplain management system that guides zoning decisions in informal settlements (Ziervogel et al., 2016).

However, Southern African cities often suffer from inadequate risk data, outdated cadastral records, and weak technical capacity to carry out such planning (UN-Habitat, 2020). This results in unregulated development in wetlands, hillsides, and floodplain areas that should serve as natural hazard buffers (IPCC, 2014). Risk-informed planning thus necessitates a shift in institutional behaviour, capacity building, and political will to prioritise resilience over short-term economic gain (Pelling & Wisner, 2009).

5.2.2 *Green Infrastructure and Ecosystem-Based DRR*

Green infrastructure refers to natural and semi-natural systems that deliver ecosystem services such as flood attenuation, water purification, and climate regulation (UNEP, 2018). Examples include wetlands, urban forests, bioswales, and permeable surfaces. These features reduce disaster risk by absorbing stormwater, mitigating heat, and stabilising soils (Elmqvist et al., 2013). Cities like Rotterdam have embedded green infrastructure into their flood management strategies, converting public plazas into water squares that store excess rainwater during storms (Aerts et al., 2014). In the African context, Durban has become a leader in ecosystem-based adaptation, integrating environmental management into its spatial planning frameworks (Roberts & Diederichs, 2002; Roberts et al., 2012). Southern African cities face mounting challenges due to the loss of green spaces to informal housing and commercial expansion. Urban deforestation, wetland encroachment, and river pollution not only degrade the environment but also magnify exposure to hazards (Mather & Stretch, 2012). Therefore, mainstreaming green infrastructure in land-use planning can serve dual objectives of urban resilience and ecological sustainability (Folke et al., 2010).

5.2.3 *Participatory Planning and Community Engagement*

Effective land-use planning is not merely technical; it is profoundly political and social. Participatory planning engages communities in the design, implementation, and monitoring of spatial development decisions (UN-Habitat, 2020). It empowers residents to articulate risks, co-develop solutions, and hold authorities accountable (Cornwall, 2008). Informal settlements, where formal land tenure is absent, pose unique planning challenges. However, cities like Nairobi and Maputo have piloted community mapping and enumeration processes that generate locally validated data to inform upgrading and risk reduction (Jenkins, 2000; Satterthwaite et al., 2020). Participatory land-use planning can also help navigate the tensions between eviction, regularisation, and upgrading in contexts of tenure insecurity. Moreover, the co-production of knowledge, especially involving women, youth, and persons with disabilities, is essential for inclusive DRR (Aldrich & Meyer, 2015). Local knowledge systems, such as indigenous flood early warning signs or traditional watershed management, should be integrated into formal land governance structures to ensure culturally relevant and context-specific appropriate planning.

5.3 Challenges of Land Use Management in Southern Africa

While land-use planning offers significant potential for risk reduction, its effective application in Southern African cities is hindered by multiple, deeply entrenched challenges. These include the rapid growth of informal settlements, weak institutional capacity, fragmented governance, and the compounding effects of climate change.

5.3.1 Rapid Urbanisation and Informal Settlements

Southern Africa's urban population has grown exponentially over the past four decades, with urbanisation rates now exceeding 60% in countries like South Africa and Botswana (UN-Habitat, 2020). This growth has often outpaced the capacity of local governments to provide land, housing, and services in a planned manner. As a result, informal settlements have proliferated, housing between 30% and 70% of urban residents in cities such as Harare, Lusaka, and Maputo (Huchzermeyer, 2011; Satterthwaite et al., 2020). These informal settlements are frequently located in high-risk areas, such as floodplains, steep slopes, and reclaimed wetlands, due to the affordability and availability of land in such locations (Mususa, 2012; Mavhura et al., 2013). Without secure tenure or formal planning, residents build structures with inadequate materials and minimal technical guidance, further exacerbating their vulnerability to hazards.

Efforts to formalise or upgrade these areas are often undermined by legal ambiguity, contested claims over land, and community mistrust of authorities due to documented histories of eviction and exclusion (Kamete, 2006; Patel & Nosal, 2015). Moreover, planning institutions frequently lack the mechanisms to meaningfully engage with informal communities, resulting in top-down approaches that fail to address local needs. Addressing the risks associated with informal urbanisation thus requires integrated strategies that combine tenure regularisation, infrastructure upgrading, and inclusive planning processes (Roy, 2005; Huchzermeyer, 2011).

5.3.2 Weak Governance and Institutional Fragmentation

Governance failures are a major impediment to effective land use management in Southern Africa. Responsibilities for urban planning, environmental protection, housing, and disaster management are often dispersed across multiple, poorly coordinated institutions (Goodfellow, 2013; Cirolia, 2017). This fragmentation leads to overlaps in authority, gaps in service delivery, and regulatory ambiguity that can be exploited by political or commercial interests. For instance, in Zambia and Zimbabwe, urban land allocation often occurs through both formal (state-led) and informal (traditional leadership or political patronage) channels. This results in conflicting land claims and unplanned settlement expansion (Jenkins, 2001; Kamete, 2006). In Mozambique, decentralisation efforts have transferred responsibilities to municipal authorities without adequate resourcing or technical support, leading to paralysis in planning implementation (Jenkins, 2013).

Political interference further weakens the autonomy of planning institutions. Local governments may be pressured to approve developments in ecologically sensitive or hazard-prone areas for political expediency or short-term economic gains (Pieterse & Parnell, 2014). Moreover, corruption in land administration undermines trust in public institutions and deters private investment in risk-reducing infrastructure (Transparency International, 2019). Institutional capacity is also undermined by budgetary constraints and high staff turnover. Many planning departments lack qualified personnel, updated equipment, and continuous training programmes, leaving them ill-equipped to undertake risk-sensitive planning (UN-Habitat, 2020). Strengthening governance requires reforms that clarify institutional mandates, promote accountability, and build human and technical capacity across all tiers of government.

5.3.3 Climate Change and Environmental Degradation

Climate change presents a rapidly escalating challenge for land use management in Southern Africa. The region is projected to experience increased temperatures, erratic rainfall, prolonged droughts, and more frequent extreme weather events, including tropical cyclones and urban flooding (IPCC, 2022; Niang et al., 2014). These changes place immense pressure on urban systems, particularly those that are already under stress from poverty and infrastructural deficits. For instance, Beira, Mozambique, has experienced repeated cyclones (for instance, Cyclone Idai in 2019) that have devastated housing, transport, and sanitation infrastructure, especially in unplanned settlements built on low-lying coastal zones (GFDRR, 2020). In Harare and Lusaka, intense rainfall events frequently lead to flooding due to blocked drainage systems, informal constructions in waterways, and inadequate stormwater infrastructure (Mususa, 2012; Chigudu, 2020).

Environmental degradation, including deforestation, loss of wetlands, and pollution of rivers, further increases disaster risks. Urban expansion into ecological buffers eliminates the natural services that previously reduced risk, such as water absorption and flood mitigation (Elmqvist et al., 2013; Mather & Stretch, 2012). In many cases, such degradation is directly linked to unregulated land use and weak environmental enforcement. Adaptation to climate change requires spatial plans that preserve and restore ecosystems, protect water catchments, and enhance climate resilience across the built environment. However, climate data is often unavailable or not downscaled to the city level, making it difficult to design locally appropriate or context-specific land use responses (Ziervogel et al., 2016).

5.4 Case Studies: Land Use and DRR in Southern African Cities

Case studies provide valuable insights into the successes, innovations, and limitations of land use management as a tool for DRR. While the urban contexts across Southern African cities differ markedly, common patterns of informality, institutional weakness, and climate risk present shared challenges. The cities of Cape Town, Lusaka, Beira, and Harare illustrate diverse approaches and outcomes.

5.4.1 Cape Town, South Africa: Formal Systems, Climate-Sensitive Planning

Cape Town offers one of the most advanced examples of integrated land-use planning in the region. As a metropolitan municipality with relatively high institutional capacity and data availability, it has made significant strides in aligning urban planning with climate adaptation and disaster risk reduction (Cartwright et al., 2012). The city's Spatial Development

Framework (SDF) and Integrated Development Plan (IDP) include clear guidelines for managing urban expansion, conserving ecological infrastructure, and identifying risk-prone areas. Critical to this process has been the development of risk overlays, mapping floodplains, wildfire zones, and sea-level rise projections to guide land-use zoning and infrastructure placement (Ziervogel et al., 2016). Cape Town's efforts also include the use of green infrastructure. The Zandvlei Estuary Nature Reserve, for example, not only provides biodiversity benefits but also acts as a natural flood buffer. The city's Disaster Risk Management Centre works closely with spatial planners to assess land development applications and ensure compliance with safety standards (CoGTA, 2019).

Despite these advances, Cape Town still faces challenges with spatial inequality and informal settlement growth on risk-prone land. Many lower-income communities reside in areas such as Khayelitsha and Philippi, which face recurring floods and fires. Nevertheless, the city's relatively strong governance and forward-thinking policies offer valuable lessons for DRR integration in urban planning.

5.4.2 *Lusaka, Zambia: The Costs of Informality and Weak Enforcement*

Lusaka exemplifies the difficulties of managing urban land in the face of rapid population growth and limited planning capacity. With over 70% of its population living in informal settlements, the city struggles to enforce zoning regulations or implement comprehensive land use plans (Mususa, 2012; Jenkins, 2001). Unregulated construction on drainage channels and wetlands has contributed to frequent urban floods. The Kanyama and George compounds, large informal settlements, are particularly vulnerable, experiencing regular inundation due to blocked waterways and insufficient stormwater infrastructure (World Bank, 2017). While the city's planning statutes technically prohibit development in these areas, a lack of enforcement mechanisms and political resistance to relocation have allowed expansion to continue.

The Lusaka City Council, working with international partners, has attempted to introduce participatory enumeration and upgrading initiatives. Projects like the Peri-Urban Self-Help Project have helped to map informal areas and pilot basic services, such as toilets and drainage (Jenkins, 2000). However, without systemic reform of land allocation processes and greater institutional coordination, these efforts remain piecemeal. Lusaka's situation highlights how weak land governance, when combined with informality, increases disaster risk and undermines resilience planning. It also points to the importance of engaging with informal communities as legitimate urban actors rather than temporary encroachers.

5.4.3 *Beira, Mozambique: Land-Use Planning in a Cyclone Hotspot*

Beira has become internationally recognised for its vulnerability to climate hazards, particularly tropical cyclones and coastal flooding. Cyclone Idai in 2019 devastated the city, displacing hundreds of thousands and damaging key infrastructure, including roads, drainage systems, and housing (GFDRR, 2020). In the wake of the cyclone, Beira launched a major urban resilience initiative, the Beira Master Plan 2035, with support from the World Bank and Dutch partners. The plan integrates land-use zoning with hydrological modelling, identifying safe areas for expansion and high-risk zones requiring conservation or resettlement (World Bank, 2020).

One of the flagship interventions has been the creation of a green corridor: a series of flood retention basins and reforested wetlands that both store excess water and provide ecosystem services. The plan also proposes road alignments and urban density thresholds that support climate resilience (UN-Habitat, 2021). Despite this progress, implementation faces several challenges. Land tenure insecurity, limited local technical expertise, and competing priorities often delay or dilute interventions. Many residents have rebuilt in high-risk zones due to the lack of affordable alternatives, underscoring the importance of coupling land-use planning with housing and livelihood strategies. Beira's experience demonstrates both the urgency and potential of integrating DRR into spatial planning in high-risk coastal cities. Its model is replicable across similarly exposed Southern African urban centres, provided that local governments are adequately supported.

5.4.4 *Harare, Zimbabwe: Political Economy of Land and Risk*

Harare offers a cautionary tale of how political contestation over land undermines DRR. The city's land use is characterised by informality, unplanned peri-urban growth, and a dual governance system in which both state and political actors allocate land (Kamete, 2006; Chigudu, 2020). Many informal settlements, such as Hopley Farm and Epworth, have emerged through politically mediated land occupations. These areas lack proper drainage, waste management, and roads, making them extremely vulnerable to flooding and disease outbreaks. The 2008–2009 cholera epidemic, which killed over 4,000 people, was largely attributed to urban service collapse and unregulated land use (Chigudu, 2020).

While Harare's formal planning instruments, such as the Regional, Town, and Country Planning Act, remain in place, their implementation is weak. Planning permissions are often issued retroactively or circumvented altogether due to political interference or corruption (Goodfellow, 2013). Efforts to upgrade informal areas have been sporadic and contentious. Operation Murambatsvina in 2005 saw the demolition of over 700,000 homes and businesses under the guise of "cleaning up" illegal settlements, drawing widespread condemnation for violating human rights and increasing homelessness (Tibaijuka, 2005). Harare illustrates the limits of technocratic planning in politically volatile contexts. Without transparent land governance, strong institutions, and citizen participation, DRR remains elusive. However, recent civil society-led mapping and advocacy efforts suggest a growing awareness of the need for inclusive, rights-based approaches to land use and urban resilience.

5.5 Policy Recommendations for Southern Africa

The challenges facing land use management and disaster risk reduction (DRR) in Southern African cities are multifaceted and deeply rooted in historical, political, and socio-economic dynamics. However, opportunities for reform and innovation abound. This section presents key policy recommendations for building more resilient and equitable urban futures in the region.

5.5.1 Reforming Urban Planning Systems

Reforming outdated and exclusionary planning systems is central to reducing disaster risk. Many Southern African cities continue to operate under colonial-era legislation that prioritises spatial control over flexibility and inclusiveness (Todes, 2011). There is an urgent need to adopt and implement urban planning laws that reflect contemporary challenges, such as climate change, informality, and demographic shifts.

Planning reforms should:

- Require the integration of hazard and vulnerability data into land use plans and development approvals (UNDRR, 2015).
- Enable adaptive zoning regulations that accommodate incremental upgrading and informal land uses without compromising safety (Roy, 2005).
- Promote compact, mixed-use urban forms that reduce infrastructure costs and limit expansion into hazard-prone areas (UN-Habitat, 2016).

Building planning capacity at the local level is also critical. This includes training urban planners in risk assessment, GIS, and participatory methods, as well as equipping municipalities with the tools and resources to enforce plans effectively (Satterthwaite et al., 2020).

5.5.2 *Upgrading Informal Settlements and Securing Tenure*

Given the scale of informal urbanisation in the region, reducing risk in informal settlements must be a core priority. Blanket evictions or forced relocations rarely yield positive outcomes. Instead, incremental upgrading, coupled with basic service provision and tenure regularisation, can substantially reduce vulnerability (Patel & Nosal, 2015; Huchzermeyer, 2011).

Key steps include:

- Providing legal recognition or occupancy certificates to informal residents to incentivise investment in safer housing.
- Co-designing infrastructure improvements (for example, stormwater drainage, footpaths, sanitation) with residents to enhance relevance and ownership.
- Establishing local upgrading committees that facilitate communication between communities, municipal departments, and NGOs.

Where relocation is unavoidable due to extreme risk (for example, in floodplains or unstable slopes), authorities must ensure that it is voluntary, transparent, and accompanied by adequate compensation and livelihood support (UN-Habitat, 2020).

5.5.3 *Integrating Ecosystem-Based Approaches*

Natural systems are critical buffers against climate-related disasters, yet they are often undervalued or destroyed in the urbanisation process. Ecosystem-based approaches can complement conventional infrastructure while delivering co-benefits for biodiversity, health, and food security (Elmqvist et al., 2013).

Recommendations include:

- Protecting and restoring wetlands, river buffers, and urban forests as part of zoning plans and development guidelines (Roberts et al., 2012).
- Incentivising green infrastructure (for example, green roofs, permeable pavements) through development codes and tax rebates.
- Embedding ecosystem services mapping in spatial planning tools to identify areas of ecological and risk-reducing importance (UNEP, 2018).

These approaches are particularly relevant in peri-urban areas, where urban expansion threatens catchments and biodiversity corridors critical for long-term sustainability.

5.5.4 *Strengthening Urban Governance, Finance, and Participation*

DRR and sustainable land use require responsive, transparent, and well-resourced institutions. Governance reforms should aim to strengthen coordination among urban departments, clarify roles and mandates, and support long-term planning over short-term political gains (Goodfellow, 2013; Cirolia, 2017).

To this end:

- National governments must devolve adequate resources and authority to municipal governments to manage land and implement resilience strategies.
- Cities should explore innovative financing mechanisms, including land value capture, resilience bonds, and climate funds.

- Civil society organisations and community groups should be embedded in decision-making structures, such as resilience councils or land governance boards (Mitlin, 2008).

Participatory processes not only improve policy relevance but also build trust, an essential ingredient in contexts with legacies of marginalisation and eviction. Public awareness campaigns and school-based education can also play a role in fostering a culture of risk reduction.

5.6 Conclusion

The relationship between land use management and disaster risk reduction (DRR) is fundamental to advancing urban resilience across Southern Africa. In the face of intensifying climate threats, rapid informal urbanisation, and fragmented governance, this chapter has underscored that spatial planning must evolve beyond its conventional regulatory scope. Instead, it must become a proactive, integrated strategy for promoting sustainability, equity, and long-term risk mitigation. Effective land-use planning plays a pivotal role in minimising hazard exposure, reducing urban vulnerability, and strengthening adaptive capacity. Approaches such as risk-sensitive zoning, ecosystem-based infrastructure, and participatory upgrading are not merely technical interventions; they are essential responses to entrenched spatial inequalities and the structural legacies of colonial and post-colonial urban development. These approaches hold transformative potential if embedded within inclusive planning frameworks.

The chapter's case studies reveal a range of outcomes. Cape Town's integrated, climate-resilient strategies showcase the success of institutional alignment and forward-looking planning. Conversely, Lusaka and Harare illustrate how weak institutional capacity and uncontrolled urban expansion perpetuate risk. Beira's experience demonstrates how international partnerships and investments in green infrastructure can enhance urban resilience in the face of repeated climate shocks. To move towards more resilient and just cities, there is a pressing need for coordinated legal, institutional, and financial reforms. Planning frameworks must actively engage marginalised communities, particularly those living in informal settlements, whose exclusion continues to drive urban risk. Addressing land tenure security, decentralising planning authority, and investing in climate-resilient infrastructure must be central to this agenda. Sustainable urban development in Southern Africa hinges on reimagining land use management not as a static regulatory mechanism, but as a dynamic instrument for social transformation, ecological stewardship, and disaster risk reduction in a rapidly changing urban landscape.

References

Aerts, J., Botzen, W., Bowman, M., Dircke, P., & Ward, P. (2014). *Climate adaptation and flood risk in coastal cities*. Routledge.

Aldrich, D. P., & Meyer, M. A. (2015). Social capital and community resilience. *American Behavioral Scientist, 59*(2), 254–269.

Cartwright, A., Oelofse, G., Parnell, S., & Ward, S. (2012). Climate at the city scale 1: The Cape Town climate think tank. *Climate change at the City Scale*, 1–8.

Chigudu, S. (2020). *The political life of an epidemic: Cholera, crisis and citizenship in Zimbabwe*. Cambridge University Press.

Cirolia, L. R. (2017). Fractured fiscal authority and fragmented infrastructures. *Urban Forum, 28*(3), 291–307.

Cornwall, A. (2008). Unpacking 'participation': Models, meanings and practices. *Community Development Journal, 43*(3), 269–283.

Dodman, D., Brown, D., Francis, K., Hardoy, J., Johnson, C., & Satterthwaite, D. (2013). *Understanding the nature and scale of urban risk in low-and middle-income countries and its implications for humanitarian preparedness, planning and response*. International Institute for Environment and Development.

Elmqvist, T., Fragkias, M., Goodness, J., Güneralp, B., Marcotullio, P. J., McDonald, R. I., Parnell, S., Schewenius, M., Sendstad, M., Seto, K. C., & Wilkinson, C. (2013). *Urbanization, biodiversity and ecosystem services: Challenges and opportunities: a global assessment*. Springer Nature.

Folke, C., Carpenter, S. R., Walker, B., Scheffer, M., Chapin, T., & Rockström, J. (2010). Resilience thinking: Integrating resilience, adaptability and transformability. *Ecology and Society, 15*(4).

Global Facility for Disaster Reduction and Recovery (GFDRR). (2020). *Beira recovery and resilience strategy*. GFDRR.

Goodfellow, T. (2013). The institutionalisation of "noise" and "silence" in urban politics: Riots and compliance in Uganda and Rwanda. *Oxford Development Studies, 41*(4), 436–454.

Huchzermeyer, M. (2011). *Cities with 'Slums': From informal settlement eradication to a right to the city in Africa*. UCT Press.

Intergovernmental Panel on Climate Change (IPCC). (2022). *Climate change 2022: Impacts, adaptation and vulnerability*. Intergovernmental Panel on Climate Change.

IPCC. (2014). *Fifth assessment report: Impacts, adaptation, and vulnerability*. IPCC.

Jenkins, P. (2000). Urban management, urban poverty and urban governance. *International Development Planning Review, 22*(2), 137–164.

Jenkins, P. (2001). Strengthening access to land for housing for the poor in Africa. *International Journal of Urban and Regional Research, 25*(3), 629–648.

Jenkins, P. (2013). *Urbanization, urbanism and urbanity in an African city: Home spaces and house cultures*. Palgrave.

Kamete, A. Y. (2006). The return of the jekemu: Governance in Harare's periphery. *Habitat International, 30*(4), 101–111.

Marks, D., & Lebel, L. (2016). Disaster governance and the scalar politics of incomplete decentralization. *Disasters, 40*(4), 491–516.

Mather, A. A., & Stretch, D. D. (2012). A perspective on sea level rise and coastal storm surge from Southern and Eastern Africa. *African Journal of Marine Science, 34*(3), 327–332.

Mavhura, E., Manyena, S. B., Collins, A. E., & Manatsa, D. (2013). Indigenous knowledge, coping strategies and resilience to floods in Muzarabani, Zimbabwe. International Journal of Disaster Risk Reduction, 5, 38-48. https://doi.org/10.1016/j.ijdrr.2013.07.001

Mitlin, D. (2008). With and beyond the state—Co-production as a route to political influence. *Environment and Urbanization, 20*(2), 339–360.

Mususa, P. (2012). Contested urbanism in Lusaka. *Urban Forum, 23*(1), 63–78.

Niang, I., et al. (2014). Africa. In *Climate change 2014: Impacts, adaptation and vulnerability*. IPCC Working Group II.

Patel, R., & Nosal, L. (2015). *Defining the resilient city*. United Nations University Centre for Policy Research.

Pelling, M., & Wisner, B. (2009). *Disaster risk reduction: Cases from urban Africa*. Earthscan.

Pieterse, E., & Parnell, S. (2014). *Africa's urban revolution*. Zed Books.

Republic of South Africa, Department of Cooperative Governance. (2023). National disaster management framework, 2023 (Government Gazette No. 48874, Notice No. 3635, 30 June 2023). Government Printing Works.

Roberts, D., Boon, R., Diederichs, N., Douwes, E., Govender, N., Mcinnes, A., Mclean, C., O'Donoghue, S., & Spires, M. (2012). Exploring ecosystem-based adaptation in Durban, South Africa: "Learning-by-doing" at the local government coal face. *Environment and Urbanization, 24*(1), 167–195.

Roberts, D., & Diederichs, N. (2002). Durban's climate protection programme. *Environment and Urbanization, 14*(1), 159–168.

Roy, A. (2005). Urban informality: Toward an epistemology of planning. *Journal of the American Planning Association, 71*(2), 147–158.

Satterthwaite, D., Archer, D., Colenbrander, S., Dodman, D., Hardoy, J., Mitlin, D., & Patel, S. (2020). Building resilience to climate change in informal settlements. *One Earth, 2*(2), 143–156.

Tibaijuka, A. (2005). *Report of the fact-finding mission to Zimbabwe on operation Murambatsvina*. United Nations.

Todes, A. (2011). Reinventing planning: Critical reflections. *Urban Forum, 22*(2), 115–133.

Transparency International. (2019). *Corruption perceptions index 2019*. Transparency International.

UNEP. (2018). *Making the case for ecosystem-based adaptation: The global mountain EbA programme*. United Nations Environment Programme.

UN-Habitat. (2016). *New urban agenda*. UN-Habitat.

UN-Habitat. (2020). *World cities report 2020: The value of sustainable urbanization*. UN-Habitat.

UN-Habitat. (2021). *Beira recovery and resilience strategy*. UN-Habitat.

UNISDR. (2015). *Sendai framework for disaster risk reduction 2015–2030*. UNISDR.

United Nations Office for Disaster Risk Reduction. (2015). Sendai framework for disaster risk reduction 2015–2030. Geneva United Nations.

World Bank. (2017). *Zambia climate risk profile*. World Bank.

World Bank. (2019). *Urban flood risk management: A guide for integrated flood risk management*. World Bank.

World Bank. (2020). *Beira master plan 2035*. World Bank.

Ziervogel, G., et al. (2016). Inserting rights and justice into urban resilience. *Environment and Urbanization, 29*(1), 123–138.

CHAPTER 6

Infrastructure Planning for Resilience: Challenges and Opportunities

6.1 Introduction

Infrastructure plays a pivotal role in the resilience and sustainability of urban environments, especially in regions such as Southern Africa, which face an array of interlinked challenges, including rapid urbanisation, climate change, and institutional fragility. Infrastructure systems comprising transportation, water supply, sanitation, energy, communication networks, and waste management form the backbone of urban life. They determine the capacity of cities not only to deliver essential services under normal conditions, but also to withstand, absorb, and recover from the shocks and stresses induced by disasters and environmental change (World Bank, 2019; UN-Habitat, 2020).

The importance of resilient infrastructure in the urban context has gained prominence globally, as seen in the Sendai Framework for Disaster Risk Reduction 2015–2030 and the Sustainable Development Goals (particularly Sustainable Development Goal 9 and Sustainable Development Goal 11), which underscore the need for sustainable, inclusive, and risk-informed infrastructure planning (United Nations, 2015). In the Global South, and more acutely in Southern Africa, the gaps in resilient infrastructure are not just technical but systemic, shaped by socio-political histories, unequal spatial development, and chronic underinvestment in urban services.

F. Mangara, N. Dorasamy, *Sustainable Urban Development in Southern Africa*, https://doi.org/10.1007/978-3-032-08286-2_6

Urban infrastructure in many Southern African cities is increasingly exposed to climate-induced hazards such as flooding, cyclones, and droughts. These are compounded by anthropogenic risks, including informal settlements encroaching on critical infrastructure corridors, poorly maintained systems, and unregulated urban sprawl. For example, cities like Beira and Durban have repeatedly experienced destructive storms and coastal inundation, exposing the fragility of both new and legacy infrastructure (Mather & Stretch, 2012; World Bank, 2020). Infrastructure failures during such events often cascade, disrupting transport, energy supply, healthcare, and livelihoods simultaneously, thereby exacerbating urban vulnerability (UNEP, 2018).

Moreover, the growing urban population in the region exerts enormous pressure on existing infrastructure, much of which was never designed for the scale and complexity of modern urban life. As of 2022, over 50% of the Southern African population resides in urban areas, a proportion expected to increase significantly by 2050 (UN-Habitat, 2020). Many of these cities suffer from outdated infrastructure systems that are spatially biased towards affluent, historically advantaged urban cores, while low-income and informal settlements remain severely underserved (Beall et al., 2002; Chigudu, 2020).

Addressing these challenges requires a shift from reactive, ad hoc infrastructure interventions to proactive, integrated, and forward-looking planning models that prioritise resilience and equity. This entails not only technical improvements, such as climate-resilient design standards, but also reforms in urban governance, financing, and community engagement (Satterthwaite et al., 2020). The concept of "resilient infrastructure" must be situated within the broader agenda of sustainable urban development and disaster risk reduction (DRR), recognising that infrastructure systems are both physical and institutional, and their performance is deeply shaped by socio-political dynamics (Folke et al., 2010).

This chapter explores the role of infrastructure planning in enhancing urban resilience across Southern Africa. It begins by unpacking the theoretical frameworks that underpin resilient infrastructure planning, including systems thinking, critical infrastructure theory, and climate adaptation perspectives. The chapter then examines the existing infrastructure landscape in selected Southern African cities, identifying key vulnerabilities and resilience gaps across water, transport, energy, and waste sectors. Through case studies from Maputo, Durban, and Johannesburg, the chapter highlights innovative practices and pilot projects that demonstrate the potential for resilience-oriented planning.

The chapter also addresses the barriers to effective implementation, including financial constraints, institutional fragmentation, corruption, and limited technical capacity. Recognising the importance of context-specific strategies, the discussion draws on global best practices while emphasising the need for locally grounded solutions. Finally, the chapter concludes with policy recommendations aimed at mainstreaming resilience into infrastructure planning processes, leveraging partnerships, and mobilising resources for inclusive and sustainable urban futures.

In essence, resilient infrastructure is not a luxury but a necessity for Southern African cities seeking to break cycles of vulnerability and build capacity for transformation. By viewing infrastructure through the dual lenses of risk and equity, planners and policymakers can help create cities that not only survive disasters but also thrive in their aftermath, ensuring that all urban residents, especially the most marginalised, are protected and empowered.

6.2 Theoretical and Conceptual Frameworks for Infrastructure Resilience

Understanding the theoretical foundations of infrastructure resilience is critical to designing systems that can withstand and recover from disruptions. In the context of Southern African cities, which are characterised by overlapping vulnerabilities and institutional fragmentation, a multidisciplinary and systems-based understanding of infrastructure planning is essential. This section explores five dominant conceptual approaches: systems thinking, critical infrastructure theory, socio-ecological resilience, climate adaptation frameworks, and the "build back better" principle in post-disaster recovery.

6.2.1 *Systems Thinking and Interdependency*

Modern urban infrastructure operates as a complex, interdependent system of systems. Transportation networks, water supply, electricity grids, and communication services are increasingly interconnected, meaning that disruptions in one sector often trigger cascading failures in others (Pescaroli & Alexander, 2015). For instance, a power outage can disable traffic lights, water pumps, and hospital systems, amplifying the impacts of a disaster.

Systems thinking encourages planners to move beyond siloed approaches and adopt integrated models that account for feedback loops, dependencies, and vulnerabilities across networks (Sterman, 2000). In Southern Africa, where institutional silos are common, this approach can help identify points of systemic weakness and prioritise multi-functional infrastructure interventions. Tools such as network mapping and resilience stress-testing are used in cities like Cape Town and Johannesburg to visualise and manage these interconnections (Cartwright et al., 2012a, b).

6.2.2 Critical Infrastructure Theory

Critical infrastructure theory refers to the idea that certain physical systems, such as electricity grids, transport corridors, and water supply networks, are essential to the functioning of society, and their disruption poses significant threats to national security, economic stability, and public health (Rinaldi et al., 2001). This theory informs policy approaches to infrastructure protection and prioritisation. In the Southern African context, where infrastructure is often concentrated in a few high-density urban cores, the failure of a single node can have disproportionately large consequences. The 2008 power crisis in Zimbabwe, for example, crippled municipal water supply systems in Harare, contributing to a deadly cholera outbreak (Chigudu, 2020). Protecting and redundantly designing these "critical nodes" is essential to minimising systemic risk. The theory also highlights the importance of governance and information flows. Critical infrastructure systems must be managed by institutions capable of real-time monitoring, maintenance, and adaptive response—a major challenge for under-resourced municipalities in the region (UNDRR, 2019).

6.2.3 Socio-Ecological Resilience and Infrastructure

The socio-ecological resilience framework expands the focus of resilience beyond engineering robustness to encompass adaptability, transformability, and social learning. It recognises that infrastructure systems are embedded within broader ecological and social contexts and that resilience emerges from the ability to absorb disturbances while reorganising and adapting (Folke et al., 2010). Applying this lens to infrastructure planning in Southern Africa means acknowledging that informal settlements, traditional governance structures, and ecosystem services are part of the urban fabric. For instance, in Durban, wetland conservation is integrated into urban flood management, providing both ecological and infrastructural benefits (Roberts & Diederichs, 2002). Similarly, community water harvesting systems in rural-urban transition zones reflect local adaptive strategies that contribute to overall system resilience (Munang et al., 2013). This framework promotes diversity, redundancy, and decentralisation, which are key characteristics of resilient systems. Rather than concentrating services in a few centralised assets, cities are encouraged to develop modular and flexible infrastructure systems that can fail gracefully and be repaired quickly (Ahern, 2011).

6.2.4 *Climate Adaptation and Risk-Informed Planning*

The climate adaptation literature provides specific guidance on how infrastructure planning must respond to projected climate risks. The Intergovernmental Panel on Climate Change (IPCC) emphasises the need for anticipatory, rather than reactive, infrastructure planning based on downscaled climate models, vulnerability assessments, and local knowledge (IPCC, 2022). Risk-informed infrastructure planning incorporates flood risk zones into road alignment decisions, designs drainage systems based on future rainfall patterns, and prioritises green infrastructure in urban expansion areas (UN-Habitat, 2020). For example, Beira's Master Plan 2035 integrates sea-level rise projections into the zoning of transport and housing infrastructure (World Bank, 2020). Adaptation planning also calls for cross-sectoral governance, flexible financing, and inclusive stakeholder processes, especially in cities with high levels of informality and tenure insecurity (Satterthwaite et al., 2020).

6.2.5 *"Build Back Better" and Post-disaster Recovery*

The "build back better" (BBB) concept, popularised in the aftermath of the 2004 Indian Ocean tsunami, emphasises the use of post-disaster recovery periods as opportunities to enhance resilience and correct pre-existing vulnerabilities (Clinton, 2006). Rather than simply restoring damaged infrastructure to its previous condition, BBB advocates for improvements in design standards, hazard mitigation, land use, and governance. In Southern Africa, Cyclone Idai's devastation in Mozambique and Zimbabwe highlighted both the potential and limitations of BBB. While international aid helped rebuild roads, schools, and drainage systems, many reconstruction projects failed to integrate hazard data or community feedback, resulting in repeated losses during subsequent events (GFDRR, 2020). To be effective, BBB must be institutionalised within disaster management frameworks, backed by contingency funding, and implemented through transparent and participatory mechanisms. It also requires coordination across infrastructure, housing, and social services to ensure holistic recovery.

6.3 Infrastructure Vulnerabilities in Southern African Cities

Southern African cities face deep-rooted infrastructure vulnerabilities that stem from a combination of colonial legacies, rapid population growth, weak institutional capacity, and insufficient investment in maintenance and upgrading. These vulnerabilities are not just physical but are embedded in socio-economic structures, governance arrangements, and policy choices that often prioritise short-term development over long-term resilience (UN-Habitat, 2020; Satterthwaite et al., 2020).

6.3.1 Water Supply and Sanitation

Access to safe water and adequate sanitation remains a critical challenge in many cities across the region. Infrastructure networks are typically aged, poorly maintained, and unable to meet the demands of rapidly growing populations. In Harare, for instance, intermittent water supply is exacerbated by ageing pipelines, high levels of non-revenue water, and energy supply disruptions (Chigudu, 2020). The resulting reliance on unsafe water sources contributes to recurrent cholera outbreaks, especially in informal settlements. In Lusaka, groundwater pollution from unregulated pit latrines and poor sanitation infrastructure has led to the contamination of aquifers that serve nearly half the population. Many peri-urban areas lack any formal water connection, relying on private boreholes and informal vendors. These systems are vulnerable to droughts, contamination, and pricing shocks.

Climate change further stresses water supply systems by altering rainfall patterns, reducing reservoir recharge rates, and intensifying competition between domestic, industrial, and agricultural users (Niang et al., 2014).

Cities like Windhoek and Gaborone, located in semi-arid zones, face acute water scarcity and rely heavily on cross-border transfers and emergency supply measures, which are not always reliable. Sanitation infrastructure is similarly weak. In many informal settlements, sewerage systems are non-existent, leading to reliance on unsafe disposal methods that create health and environmental risks. The lack of coordinated waste and sanitation management also contributes to blocked drains and flooding during heavy rains.

6.3.2 Energy Infrastructure

Energy systems in Southern African cities are often unreliable, unaffordable, and unevenly distributed. While formal urban areas typically have access to grid electricity, informal settlements and rural-urban fringes remain underserved. Frequent load-shedding, ageing transmission infrastructure, and dependence on fossil fuels limit the capacity of cities to power essential services, including hospitals, water treatment plants, and emergency systems (Matinga et al., 2013). South Africa's electricity crisis, marked by repeated power cuts due to ageing infrastructure and governance failures at Eskom, exemplifies the systemic nature of energy insecurity in the region (Baker et al., 2014). These disruptions reduce productivity, hinder service delivery, and increase reliance on expensive and polluting diesel generators.

Moreover, the energy mix in many cities is poorly aligned with climate goals. Investments in renewable energy remain low, despite abundant solar and wind resources across the region. Barriers include a lack of policy coherence, limited financing mechanisms, and weak regulatory frameworks (REN21, 2022). In disaster contexts, the fragility of energy infrastructure has immediate consequences. Cyclone Idai damaged transmission lines and substations in Beira, delaying rescue efforts and water-pumping operations (GFDRR, 2020). Ensuring the resilience of energy infrastructure is thus vital for both daily operations and emergency response.

6.3.3 Urban Transport Networks

Transport infrastructure in many Southern African cities is underdeveloped, congested, and poorly maintained. Road networks are often unpaved or inadequately designed for current traffic volumes, while public transport systems are largely informal and unregulated (Porter, 2014). In

Harare, Lusaka, and Maputo, minibuses and motorcycles dominate mobility but operate with minimal oversight, safety regulations, or integration with formal transport systems. During disaster events, the limitations of urban transport are starkly visible. Flooded roads hinder evacuation, delay emergency services, and isolate vulnerable communities (Cartwright et al., 2012a, b). The lack of multi-modal transport options further reduces the resilience of mobility systems.

Poor road drainage infrastructure and informal settlement encroachment onto transport corridors also increase risk. In Cape Town, for instance, flooding along major roads has been linked to inadequate stormwater management systems that fail under increasing rainfall intensities (Ziervogel et al., 2017). Investments in climate-resilient transport infrastructure, such as elevated roads, improved culverts, and permeable paving, are limited. Institutional bottlenecks, including fragmented mandates across transport, planning, and environment departments, often delay or derail resilience-focused transport interventions (UN-Habitat, 2020).

6.3.4 *Solid Waste and Drainage Infrastructure*

Waste management systems in the region are generally weak, with significant implications for disaster risk. In many cities, solid waste collection coverage is low, especially in informal settlements, leading to illegal dumping in waterways, drains, and open spaces (UNEP, 2018). This not only poses health risks but also contributes directly to urban flooding when blocked drainage systems overflow. For example, in Dar es Salaam and Lusaka, studies have shown a clear correlation between uncollected waste, clogged drains, and flood intensity (Douglas et al., 2008). Efforts to formalise waste systems through municipal service delivery are constrained by limited budgets, lack of equipment, and weak enforcement mechanisms.

Decentralised waste collection systems and community-led initiatives have emerged in some cities, often supported by NGOs and international donors. However, these remain fragmented and underfunded. Integrated waste and drainage planning is rare, and urban flood risk assessments often overlook waste-related drivers. The case of Beira demonstrates how climate-induced flooding is intensified by clogged and undersized drains that cannot handle increasing rainfall volumes, particularly when combined with uncollected solid waste (World Bank, 2020).

6.4 Case Studies: Resilient Infrastructure Planning in Practice

Southern Africa presents diverse urban contexts, ranging from coastal lowlands to highland cities, each with distinct infrastructure challenges and innovations. The following case studies illustrate how cities are attempting to integrate resilience into infrastructure planning, highlighting both the progress made and the barriers that persist.

6.4.1 *Durban, South Africa: Nature-Based Infrastructure and Governance Integration*

Durban (eThekwini Municipality) is widely regarded as a pioneer in ecosystem-based approaches to urban resilience in Africa. Facing risks from sea-level rise, coastal erosion, and flash floods, Durban has responded with a range of infrastructure innovations that combine grey and green systems (Roberts & Diederichs, 2002). One flagship project is the uMngeni Ecological Infrastructure Partnership, which restores degraded catchment areas to improve water security and reduce flood risks (Sutherland et al., 2015). Wetlands and riparian buffers are integrated into the city's stormwater infrastructure to manage runoff and prevent erosion.

The Municipal Climate Protection Programme (MCPP) established a cross-departmental governance platform to mainstream climate adaptation into infrastructure planning. This includes guidelines for climate-proofing roads, housing, and public buildings, as well as zoning overlays that restrict development in ecologically sensitive areas (Roberts et al., 2012). Durban's experience demonstrates the importance of political leadership, interdepartmental coordination, and knowledge co-production with academic partners like the University of KwaZulu-Natal. However, scaling ecosystem-based infrastructure remains limited by land tenure conflicts and the marginalisation of informal settlements from formal planning systems (Taylor et al., 2016).

6.4.2 *Maputo, Mozambique: Post-disaster Infrastructure Resilience*

Maputo, Mozambique's capital, has increasingly faced the impacts of coastal flooding, cyclones, and unregulated urban growth. The devastating effects of Cyclone Idai in 2019 spurred renewed attention to infrastructure resilience across coastal cities like Maputo and Beira (GFDRR, 2020).

In response, the city developed a Climate Resilient Infrastructure Development Plan supported by the World Bank. The plan integrates hydrological modelling and risk mapping into infrastructure investment decisions, prioritising elevated road alignments, flood-resilient schools, and protective sea barriers (World Bank, 2020). Drainage improvements and road rehabilitation projects now include climate risk screening to ensure long-term functionality. A notable innovation is the use of modular culvert designs that allow easy scaling based on future rainfall projections. Despite this progress, implementation is hampered by weak institutional capacity, under-resourced municipalities, and difficulties in engaging vulnerable communities in infrastructure co-design. The case of Maputo illustrates both the opportunities and constraints of using disaster recovery to advance resilient infrastructure planning.

6.4.3 Johannesburg, South Africa: Critical Infrastructure Assessment and Stress Testing

Johannesburg, the economic hub of South Africa, faces multiple stressors, including ageing infrastructure, flash flooding, and energy instability. The city has begun using critical infrastructure stress testing as a method to prioritise resilience investments and improve inter-agency coordination (CoGTA, 2019). Through its Integrated Infrastructure Master Plan, Johannesburg identified vulnerable assets, such as bridges, electricity substations, and hospitals, located in flood-prone or geotechnically unstable zones. The city is now phasing in climate-resilient road materials and improved maintenance systems for stormwater channels.

Digital tools such as geographic information systems (GIS) and asset management software are being deployed to monitor infrastructure performance and anticipate failures (Ziervogel et al., 2017). The city also piloted a resilience scoring framework in partnership with the 100 Resilient Cities initiative, helping align budget allocations with climate risk priorities. However, legacy spatial inequalities and high levels of informality in townships like Alexandra and Soweto continue to challenge equitable service delivery. While the city has technical capacity, resource allocation remains biased towards high-income suburbs, and informal areas often fall outside the scope of resilience-focused investments.

6.4.4 *Windhoek, Namibia: Water Infrastructure Innovation in a Semi-Arid City*

Windhoek offers a unique example of water infrastructure resilience in a region highly vulnerable to drought. As one of the driest capitals in the world, Windhoek has pioneered direct potable water reuse, blending recycled wastewater into the city's drinking water supply since the 1960s (Lahnsteiner & Lempert, 2007). Faced with recurrent droughts and limited surface water, the city developed a Diversified Water Supply Strategy, combining aquifer recharge, groundwater extraction, desalination, and rainwater harvesting. The Goreangab Water Reclamation Plant is a central component, allowing the city to sustain its water supply during multi-year droughts (Schreiner & Baleta, 2015).

This approach is supported by strict water conservation campaigns, tiered pricing models, and stakeholder engagement to ensure public acceptance. Resilience is further enhanced by integrating water risk assessments into urban land-use planning and restricting development in recharge zones. While Windhoek has set a regional benchmark for drought resilience, scaling similar technologies in less-capacitated cities requires significant investment, governance reform, and public education.

6.5 Barriers to Resilient Infrastructure Implementation in Southern Africa

Despite the growing policy emphasis on resilience and numerous pilot initiatives across the region, the effective implementation of resilient infrastructure remains limited in scope and scale. This section examines the key barriers—financial, institutional, technical, political, and social—that constrain the development and sustainability of resilient infrastructure systems in Southern African cities.

6.5.1 *Financial Constraints and Inadequate Investment*

One of the most pervasive barriers to resilient infrastructure implementation is the chronic underfunding of urban services. Municipal budgets in Southern Africa are often heavily constrained, with limited capacity to mobilise revenue or access long-term capital markets (Cirolia, 2017). Infrastructure investment tends to prioritise economic growth and expansion, rather than risk reduction and adaptation. Where donor funding is available, it is frequently project-based, fragmented, and donor-driven, limiting continuity and alignment with long-term city plans (Khan, 2021). In Mozambique, for example, resilience-focused infrastructure projects launched after Cyclone Idai were partially funded by international aid but lacked domestic financing mechanisms to ensure operation and maintenance (GFDRR, 2020).

Accessing climate finance remains especially challenging for municipalities. Funds such as the Green Climate Fund and Adaptation Fund often require technical proposals, fiduciary compliance, and institutional frameworks that local governments lack. As a result, African cities secure only a fraction of available global climate finance, despite being disproportionately vulnerable (Watkiss & Klein, 2019).

6.5.2 Institutional Fragmentation and Poor Coordination

Urban infrastructure systems are typically managed by multiple departments, agencies, and levels of government, often with overlapping or poorly defined mandates. This institutional fragmentation undermines coordination, delays project implementation, and hampers cross-sectoral resilience planning (Goodfellow, 2013). For instance, in Harare, responsibilities for drainage, housing, and waste management are split across local authorities, parastatals, and line ministries, with little communication or shared data systems (Kamete, 2006). The result is disjointed planning and service duplication or gaps, especially in informal areas.

In some cities, central governments retain control over strategic infrastructure (for example, highways, power grids) while devolving responsibilities for maintenance and delivery to under-resourced local governments. This leads to mismatches in capacity and accountability, weakening resilience outcomes (UN-Habitat, 2020). Integrated development planning tools, such as spatial development frameworks, integrated infrastructure plans, and resilience strategies, are often absent or poorly implemented, especially in secondary and tertiary cities (Todes, 2011).

6.5.3 Technical Capacity Gaps

Technical knowledge and data availability are fundamental to resilience planning, yet many Southern African cities lack the tools, expertise, and systems to develop and maintain resilient infrastructure. Planners and engineers may be unfamiliar with risk modelling, climate projections, or green infrastructure design (World Bank, 2019). Data gaps are especially acute. Hazard maps, infrastructure audits, and risk assessments are often outdated or non-existent. For example, many cities do not have accurate maps of underground utilities, which complicates retrofitting or expanding resilient infrastructure (UNDRR, 2019).

The loss of skilled personnel due to migration ("brain drain"), poor salaries, and political interference further erodes institutional capacity. Moreover, procurement systems often prioritise the lowest-cost bids, rather than resilience or long-term quality, incentivising substandard construction and materials (Transparency International, 2019). Addressing these gaps requires sustained investment in training, local research, and partnerships with academic institutions and technical organisations.

6.5.4 *Political Economy and Elite Capture*

Infrastructure decisions are shaped not only by technical needs but also by political and economic interests. In many Southern African cities, infrastructure projects are influenced by electoral cycles, patronage networks, or private sector lobbying, rather than evidence-based assessments of risk and need (Pieterse & Parnell, 2014). High-profile "prestige" projects, such as stadia, highways, or shopping malls, may receive disproportionate funding, while low-income neighbourhoods remain underserved. Similarly, corruption in procurement processes can inflate costs, compromise quality, and divert funds from essential infrastructure upgrades (Transparency International, 2019).

Efforts to enhance resilience may be resisted by vested interests, particularly when they involve relocating settlements, enforcing building codes, or regulating land use in informal markets (Roy, 2005). Planning systems often lack the political independence to challenge these interests. Public participation mechanisms are often weak or tokenistic, excluding communities from decisions that affect their access to services and exposure to risk (Cornwall, 2008). This undermines trust and reduces the uptake and sustainability of resilience interventions.

6.5.5 *Socio-Spatial Inequality and Informality*

Infrastructure resilience is deeply affected by patterns of spatial inequality. In most Southern African cities, infrastructure investment has historically favoured formal, central, and affluent areas, while informal settlements on the urban periphery remain marginalised and exposed to hazards (Huchzermeyer, 2011). Informal areas often lack legal recognition, making it difficult to deliver public infrastructure without formal tenure. Residents may fear eviction, leading to resistance against formal upgrading. Meanwhile, informal systems of service delivery (for example, boreholes, community electricity) operate outside regulatory frameworks, making resilience planning difficult (Satterthwaite et al., 2020).

Socio-economic exclusion also limits the ability of low-income communities to invest in infrastructure or participate in planning processes. Gender dynamics further exacerbate this, as women often face greater burdens during disasters (for example, accessing water, caring for children), yet are underrepresented in infrastructure governance (Bradshaw, 2013). Addressing these issues requires not only technical solutions but also rights-based approaches that foreground equity, inclusion, and social justice in infrastructure planning.

6.6 Policy Recommendations for Advancing Resilient Infrastructure in Southern Africa

Building resilient infrastructure in Southern African cities requires a multifaceted approach that integrates technical, financial, institutional, and social considerations. Based on the vulnerabilities and lessons discussed throughout this chapter, the following recommendations are proposed to guide policymakers, urban planners, donors, and civil society in advancing resilient infrastructure agendas.

6.6.1 Mainstream Risk and Resilience into Infrastructure Planning

Disaster and climate risk must be integrated from the earliest stages of infrastructure planning. This includes:

- *Mandatory climate risk assessments* for all major infrastructure projects using downscaled climate models and vulnerability maps (IPCC, 2022).
- *Integration of resilience criteria into design codes*, procurement processes, and environmental impact assessments (UNDRR, 2019).

- *Development of city-level infrastructure resilience frameworks* that prioritise investments based on risk exposure, criticality, and equity.

Planning tools such as integrated development plans (IDPs), spatial development frameworks (SDFs), and infrastructure asset registers should include resilience indicators and be regularly updated in response to emerging hazards.

6.6.2 Prioritise Nature-Based and Hybrid Infrastructure Solutions

Green and hybrid infrastructure can complement conventional engineering approaches while offering long-term cost and environmental benefits. Municipalities should:

- *Protect and restore wetlands, riverbanks, and green corridors* as natural buffers against floods and heatwaves (Elmqvist et al., 2013; Roberts et al., 2012).
- *Incorporate nature-based solutions* into water, drainage, and transport systems (for example, bioswales, rain gardens, and permeable pavements).
- *Update building regulations* to incentivise rooftop gardens, green walls, and urban forestry, especially in dense informal areas.

Such approaches are especially important in flood-prone and drought-affected cities and are often more cost-effective and scalable than grey infrastructure alone.

6.6.3 Expand Access to Resilience Financing

Financing is a major bottleneck. Governments and development partners must:

- *Strengthen municipal financial systems* to enhance creditworthiness, improve revenue collection, and reduce dependency on national transfers (Cirolia, 2017).
- *Support city-level access to international climate funds* through technical assistance, proposal writing, and fiduciary training (Khan, 2021).

- *Leverage public–private partnerships (PPPs)* for resilient infrastructure, especially in energy and transport sectors, while ensuring affordability and public accountability.

Innovative financing mechanisms, such as municipal resilience bonds, green infrastructure levies, and land value capture, can also be explored.

6.6.4 Improve Intersectoral and Intergovernmental Coordination

Effective infrastructure resilience demands collaboration across departments and levels of government. Recommendations include:

- *Establishing urban resilience units* within city administrations with a cross-sectoral mandate.
- *Creating national coordination platforms* to align infrastructure, climate, and disaster policies (for example, ministries of public works, environment, and local government).
- *Developing shared data platforms* to facilitate planning, monitoring, and accountability across institutions (World Bank, 2019).

Integrated planning reduces duplication, ensures that investments serve multiple objectives, and enhances adaptive capacity.

6.6.5 Invest in Capacity Building and Local Innovation

Resilience is not only about physical assets; it also depends on the knowledge, skills, and creativity of people managing and using infrastructure. Governments and donors should:

- *Train engineers, planners, and project managers* in climate resilience, risk modelling, and community engagement techniques (UN-Habitat, 2020).
- *Support partnerships with universities and technical institutions* to develop context-appropriate tools and curricula.
- *Promote pilot projects* in low-income and informal areas to test scalable, community-driven infrastructure solutions (for example, off-grid energy, modular sanitation, and low-cost flood defences).

These initiatives can help reduce reliance on foreign consultants and build endogenous expertise.

6.6.6 *Promote Equity, Inclusion, and Accountability*

Infrastructure resilience must centre on the needs of the most vulnerable. To ensure this:

- *Resilience investments should prioritise underserved areas*, such as informal settlements, with strong community participation in design and monitoring.
- *Gender-sensitive infrastructure design* should be standardised, recognising different needs in access, safety, and use (Bradshaw, 2013).
- *Citizen feedback mechanisms* (for example, mobile reporting, and social audits) should be institutionalised to track service delivery and project quality (Cornwall, 2008).

A rights-based approach helps ensure that infrastructure contributes to justice and human dignity, not just physical survival.

6.7 Conclusion

Infrastructure systems are the backbone of urban resilience. In Southern African cities, where the effects of climate change, socio-economic inequality, and rapid urbanisation converge, the need to design, invest in, and manage resilient infrastructure has never been more urgent. Infrastructure not only enables daily urban functions but also determines how well cities can withstand and recover from shocks, whether natural disasters, pandemics, or economic disruptions. This chapter has explored the complex and interdependent nature of infrastructure resilience, emphasising that solutions must move beyond technical fixes to embrace systemic, inclusive, and adaptive approaches. By reviewing theoretical frameworks, current vulnerabilities, case studies, and implementation barriers, it has become evident that infrastructure resilience in Southern Africa is both a developmental challenge and an opportunity for transformation.

Durban's ecosystem-based infrastructure, Windhoek's water reuse systems, Maputo's post-cyclone rebuilding, and Johannesburg's risk assessments provide concrete examples of what is possible when planning aligns with resilience goals. However, these examples remain exceptions in a region where infrastructure is still largely reactive, underfunded, and unequal. To mainstream resilience, cities must overcome structural barriers, including limited finance, fragmented institutions, weak technical capacity, and political capture. This requires coordinated policy reform, stronger partnerships, improved data and training, and a firm commitment to inclusion, particularly for informal and marginalised communities who often bear the brunt of infrastructural failure. Looking ahead, infrastructure planning must be central to Southern Africa's resilience agenda. It must anticipate future risks, incorporate nature-based solutions, prioritise equity, and be guided by long-term visions that put people—and especially the most vulnerable—at the heart of urban development.

References

Ahern, J. (2011). From fail-safe to safe-to-fail: Sustainability and resilience in the new urban world. *Landscape and Urban Planning, 100*(4), 341–343.

Baker, L., Newell, P., & Phillips, J. (2014). The political economy of energy transitions: The case of South Africa. *New Political Economy, 19*(6), 791–818.

Beall, J., Crankshaw, O., & Parnell, S. (2002). *Uniting a divided city: Governance and social exclusion in Johannesburg*. Earthscan.

Bradshaw, S. (2013). Gender, development and disasters. In P. Delaney & E. Shrader (Eds.), *Gender and post-disaster reconstruction*. World Bank.

Cartwright, A., Cohen, B., & Liddell, D. (2012a). Supporting city-scale decisions in the context of climate change: The case of the City of Cape Town. In *Climate change at the city scale* (pp. 202–222). Routledge.

Cartwright, A., Cohen, B., & Liddell, D. (2012b). *Climate change at the city scale: Impacts, mitigation and adaptation in Cape Town*. Earthscan.

Chigudu, S. (2020). *The political life of an epidemic: Cholera, crisis and citizenship in Zimbabwe*. Cambridge University Press.

Cirolia, L. R. (2017). Fractured fiscal authority and fragmented infrastructures: Financing sustainable urban development in sub-Saharan Africa. *Cities, 70*, 1–10.

Clinton, W. J. (2006). *Lessons learned from tsunami recovery*. United Nations Secretary-General's Special Envoy for Tsunami Recovery. United Nations.

Cornwall, A. (2008). Unpacking "Participation": Models, meanings and practices. *Community Development Journal, 43*(3), 269–283.

Department of Cooperative Governance and Traditional Affairs (CoGTA). (2019). *National Disaster Management Framework (NDMF) 2019–2024*. Pretoria: Government of South Africa.

Douglas, I., Alam, K., Maghenda, M., Mcdonnell, Y., McLean, L., & Campbell, J. (2008). Unjust waters: Climate change, flooding and the urban poor in Africa. *Environment and Urbanization, 20*(1), 187–205.

Elmqvist, T., Fragkias, M., Goodness, J., Güneralp, B., Marcotullio, P. J., McDonald, R. I., Parnell, S., Schewenius, M., Sendstad, M., Seto, K. C., & Wilkinson, C. (2013). *Urbanization, biodiversity and ecosystem services: Challenges and opportunities: A global assessment*. Springer Nature.

Folke, C., Carpenter, S. R., Walker, B., Scheffer, M., Chapin, T., & Rockström, J. (2010). Resilience thinking: Integrating resilience, adaptability and transformability. *Ecology and Society, 15*(4).

Global Facility for Disaster Reduction and Recovery (GFDRR). (2020). *Beira recovery and resilience strategy*. GFDRR.

Goodfellow, T. (2013). The institutionalisation of "noise" and "silence" in urban politics: Riots and compliance in Uganda and Rwanda. *Oxford Development Studies, 41*(4), 436–454.

Huchzermeyer, M. (2011). *Cities with 'Slums': From informal settlement eradication to a right to the city in Africa*. UCT Press.

Intergovernmental Panel on Climate Change (IPCC). (2022). *Climate change 2022: Impacts, adaptation and vulnerability*. Intergovernmental Panel on Climate Change.

Kamete, A. Y. (2006). The return of the jekemu: Governance in Harare's periphery. *Habitat International, 30*(4), 101–111.

Khan, M. R. (2021). Unlocking climate finance for city resilience: Unlocking climate finance. *Cities, 117*, 103–291.

Lahnsteiner, J., & Lempert, G. (2007). Water management in Windhoek, Namibia. *Water Science and Technology, 55*(1–2), 441–448.

Mather, A. A., & Stretch, D. D. (2012). A perspective on sea level rise and coastal storm surge from Southern and Eastern Africa. *African Journal of Marine Science, 34*(3), 327–332.

Matinga, M. N., Clancy, J. S., & Annegarn, H. (2013). Explaining the non-implementation of health-improving policies in electricity generation: Indoor air pollution in South Africa. *Energy Policy, 58*, 163–170.

Munang, R., Thiaw, I., Alverson, K., Liu, J., & Han, Z. (2013). The role of ecosystem services in climate change adaptation and disaster risk reduction. *Current Opinion in Environmental Sustainability, 5*(1), 47–52.

Niang, I., Ruppel, O. C., Abdrabo, M. A., Essel, A., Lennard, C., Padgham, J., & Urquhart, P. (2014). Africa. In V. R. Barros, C. B. Field, D. J. Dokken, M. D. Mastrandrea, K. J. Mach, T. E. Bilir, … L. L. White (Eds.), *Climate change 2014: Impacts, adaptation, and vulnerability. Part B: Regional aspects. Contribution of Working Group II to the Fifth Assessment Report of the Intergovernmental Panel on Climate Change* (pp. 1199–1265). Cambridge University Press.

Pescaroli, G., & Alexander, D. (2015). A definition of cascading disasters and cascading effects: Going beyond the "toppling dominos" metaphor. *Planet@ Risk, 3*(1), 58–67.

Pieterse, E., & Parnell, S. (2014). *Africa's urban revolution*. Zed Books.
Porter, G. (2014). Transport services and their impact on poverty and growth in rural sub-Saharan Africa. *Transport Reviews, 34*(1), 25–45.
Renewable Energy Policy Network for the 21st Century (REN21). (2022). *Renewables 2022 global status report*. REN21.
Rinaldi, S. M., Peerenboom, J. P., & Kelly, T. K. (2001). Identifying, understanding, and analyzing critical infrastructure interdependencies. *IEEE Control Systems Magazine, 21*(6), 11–25.
Roberts, D., Boon, R., Diederichs, N., Douwes, E., Govender, N., Mcinnes, A., Mclean, C., O'Donoghue, S., & Spires, M. (2012). Exploring ecosystem-based adaptation in Durban, South Africa: "Learning-by-doing" at the local government coal face. *Environment and Urbanization, 24*(1), 167–195.
Roberts, D., & Diederichs, N. (2002). Durban's climate protection programme: Climate change and urban resilience in South Africa. *Environment and Urbanization, 14*(1), 159–168.
Roy, A. (2005). Urban informality: Toward an epistemology of planning. *Journal of the American Planning Association, 71*(2), 147–158.
Satterthwaite, D., Archer, D., Colenbrander, S., Dodman, D., Hardoy, J., Mitlin, D., & Patel, S. (2020). Building resilience to climate change in informal settlements. *One Earth, 2*(2), 143–156.
Schreiner, B., & Baleta, H. (2015). Broadening the lens: A regional perspective on water, food and energy integration in SADC. *Aquatic Procedia, 5*, 90–103.
Sterman, J. D. (2000). *Business dynamics: Systems thinking and modeling for a complex world*. McGraw-Hill.
Sutherland, C., Roberts, D., & Douwes, J. (2015). Constructing resilience at three scales: The 100 Resilient Cities programme, Durban and the uMngeni catchment. *Environment and Urbanization, 27*(2), 1–18.
Taylor, A., Cartwright, A., & Sutherland, C. (2016). Institutional pathways for local climate adaptation: A comparison of three South African municipalities. *Environment and Planning. C, Government & Policy, 34*(6), 1135–1153.
Todes, A. (2011). Reinventing planning: Critical reflections. *Urban Forum, 22*(2), 115–133.
Transparency International. (2019). *Corruption perceptions index 2019*. [online] www.transparency.org
UN-Habitat. (2020). *World cities report 2020: The value of sustainable urbanization*. UN-Habitat.
United Nations. (2015). *Transforming our world: The 2030 agenda for sustainable development*. United Nations.
United Nations Environment Programme (UNEP). (2018). *Making the case for ecosystem-based adaptation: The global mountain EbA programme*. United Nations Environment Programme.

United Nations Office for Disaster Risk Reduction (UNDRR). (2019). *Global Assessment report on disaster risk reduction*. United Nations Office for Disaster Risk Reduction.

Watkiss, P., & Klein, R. J. T. (2019). Financing climate resilience in cities. *Current Opinion in Environmental Sustainability, 39*, 77–84.

World Bank. (2019). *Lifelines: The resilient infrastructure opportunity*. World Bank.

World Bank. (2020). *Beira master plan 2035: Building a resilient city*. World Bank Group.

Ziervogel, G., Pelling, M., Cartwright, A., Chu, E., Deshpande, T., Harris, L., Hyams, K., Kaunda, J., Klaus, B., Michael, K., & Pasquini, L. (2017). Inserting rights and justice into urban resilience: A focus on everyday risk. *Environment and Urbanization, 29*(1), 123–138.

CHAPTER 7

Climate Change Adaptation and Urban Resilience in Southern Africa

7.1 Introduction

Southern Africa's urban centres are growing rapidly against the backdrop of intensifying climate risks. With global urban populations expected to reach 68% by 2050, cities such as Johannesburg, Durban, Maputo, and Harare reflect the pressures of fast-paced, often unplanned urbanisation. This growth has produced sprawling informal settlements, strained infrastructure, and environmental degradation, all of which heighten exposure to climate-induced hazards like floods, cyclones, and droughts (UN-Habitat, 2020). The effects of climate change are increasingly evident, with the region experiencing more frequent droughts, erratic rainfall, and extreme weather events (IPCC, 2022). Cyclone Idai, for example, caused over US$1.4 billion in damages in Mozambique, exposing the vulnerability of urban systems to climate shocks.

This reality demands urgent alignment between climate change adaptation, disaster risk reduction (DRR), and sustainable urban development. Unregulated expansion into floodplains and drought-prone areas compounds risks but simultaneously opens opportunities to embed resilience into planning systems (Satterthwaite et al., 2020). Cities in Southern Africa can lead by example in integrating adaptation into urban governance, land use management, and infrastructure investment. This

F. Mangara, N. Dorasamy, *Sustainable Urban Development in Southern Africa*, https://doi.org/10.1007/978-3-032-08286-2_7

chapter explores how Southern African cities are responding to climate risks through integrated adaptation and DRR strategies. It maps the regional climate risk landscape, examines institutional and policy frameworks, and reviews adaptation efforts across key sectors water, housing, health, and infrastructure drawing on case studies from Lusaka, Gaborone, Maputo, and Windhoek. The discussion further identifies governance, financing, and community participation as critical enablers or barriers to effective adaptation. Ultimately, the chapter positions climate adaptation as a driver of inclusive, sustainable urban development. In a region where climate change threatens to deepen inequality and disrupt livelihoods, resilience-building through risk-informed planning is essential for achieving Sustainable Development Goal 11 and safeguarding urban futures (Revi et al., 2014; UN-Habitat, 2020).

7.2 Climate Risk Landscape in Southern African Cities

Southern African cities face a multifaceted climate risk landscape defined by rising temperatures, shifting rainfall patterns, and an increasing frequency of extreme weather events. Over the past century, the region has warmed by over 0.5 °C, with parts of the Indian Ocean warming by more than 1 °C since the 1950s (IPCC, 2022). Rainfall trends have become more erratic, generally declining in many regions while being punctuated by intense storms and severe droughts. Since the early 1980s, stronger El Niño events have resulted in widespread climatic disruptions, including the 1988–1992 drought across Southern Africa and periodic floods linked to La Niña phases.

These below-average rainfall years now occur more frequently, straining water supplies and diminishing rain-fed agriculture. Simultaneously, when rainfall does occur, it often comes in short, heavy bursts that overwhelm urban drainage systems, triggering flash floods, particularly in informal settlements with poor infrastructure (Satterthwaite et al., 2020). These compounding climate trends prolonged droughts punctuated by extreme rainfall have intensified urban exposure to climate-related hazards.

7.3 Key Climate Hazards Affecting Southern African Cities Include

7.3.1 *Droughts and Water Scarcity*

Recurring droughts impact both interior and coastal cities, leading to declining river flows and depleted reservoirs. Cities such as Gaborone and Windhoek, two of the driest capitals globally, have experienced severe water shortages in recent decades. Between 2015 and 2018, Cape Town faced the well-publicised "Day Zero" crisis, where water supplies nearly ran dry, underscoring urban vulnerability to prolonged dry spells. Many cities depend on a limited number of large dams or aquifers; when these sources are compromised, water rationing, supply disruptions, and economic losses follow. In regions where hydropower is prominent, such as the Kariba Dam in Zambia and Zimbabwe, drought also threatens energy security. Without adaptive interventions, increasing evaporation and temperature stress may render current water systems insufficient (IPCC, 2022).

7.3.2 *Flooding and Extreme Rainfall*

Intense rainfall and cyclonic activity frequently cause urban flooding, posing significant risks to cities such as Lusaka, Maputo, and Dar es Salaam. Many urban areas in Southern Africa contain informal settlements in low-lying or swampy zones, where poorly planned construction and limited drainage make them especially vulnerable. In Lusaka, for instance, unplanned compounds built on former wetlands suffer regular floods during heavy rains (Chikodzi, 2020). Cyclone Idai in 2019 devastated urban areas in Mozambique, Zimbabwe, and Malawi, destroying over 90,000 homes and paralysing urban infrastructure such as roads, bridges, and power grids. More recently, in April 2022, catastrophic floods in eThekwini (Durban) claimed over 430 lives and inflicted billions of rands in damages, disrupting port and transportation operations. Climate models predict increased intensity and frequency of such events in the future (IPCC, 2022).

7.3.3 Cyclones and Coastal Storms

The southwestern Indian Ocean has recorded a rise in high-intensity cyclones, significantly threatening coastal cities such as Maputo, Beira, and Durban. These cities are exposed to storm surges, extreme winds, and flooding. Cyclones Idai and Eloise (2019 and 2021, respectively) resulted in extensive coastal inundation and wind damage in Mozambique, with impacts reaching as far inland as Harare. The threat is worsened by sea-level rise, which increases base water levels and exacerbates coastal erosion and flooding. Without adequate adaptation measures, such as mangrove restoration, elevated embankments, or managed retreat, infrastructure and livelihoods in coastal zones remain highly vulnerable (Cartwright et al., 2021).

7.3.4 Heatwaves and Urban Heat Islands

As global temperatures rise, heatwaves are becoming more frequent and intense. Urban areas often experience higher temperatures than their rural surroundings—a phenomenon known as the urban heat island effect. Cities like Harare, Lusaka, and Pretoria have reported increased incidences of heat-related illness during peak summer periods, especially among low-income populations lacking access to cooling systems or green spaces. Infrastructural stress is also evident, as extreme heat softens road surfaces and affects energy demand. Projections indicate a significant increase in days exceeding 35 °C by mid-century unless emissions are curtailed (IPCC, 2022).

7.3.5 Secondary and Compounding Risks

Climate risks often intersect with other vulnerabilities. Floods and heat-waves exacerbate public health issues, such as cholera outbreaks following flooding in Lusaka or malaria surges in Maputo (WHO, 2021). Drought-related crop failures drive rural-to-urban migration, further stressing city infrastructure and services. These cascading impacts highlight the systemic nature of climate risk: a flood event can simultaneously affect transport, sanitation, education, healthcare, and social cohesion (Revi et al., 2014; UNDRR, 2015).

Vulnerability is unevenly distributed. The urban poor, often residing in informal settlements, are most exposed to climate hazards and least equipped to recover. In Lusaka's Kanyama settlement, for example, moderate rains frequently flood homes and pit latrines, posing severe health threats (Nchito, 2021). These households lack the financial means to adapt or rebuild after disasters, and responses often lead to maladaptation, such as relocation to equally unsafe areas (Pelling & Garschagen, 2019). Southern African cities are on the frontlines of climate change. The convergence of rising hazard exposure and socio-economic vulnerability demands urgent and context-specific adaptation strategies. The next section will explore how international, national, and local frameworks can guide such efforts.

7.4 Conceptual and Policy Frameworks for Urban Adaptation

Climate change adaptation in urban areas is shaped by an evolving body of conceptual frameworks and policy instruments at the global, national, and local levels. In recent years, there has been a convergence of agendas across international climate policy, disaster risk reduction (DRR), and sustainable development, all of which emphasise the centrality of climate adaptation for cities. This section reviews the principal frameworks guiding adaptation in Southern Africa and examines how well these integrate climate action with DRR in urban governance.

7.5 International Frameworks and Agreements

The Paris Agreement (2015), adopted under the United Nations Framework Convention on Climate Change (UNFCCC), provides a foundational international commitment to adaptation. It establishes a Global Goal on Adaptation aimed at enhancing adaptive capacity, strengthening resilience, and reducing vulnerability to climate change (UNFCCC, 2015). Southern African nations, as signatories, have articulated adaptation goals through Nationally Determined Contributions (NDCs), focusing on sectors such as agriculture, water, and infrastructure.

For example, Botswana's climate policy positions adaptation as a developmental priority, aiming to mainstream it across sectors to protect economic progress from climate disruption. Similarly, South Africa's National Climate Change Adaptation Strategy (NCCAS) (2019) outlines a 10-year roadmap to embed adaptation into planning at national, provincial, and municipal levels (DEA, 2019). It links directly to global frameworks, including the Paris Agreement, the 2030 Agenda for Sustainable Development, the United Nations Convention to Combat Desertification, and the Sendai Framework for Disaster Risk Reduction (2015–2030) (UNDRR, 2015). These linkages reflect an increasing effort to localise global adaptation mandates through national strategies.

The Sendai Framework for DRR plays a pivotal role in bridging climate adaptation and conventional DRR. It emphasises four priorities: understanding risk, strengthening disaster governance, investing in resilience, and enhancing preparedness. These priorities intersect closely with adaptation goals. Sendai advocates integrating DRR into development at all levels, from national to local, and Southern African countries have begun to align their disaster management legislation and climate policies accordingly (UNDRR, 2015). For instance, South Africa's Disaster Management Act and its Climate Change Bill mandate risk-based planning and proactive adaptation to reduce future losses (Government of South Africa, 2021).

Many countries in the region are also formulating National Adaptation Plans (NAPs), for example, Zimbabwe's National Climate Policy (2016) and Botswana's NAP Framework (2020), which are increasingly aligned with their national DRR strategies. These plans typically prioritise urban areas due to their high concentrations of people and assets at risk. In addition, international initiatives such as the UNDRR Making Cities Resilient Campaign and the 100 Resilient Cities Programme have encouraged Southern African cities to craft resilience strategies consistent with the Sendai Framework and Sustainable Development Goal 11 (UNDRR, 2017).

7.5.1 *Sustainable Development Goals (SDGs) and the New Urban Agenda*

The 2030 Agenda for Sustainable Development integrates climate resilience into its urban vision, especially through SDG 11 ("Make cities inclusive, safe, resilient, and sustainable"). This goal calls for reducing the adverse impacts of disasters, improving urban infrastructure, and integrating climate adaptation and mitigation into broader development planning (UN, 2015). Targets include upgrading informal settlements, ensuring access to green spaces, and developing climate-resilient infrastructure.

The New Urban Agenda, adopted at Habitat III in 2016, reinforces the need for holistic, participatory urban planning that embeds both adaptation and DRR. It urges cities to employ inclusive approaches that engage communities and incorporate local knowledge. These global agendas have influenced urban policy discourse in Southern Africa. For instance, Namibia's national development plans and Zambia's urban policy explicitly reference SDGs and commit to climate-resilient infrastructure and settlement development (Republic of Namibia, 2017). However, actual implementation remains uneven, constrained by limited financial resources and institutional capacity.

7.5.2 *National Urban and Climate Policies*

At the national level, many Southern African states have developed climate change strategies or policies that identify priority adaptation areas, such as improving urban water security, climate-resilient housing, or early warning systems. South Africa offers one of the most advanced examples: in addition to the NCCAS, it has provided guidance for local municipalities to prepare Climate Change Adaptation Plans. Major cities like Durban, Cape Town, and Johannesburg have also adopted standalone climate strategies. Durban (eThekwini), for instance, pioneered the Municipal Climate Protection Programme in the early 2000s, integrating adaptation, particularly ecosystem-based approaches, into city-wide planning (Roberts & O'Donoghue, 2013). The programme combines scientific assessments, green infrastructure projects, and cross-departmental coordination and is widely cited as a model of municipal-level adaptation mainstreaming in Africa (Pasquini et al., 2015).

Other countries are also advancing urban-relevant climate policies. Zimbabwe's Climate Policy (2016) emphasises resilient infrastructure and housing, while Mozambique's National Strategy for Adaptation and Mitigation (2013–2025) includes urban flood control and coastal protection measures. However, policy-practice gaps remain pervasive. While frameworks promote integration, implementation is often hindered by institutional fragmentation, lack of local technical expertise, and limited finance (UN-Habitat, 2020).

7.6 Conceptual Approaches to Adaptation

Two central conceptual tools guide urban adaptation: resilience and transformative adaptation. Urban resilience refers to a city's ability to absorb and recover from shocks while maintaining essential functions. It underpins both adaptation and DRR by focusing on robustness, redundancy, and flexibility. This has been applied in infrastructure design (for example, modular systems) and community initiatives (for example, social capital-building for faster recovery). Transformative adaptation extends this further by advocating structural changes in governance, planning, and social arrangements to tackle the root causes of vulnerability. For instance, reconfiguring urban layouts to avoid high-risk zones or reforming land tenure systems to empower informal residents represents transformative shifts. In Southern Africa, Durban's ecosystem-based adaptation and Harare's wetland advocacy movement offer contrasting models: one led by formal governance, the other by civil society (Cartwright et al., 2021). Transformative adaptation is particularly relevant where incremental adjustments are insufficient in the face of escalating climate risks. It aligns strongly with DRR's "Build Back Better" agenda and with sustainable development goals that require systemic change rather than isolated interventions.

7.7 Integration of Adaptation and DRR in Urban Planning

Historically, climate change adaptation (CCA) and DRR evolved separately, with CCA within environmental governance and DRR within emergency management. However, their objectives increasingly converge. Both aim to reduce vulnerability and build resilience to environmental shocks (Revi et al., 2014). Cities are beginning to integrate the two through risk-informed development planning, applying hazard and climate data to zoning, infrastructure design, and investment prioritisation. In Durban, for example, the city's disaster management unit collaborates closely with its climate adaptation team, ensuring that actions such as wetland restoration serve dual goals. Cape Town's Climate Strategy (2021) similarly aligns informal settlement upgrading and flood early warning systems under a unified resilience agenda. Nonetheless, such integration is uneven across the region. In many cities, DRR remains reactive, focused on response, while climate adaptation is siloed within environmental departments. Breaking these silos remains an urgent institutional task (IPCC, 2022). Stronger linkages in planning, budgeting, and project design are needed to realise the potential co-benefits of integration.

7.8 Urban Governance and Institutions

Ultimately, the effectiveness of adaptation frameworks depends on governance capacity. Cities require inclusive, well-coordinated institutions to translate policies into on-the-ground action. Some Southern African municipalities have established climate focal points or multi-departmental committees. Multi-level governance is also essential: national governments must support local actors through mandates, finance, and technical tools. Yet, governance barriers remain a critical bottleneck. Weak coordination, inadequate skills, and insufficient funding hamper adaptation implementation (IPCC, 2022). For example, housing departments may approve developments in hazard zones despite climate warnings. Strengthening institutions requires policy reforms, training for municipal staff, and platforms for community participation, particularly to integrate Indigenous and local knowledge into adaptation practices.

7.9 Sectoral Adaptation Strategies for Sustainable Urban Development

Climate change adaptation in cities must engage multiple sectors simultaneously, as climate impacts cut across the interconnected systems that underpin urban life. Effective adaptation strategies, therefore, involve both targeted sectoral interventions and cross-cutting approaches that generate co-benefits for sustainable development and disaster risk reduction (DRR) (Satterthwaite et al., 2020; IPCC, 2022). This section discusses climate adaptation strategies across four critical sectors: (a) water and sanitation; (b) housing and informal settlements; (c) public health; and (d) urban infrastructure. In each domain, we explore how Southern African cities are aligning adaptation initiatives with resilience-building and developmental goals.

These sectors are deeply interrelated. For instance, enhancing water security not only reduces vulnerability to drought but also improves public health and supports local economies. Likewise, upgrading housing in flood-prone areas mitigates disaster risk while improving living conditions. As such, a holistic and systems-based perspective is essential, though sectoral entry points provide practical foundations for implementation.

7.9.1 Water Security and Flood Management

Water is perhaps the most immediate and visible point of stress in Southern African cities, manifesting as both scarcity (due to drought) and excess (due to flooding). Adaptation strategies in this sector aim to ensure reliable and safe water supplies amid changing climatic conditions, while also protecting cities from water-related hazards (World Bank, 2021).

7.9.1.1 Diversifying Water Sources

Cities are increasingly diversifying their water portfolios to reduce dependence on single sources, thereby spreading climate risk. Windhoek, Namibia, is a global pioneer in this regard. Its integrated water management strategy includes surface water, groundwater, aquifer recharge, and direct reuse of treated wastewater (Lahnsteiner & Lempert, 2007). The Goreangab Water Reclamation Plant, operational since the 1960s and continuously upgraded, supplies 15–30% of the city's drinking water through advanced wastewater purification (Heyns, 2005). This innovation has allowed Windhoek to endure multiple droughts and is now a model for arid urban centres facing similar water scarcity challenges. Other cities, such as Gaborone in Botswana, are adopting comparable approaches through inter-basin water transfers, additional borehole drilling, and exploration of water reuse and desalination options. Diversified systems enhance adaptive capacity by reducing vulnerability to disruptions in any single source, a necessity as climate variability increases (IPCC, 2022).

7.9.1.2 Water Demand Management

Efforts to manage consumption are equally crucial. Measures such as public conservation campaigns, leak detection programs, and progressive water tariffs can significantly reduce overall demand. Cape Town's aggressive demand reduction campaign during the 2017–2018 drought, featuring water restrictions, pricing reforms, and extensive public outreach, halved daily water usage and delayed "Day Zero". Windhoek has similarly promoted a culture of conservation through public education and tiered pricing (Heyns, 2005). These initiatives not only address immediate shortages but also promote long-term sustainability by embedding efficient water use into urban habits and policies.

7.9.1.3 Flood Risk Management and Urban Drainage

As intense rainfall events become more frequent, many Southern African cities are overhauling outdated drainage systems and adopting comprehensive flood management strategies. Risk-sensitive land-use planning is a core component, preventing construction in floodplains and conserving natural drainage channels where possible. Lusaka, Zambia, for example, has implemented a flood management master plan with support from development partners such as GIZ, which includes the protection of urban wetlands and the construction of retention ponds and drainage canals in flood-prone communities (Nchito, 2021). In Maputo, Mozambique, the Climate Resilient Infrastructure Plan, supported by the World Bank, includes upgrades to stormwater culverts, elevated roadways, and the restoration of coastal mangroves to buffer storm surges (Cartwright et al., 2021). Such interventions not only protect against flooding but also support DRR and sustainable development objectives by safeguarding infrastructure and reducing displacement.

7.9.1.4 Early Warning Systems and Preparedness

Robust hydrometeorological monitoring and early warning systems (EWS) are essential for urban adaptation. These systems enable cities to anticipate floods and droughts and implement timely emergency measures to minimise loss. Cities like Durban and Pretoria are expanding their networks of rain gauges and river-level sensors to detect flash flood risks. National meteorological services also provide seasonal forecasts and cyclone alerts to municipalities and communities, a practice that is increasingly recognised as vital for urban resilience (WMO, 2020). Effective EWS are those that are localised and actionable—targeted alerts (for example, SMS warnings to residents of informal settlements) must be integrated with contingency plans such as evacuation routes or pre-positioned supplies (UNDRR, 2022). Linking early warning with preparedness not only saves lives but enhances community trust in climate services, which is critical for long-term adaptation.

7.9.1.5 Ecosystem-Based Adaptation in Water Management

Nature-based solutions are gaining traction in urban water management. Restoring and conserving ecosystems such as forests, wetlands, and riparian buffers can enhance water quality, reduce runoff, and provide natural flood attenuation (Seddon et al., 2020). In Harare, wetlands play a vital role in regulating water flows into Lake Chivero, the city's main reservoir.

Yet, these ecosystems face pressure from encroaching development and pollution (Chikodzi, 2020). Civil society-led efforts, like the Harare Wetlands Initiative, seek to restore and protect these landscapes as part of a broader strategy for urban water security. Durban's extensive mangrove and river buffer restoration programmes offer another example. These efforts yield co-benefits such as reduced flood risk, improved biodiversity, carbon sequestration, and recreational green space (Roberts & O'Donoghue, 2013). Ecosystem-based approaches are often more cost-effective and sustainable over the long term than purely engineered solutions and have been recognised by the IPCC as high-confidence adaptation measures that provide economic, social, and environmental gains (IPCC, 2022).

7.9.2 Housing, Land Use, and Resilient Settlements

Housing and land use are central to addressing urban vulnerability and form a crucial part of climate adaptation in Southern African cities. A substantial proportion of the population resides in substandard housing, such as informal settlements, slums, or peri-urban areas, where exposure to climate hazards is high, and coping capacities are limited (Satterthwaite et al., 2020). Adaptation strategies in this domain focus on making human settlements safer and more resilient through both physical infrastructure improvements and institutional or regulatory reforms.

7.9.2.1 Upgrading Informal Settlements

Urban climate adaptation adds urgency to the long-standing development challenge of upgrading informal settlements. Interventions typically include reinforcing housing structures, installing basic infrastructure (drainage, water, sanitation, electricity), and securing land tenure. These measures significantly reduce vulnerability to climate extremes. For example, replacing precarious dwellings with sturdier structures can prevent collapses during storms, while improved drainage mitigates flood impacts. Legal recognition of tenure often encourages residents to invest in incremental upgrades to their homes (Satterthwaite et al., 2020). Cities like Cape Town, Lusaka, and Maputo have launched upgrading initiatives, many incorporating climate resilience components. Participatory approaches, where residents co-design solutions, ensure that local knowledge informs project design. Examples include elevating floor levels in flood-prone areas and orienting buildings for natural ventilation in heat-prone regions (UN-Habitat, 2020). In Windhoek, the Community Land Trust housing programme has resulted in safer, more resilient homes. Durban's in-situ upgrades in vulnerable informal areas have also shown tangible reductions in disaster losses. Such initiatives represent a "triple win", advancing adaptation, DRR, and sustainable development goals, particularly SDG 11.1 on adequate housing.

7.9.2.2 Risk-Based Land-Use Planning and Zoning

A forward-looking adaptation strategy is to integrate climate risk data into land-use planning and zoning regulations. This involves identifying and steering urban development away from high-hazard zones, such as floodplains, unstable slopes, and wildfire-prone zones, by leveraging hazard maps, environmental assessments, and climate projections (UNDRR, 2015; Revi et al., 2014). Implementing such policies in cities with acute housing shortages and widespread informality is challenging. Often, marginalised populations settle in high-risk zones because safer land is unaffordable or unavailable. Consequently, effective enforcement must be accompanied by the provision of viable relocation options, such as serviced plots or public housing schemes (Dodman et al., 2012). Some Southern African cities have introduced hazard zoning mechanisms. Cape Town, for instance, uses coastal setback lines to restrict construction in areas vulnerable to sea-level rise. Mozambique revised its building code post-Cyclone Idai to mandate cyclone-resistant designs and minimum floor heights in flood zones. Over time, consistent enforcement of risk-informed zoning can reduce overall urban exposure and prevent the creation of new risks.

7.9.2.3 Climate-Resilient Building Design

Adaptation efforts at the individual building scale can greatly reduce household vulnerability to climate stressors. Incorporating resilience into housing design improves safety, thermal comfort, and disaster resistance. Typical measures include elevating houses on stilts or plinths in flood-prone areas, using cool or green roofs to moderate indoor temperatures, improving insulation and ventilation, and reinforcing structures to withstand high winds. In South Africa, pilot projects have tested green roofing in low-income housing to reduce indoor heat during summer peaks (Ziervogel et al., 2016). In Zambia and Malawi, floodplain housing programmes promote elevated structures. Zimbabwe's updated building standards encourage climate-appropriate materials that provide thermal comfort and structural stability (Government of Zimbabwe, 2016). In Lusaka, informal settlers in flood-prone areas have raised their foundations and added entrance steps to prevent floodwater intrusion (Nchito, 2021).

Community-driven innovations are also relevant. In Kisumu, Kenya, a local programme supplied quarry stone and rubble for households to stabilise and raise mud-floor homes. Such low-cost techniques are transferable across Southern Africa and can generate employment in construction and training in resilient methods. Climate-resilient housing improves long-term sustainability by reducing reconstruction needs after disasters and aligns with SDGs on decent housing and sustainable cities (UN, 2015).

7.9.2.4 Nature-Based Solutions for Settlements

Green infrastructure offers natural buffers against climate hazards. Planting trees and establishing green belts around settlements reduces urban heat and improves stormwater absorption, especially in areas with high runoff risk (Seddon et al., 2020). Mangrove forests, for instance, act as protective barriers against storm surges and coastal erosion—a strategy being used in parts of Mozambique and Madagascar (Cartwright et al., 2021). Permeable surfaces in cities, such as parks, greenways, or community gardens, help recharge groundwater and moderate flooding. Urban agriculture programs, like Bulawayo's, maintain green spaces in floodplains that double as farming zones and flood absorption areas (Chikodzi, 2020). These approaches improve environmental and social resilience by fostering local stewardship, providing food and income, and cooling microclimates in dense settlements (Satterthwaite et al., 2020). Nature-based solutions can be more cost-effective than hard infrastructure, particularly in resource-constrained cities, and have the added advantage of supporting biodiversity, community participation, and job creation.

7.9.2.5 Social Protection and Post-disaster Support

Housing resilience extends beyond physical structures. Social safety nets and financial support are vital for helping vulnerable urban populations recover from climate shocks. In the aftermath of disasters, small grants or materials provided to low-income families can facilitate rebuilding with more durable and resilient structures (World Bank, 2021). In Mozambique, a post-cyclone reconstruction initiative has trained local masons in cyclone-resistant construction techniques while subsidising home repairs for affected families. These interventions apply the "Build Back Better" principle, which advocates that reconstruction should enhance resilience rather than replicate existing vulnerabilities (UNDRR, 2015). Insurance also holds promise. Though uptake remains low, index-based microinsurance schemes for flood and drought losses are emerging as tools for urban resilience in the Global South (Pelling & Garschagen, 2019). Government policies supporting risk pools, subsidised premiums, or catastrophe funds could help scale such models in the region. Combining physical adaptation with financial and institutional support enables more holistic and equitable resilience in housing. Integrating community participation, secure tenure, and inclusive design ensures that vulnerable populations are protected and empowered.

7.9.3 *Public Health and Resilience of Urban Populations*

Climate change poses both direct and indirect threats to urban public health. As such, adaptation strategies must aim to protect people from illness, improve the robustness of health systems, and reduce vulnerability to disease outbreaks. In many Southern African cities, the existing health burdens, including HIV/AIDS, tuberculosis, and diarrhoeal diseases, are likely to be exacerbated by climate stressors (WHO, 2021; IPCC, 2022). Adaptation approaches in the health sector, therefore, span infrastructure improvements, early warning systems, and environmental health interventions.

7.9.3.1 Heat Health Action Plans

With extreme heat becoming more common, cities are developing heatwave early warning and response systems. These plans often include the establishment of heat-health thresholds (temperatures beyond which alerts are triggered), public cooling centres, and community outreach to prevent heatstroke, especially among vulnerable groups such as the elderly, children, and outdoor workers (Robine et al., 2008; UN-Habitat, 2020). For example, Pretoria (City of Tshwane) has begun integrating heat alerts into its disaster risk management systems, offering advice on hydration and modifying outdoor activities during extreme heat days. Some municipalities are also promoting urban greening, planting street trees, expanding parks, and introducing green roofs in informal settlements to mitigate the urban heat island effect. These measures offer co-benefits, such as improved air quality, mental well-being, and liveability, aligning with both SDG 3 (good health) and SDG 11 (inclusive, green cities).

7.9.3.2 Disease Surveillance and Control

Climate change is shifting the epidemiology of vector-borne and waterborne diseases. Warmer temperatures and altered rainfall patterns expand the geographic range and seasonality of disease vectors like mosquitoes, potentially increasing the incidence of malaria, dengue, and other illnesses in urban areas that were previously less affected (Patz et al., 2005; WHO, 2021). In addition, flooding can result in contamination of drinking water supplies, leading to outbreaks of cholera, dysentery, and typhoid. Adaptation responses include strengthening disease surveillance systems and integrating climate data into early warning mechanisms. For instance, early warning models for malaria using rainfall and temperature data to predict outbreak risks have been tested in parts of Mozambique and South Africa. Pre-emptive actions such as indoor residual spraying and community clean-up campaigns have proven effective. Moreover, cities are investing in climate-resilient health infrastructure, ensuring that clinics and hospitals are located outside flood-prone areas, have elevated foundations, and maintain backup power and water supply systems to continue functioning during extreme events. The 2022 floods in Durban highlighted the urgency of such measures. Several clinics were rendered inaccessible or non-functional due to inundated roads and facility damage. Post-disaster assessments recommended the flood-proofing of health centres and the establishment of alternative access routes for ambulances during emergencies (City of eThekwini, 2022).

7.9.3.3 Water and Sanitation Services

Safe and reliable water and sanitation systems are essential for protecting public health in a changing climate. Service interruptions during droughts or storms can rapidly escalate into health crises, increasing the risks of dehydration, poor hygiene, and disease outbreaks. Consequently, many of the water sector adaptation measures discussed earlier, such as diversification of water sources, decentralised treatment systems, and emergency provision mechanisms, also serve as public health interventions (Satterthwaite et al., 2020; IPCC, 2022). Sanitation is equally vital. In cities such as Lusaka and Harare, flooding regularly compromises pit latrines and septic tanks, contaminating water sources and residential areas

(Nchito, 2021). To address these risks, some urban authorities are promoting ecological sanitation solutions, such as urine-diverting dry toilets, that reduce reliance on sewered systems vulnerable to climate impacts. Community-scale sanitation systems, especially those adapted to informal areas with high water tables, are being piloted in Windhoek and Maputo with promising results (UN-Habitat, 2020).

7.9.4 *Urban Infrastructure and Climate-Resilient Investment*

Urban infrastructure systems such as transport networks, energy grids, and communications systems are vital to the functioning and growth of cities. However, these systems are increasingly at risk from climate hazards. In Southern African cities, infrastructure is often ageing, poorly maintained, or built without considering future climate stressors, making adaptation an urgent priority. Building climate-resilient infrastructure is essential to reduce disaster losses, ensure service continuity, and enable sustainable urban development (IPCC, 2022; Satterthwaite et al., 2020).

7.9.4.1 *Critical Infrastructure Vulnerabilities*

Climate impacts on infrastructure manifest in multiple ways. Flooding can damage roads, bridges, and rail lines, disrupting mobility and trade. Heatwaves strain electricity grids and reduce transmission efficiency, while droughts impact hydropower production. Cyclones and storms damage power lines and telecommunication towers, leaving communities disconnected during emergencies (UNDRR, 2015). In Mozambique, Cyclone Idai (2019) severely damaged Beira's port, road network, and power infrastructure, hampering response and recovery efforts. In Durban, the 2022 floods destroyed roads and bridges, affecting over 1,000 kilometres of road surface and highlighting the vulnerability of transport systems in hilly, poorly drained urban environments (City of eThekwini, 2022). Such events underline the need to assess and retrofit infrastructure to withstand projected climate extremes.

7.9.4.2 *Resilient Infrastructure Planning and Investment*

Adaptation strategies in this domain include climate-proofing new infrastructure and retrofitting existing assets. Key measures involve elevating roads in flood-prone areas, constructing culverts and stormwater detention basins, using heat-resistant materials, and decentralising energy systems to increase redundancy (World Bank, 2021). Cities such as

Johannesburg are incorporating climate resilience into their Integrated Development Plans (IDPs), ensuring that transport corridors and public buildings are designed to endure climate hazards. In Namibia, Windhoek is exploring solar-powered water pumping stations and decentralised wastewater treatment as part of its climate-resilient infrastructure package (Republic of Namibia, 2021). These innovations improve adaptive capacity and service reliability, particularly in the face of compound shocks such as droughts coinciding with power outages.

Urban infrastructure design is also shifting towards modular and flexible systems that can be upgraded as climate risks evolve. For instance, Zimbabwe's National Renewable Energy Policy promotes off-grid solar mini-grids in underserved areas, which are more resilient to extreme weather than centralised systems (Government of Zimbabwe, 2019). Such infrastructure solutions not only enhance resilience but also advance equity by extending services to previously excluded populations.

7.9.4.3 Bridging the Infrastructure-Finance Gap

Financing climate-resilient infrastructure remains a major barrier in Southern Africa. Many cities lack the fiscal space, creditworthiness, or technical capacity to access large-scale climate finance or investment capital (UN-Habitat, 2020). Even where infrastructure needs are identified, project pipelines are often underdeveloped, and feasibility studies are lacking. To address this, cities are exploring partnerships with development finance institutions, national governments, and the private sector. Blended finance, combining concessional finance with private capital, is gaining attention as a strategy for funding urban adaptation. The Green Climate Fund, the Global Environment Facility, and the African Development Bank are increasingly supporting urban infrastructure programmes in climate-vulnerable cities (AfDB, 2021). Johannesburg and Cape Town have issued green bonds to fund climate-resilient infrastructure, including stormwater upgrades and energy-efficient buildings. These instruments are also being considered in Lusaka and Harare but require robust monitoring and reporting frameworks to attract investors (World Bank, 2021). Capacity-building in financial planning, project appraisal, and climate risk assessment is essential to enable smaller municipalities to access and deploy adaptation finance effectively.

7.9.4.4 Infrastructure, DRR, and Risk-Informed Urban Development

Infrastructure investment is increasingly seen as a lever for DRR. Embedding risk assessments into infrastructure planning ensures that new developments do not exacerbate exposure or vulnerability. For example, elevating roads in flood zones improves evacuation capacity during disasters; integrating stormwater capture into transport corridors reduces urban runoff; and decentralising energy improves post-disaster recovery speed (Revi et al., 2014). Cities are beginning to apply resilience screening tools in infrastructure planning. Durban uses a "climate lens" in capital budgeting to prioritise high-risk investments, while Lusaka has introduced hazard overlays into spatial development plans to avoid siting infrastructure in flood-prone areas (Cartwright et al., 2021). Such efforts embody a shift towards risk-informed development, where infrastructure is not merely built to withstand current risks but anticipates future climate scenarios.

Urban infrastructure lies at the intersection of climate adaptation, sustainable development, and disaster risk reduction. In Southern African cities, building climate-resilient infrastructure is not a luxury but a necessity to secure growth, equity, and stability in an era of intensifying climate risk. Resilient investment must be systemic, considering land use, service access, community needs, and environmental limits. It must be financed in ways that are inclusive, accountable, and forward-looking. Integrating DRR into infrastructure planning will be essential to safeguard the region's development gains in the decades ahead.

7.10 Case Studies

To ground the preceding discussion in real-world contexts, this section presents case studies from six Southern African cities: Lusaka (Zambia), Harare (Zimbabwe), Maputo (Mozambique), Windhoek (Namibia), Johannesburg (South Africa), and Gaborone (Botswana). Each case highlights specific adaptation challenges and innovations, providing insight into how strategies discussed in earlier sections are applied on the ground. Emphasis is placed on developments post-2020 and the dynamic interplay between climate adaptation, disaster risk reduction (DRR), and broader development goals.

7.10.1 *Lusaka, Zambia: Community Flood Adaptation in Informal Settlements*

Lusaka, the capital of Zambia, is a rapidly urbanising city with an estimated population of over 3 million. Its flat terrain and karstic limestone subsoil result in poor drainage, making it highly susceptible to flooding during the rainy season from November to April (Nchito, 2021). Approximately 70% of Lusaka's population resides in informal settlements, including flood-prone areas such as Kanyama and Kalikiliki, which are situated on reclaimed wetlands and low-lying land. Unregulated urban expansion without corresponding drainage infrastructure has compounded flood risks. Heavy rains frequently turn streets into streams, inundating homes, overflowing latrines, and triggering waterborne disease outbreaks such as cholera and dysentery. Climate projections suggest increased rainfall intensity and variability for Lusaka, with more frequent flash floods and prolonged dry spells, aggravating an already fragile urban water regime (IPCC, 2022).

Adaptation Initiatives

Lusaka has adopted both institutional and community-led measures to address flood risks. One major top-down initiative is the Drainage Improvement Project, implemented by the Lusaka City Council in partnership with international donors and NGOs. The project constructed concrete drainage channels, culverts, and soak-away pits in vulnerable townships. In Kanyama, a large drainage canal completed in 2020 has reportedly reduced flooding during moderate rainfall events (LCC, 2021). The initiative also trained local maintenance committees to clear debris from the drains, an approach that embeds sustainability through community ownership.

Community-driven responses have also been significant. Residents have undertaken autonomous measures such as elevating house foundations, digging informal trenches, and relocating vending stalls to higher ground during the rainy season (Nchito, 2021). These self-initiated adaptations reflect accumulated local knowledge and practical coping strategies. Notably, community groups in Kalikiliki organised regular clean-up campaigns to remove garbage from clogged waterways, a major contributor to local flooding. This underscores the effectiveness of behavioural adaptation and low-cost solutions, even in the absence of substantial financial resources. The Lusaka case illustrates the value of multi-level adaptation.

Municipal infrastructure improvements provide systemic flood relief, while grassroots actions address localised vulnerabilities. Together, they demonstrate how hybrid governance, combining formal state support and informal citizen agency, can enhance resilience in high-risk urban environments.

7.10.2 Harare, Zimbabwe: Protecting Urban Wetlands for Water and Climate Resilience

Harare, Zimbabwe's capital with a population of approximately 2.4 million, faces escalating climate-related challenges, chief among them, water insecurity and seasonal flooding. The city has long struggled with irregular water supply, attributed both to recurring droughts that reduce inflows to Lake Chivero (its primary reservoir) and to operational inefficiencies and pollution (Chikodzi, 2020). Additionally, Harare experiences periodic flash flooding, particularly in densely populated suburbs such as Budiriro and Glen View, where poor drainage and solid waste accumulation block runoff (Mabiza et al., 2021). A defining environmental feature of Harare is its network of wetlands (locally called *dambos*), which naturally retain and filter rainfall, recharge groundwater, and mitigate floods. However, rapid urban expansion, weak land governance, and widespread encroachment have led to the degradation of these critical ecosystems. By 2015, substantial portions of the city's wetlands had been lost or altered, compromising both water quality and availability. Untreated sewage and solid waste from informal settlements and industrial areas enter Lake Chivero via wetland channels, leading to eutrophication and rising treatment costs for municipal water (Chirisa et al., 2017).

Adaptation Initiatives

A notable shift in Harare's adaptation landscape has been the embrace of ecosystem-based approaches to urban resilience, with wetland protection taking centre stage.

The Harare Wetlands Advocacy Project (HWAP), launched around 2018–2019, has emerged as a leading civil society initiative focused on wetland conservation. Spearheaded by local conservation groups and supported by national NGOs, HWAP educates communities about the ecological importance of wetlands for climate resilience. Activities include community mobilisation, monitoring of illegal construction on wetlands, and legal advocacy to prevent environmentally destructive developments

(Chikodzi, 2020). Importantly, HWAP has built public awareness around existing legal frameworks, particularly the Environmental Management Act, which requires Environmental Impact Assessments (EIAs) before developing in ecologically sensitive areas. Community organisations, empowered with legal and scientific knowledge, have successfully contested illegal developments in court, setting important legal precedents. In several cases, construction permits were revoked, and wetland areas were rehabilitated through replanting and fencing. These successes highlight the potential of legal empowerment and civic agency in advancing urban climate adaptation.

Institutional and Policy Shifts

Sustained advocacy has influenced both local and national institutions. The Environmental Management Agency (EMA), in collaboration with Harare City Council and civil society actors, initiated steps to secure Ramsar Convention status for several wetland areas, thus gaining international recognition and protection for these sites (Government of Zimbabwe, 2021). Ramsar listing not only prevents unregulated development but also opens access to international funding and technical support for conservation. Parallel efforts are underway to gazette an official wetland map for Harare, which will legally delineate no-build zones across the city. Once gazetted, these zones will be integrated into Harare's Master Plan and enforced through city bylaws. This marks a significant transition towards risk-informed land-use planning, where ecological features are formally recognised as infrastructure for resilience.

Additionally, coordination between city planning departments and environmental regulators has improved. Previously, fragmented responsibilities allowed permits to be issued without proper environmental checks. The city now aims to mainstream wetland protection into all future urban planning processes, aligning ecological, hydrological, and urban development priorities. The Harare experience shows how nature-based solutions, community engagement, and institutional reform can be combined to safeguard critical urban ecosystems. It also reinforces the idea that climate adaptation need not be infrastructure-heavy; protecting and restoring natural buffers can be equally, if not more, effective, especially in resource-constrained contexts.

7.10.3 Maputo, Mozambique: Building Resilience Through Infrastructure and Community Engagement

Maputo, Mozambique's capital, has a metropolitan population exceeding 1.1 million and lies on the coast of Maputo Bay. It faces multiple interlinked climate risks, including coastal erosion, sea-level rise, storm surges, riverine and flash flooding from intense rainfall, and urban heat stress (World Bank, 2020). As a low-lying city located at the mouths of several rivers, Maputo's vulnerabilities are exacerbated by its inadequate stormwater infrastructure, unregulated land use, and widespread informal settlements, especially in flood-prone zones such as Maxaquene and Chamanculo (Cartwright et al., 2021). While Cyclones Idai and Kenneth in 2019 did not directly impact Maputo, the scale of destruction in cities like Beira served as a wake-up call. In early 2020, Maputo experienced severe rainfall-induced flooding that displaced thousands. Climate models project increasing intensity of extreme rainfall events and rising mean sea levels by 2050, amplifying both fluvial and coastal flood risk (IPCC, 2022).

Adaptation Initiatives
Maputo has responded with a combination of infrastructure investment, spatial planning, and community engagement aimed at bolstering resilience.

Climate Resilient Infrastructure Development Plan
Supported by the World Bank and the Global Facility for Disaster Reduction and Recovery (GFDRR), Maputo launched a city-wide resilience initiative focused on risk-informed infrastructure upgrades. The plan involved hazard mapping to identify flood-prone neighbourhoods, roads, and public facilities, followed by prioritisation of protective works (World Bank, 2020). Among the key interventions:

- Elevation of arterial road segments in downtown Maputo to prevent inundation.
- Expansion of drainage culverts to cope with high-intensity rainfall.
- Construction of sea walls and rock revetments along vulnerable coastlines, such as Costa do Sol beach, to address rapid coastal erosion.

- Retrofitting of essential services: for example, relocating hospital electrical systems to higher floors and reinforcing school roofs previously damaged by storm winds.

These projects were selected not only to reduce disaster risk but also to safeguard critical services such as healthcare, education, and commerce. They reflect a shift towards integrated urban development, where adaptation is aligned with long-term service delivery goals.

Upgrading of Informal Settlements
Given that many of Maputo's informal settlements are located on marginal or ecologically sensitive land, adaptation in these areas is crucial. In Chamanculo C, a participatory upgrading project combined physical and social resilience-building. Residents were involved in the design and implementation of stormwater drains, street paving (to enable both runoff and emergency vehicle access), and the installation of communal sanitation facilities (UN-Habitat, 2020). These interventions significantly reduced flood frequency and enhanced public health outcomes. Equally important, they built trust between municipal authorities and informal communities, a prerequisite for scaling resilience initiatives city-wide. Such co-produced upgrades offer replicable models for informal settlement adaptation across Southern Africa.

Nature-Based Measures and Risk Communication
In addition to hard infrastructure, Maputo is exploring nature-based solutions. Pilot projects involve rehabilitating degraded mangrove belts along the coast, which help buffer storm surges and stabilise shorelines. These efforts contribute to ecosystem restoration while providing green jobs for local residents (Seddon et al., 2020). Risk communication has also improved. Municipal authorities now disseminate flood warnings via local radio and SMS platforms, while schools and health facilities have been integrated into emergency response networks. These soft measures complement physical investments by ensuring that communities are informed, prepared, and empowered. Maputo's experience illustrates how layered and inclusive adaptation, combining large-scale infrastructure, community-led upgrading, and ecosystem restoration, can significantly enhance urban resilience to climate shocks. The city's approach demonstrates how

proactive planning, when coupled with sustained investment and community participation, can protect both infrastructure and lives in the face of escalating climate threats.

7.10.4 Windhoek, Namibia: Innovating for Water Resilience in a Semi-Arid City

Windhoek, Namibia's capital, with a population of approximately 400,000, is among the driest capital cities in the world. Situated in a semi-arid highland zone, it receives an average of just 360 mm of rainfall annually, with high inter-annual variability (Christelis & Struckmeier, 2001). The city lacks a perennial river and has historically depended on a mix of seasonal dams and groundwater resources. Recurrent droughts, intensified by climate change, pose an existential threat to Windhoek's water security. The 2015–2016 drought brought reservoir levels to record lows, triggering water rationing and heightening awareness of Windhoek's acute climate vulnerability. While urban flooding does occur, particularly from flash floods in dry riverbeds (ephemeral streams), the city's primary climate-related concern is prolonged drought, worsened by increasing evaporation rates and population-driven water demand (IPCC, 2022).

Adaptation Initiatives
Windhoek has become internationally recognised for its pioneering water management strategies, many of which constitute proactive climate adaptation well ahead of global trends.

Direct Potable Reuse of Wastewater
Since 1968, Windhoek has operated the *Goreangab Water Reclamation Plant*, which treats municipal wastewater to drinking standards. This process, known as direct potable reuse (DPR), is globally rare and was born out of necessity due to extreme water scarcity (Lahnsteiner & Lempert, 2007). Today, Windhoek reclaims approximately 25–30% of its drinking water through DPR, which is blended with groundwater and dam water. The city has invested in high-end water quality monitoring and public transparency to ensure consumer trust and WHO compliance. While public perception posed challenges initially, robust communication strategies and the city's track record for safe water have built confidence. Windhoek's

DPR system is now being studied by water-stressed cities globally as a model for climate-resilient water supply.

Diversified Water Supply Strategy
Beyond DPR, Windhoek employs a *multi-source water strategy* involving:

- Groundwater abstraction from boreholes;
- Surface water collection from three regional dams;
- Artificial recharge of the Windhoek aquifer; and
- Long-term plans for a desalination plant on the Atlantic coast (City of Windhoek, 2020).

Of particular note is the *aquifer recharge system*. During wet years, surplus surface water is treated and injected into underground aquifers for storage, effectively "banking" water for future droughts. During dry years, the city draws from this banked supply. This system proved invaluable during the 2019–2020 dry season when stored aquifer water bridged supply gaps. It exemplifies anticipatory adaptation—investing during surplus periods to build resilience for future scarcity (Jacobsen et al., 2012).

Water Demand Management and Innovation
Windhoek also leads in water demand management, having introduced tiered pricing, public awareness campaigns, greywater recycling in households, and mandatory water-efficient fixtures in building codes. Per capita consumption has declined steadily as a result. Businesses and institutions are incentivised to harvest rainwater and install water reuse systems. Moreover, Windhoek's policies have embedded water resilience into broader urban development. Urban planning considers hydrological constraints, and coordination between utilities, planners, and environmental authorities has strengthened institutional governance over water resources. Windhoek's experience demonstrates that even in highly water-stressed environments, innovation, public engagement, and long-term planning can transform existential climate risks into manageable challenges. Its strategies offer valuable lessons for other Southern African cities confronting water insecurity under climate change.

7.10.5 Johannesburg, South Africa: Mainstreaming Climate Risk in a Major Metropolis

Johannesburg, South Africa's largest city with a metropolitan population of approximately 5.6 million, is the country's economic powerhouse. The city has a subtropical highland climate and experiences summer thunderstorms that frequently trigger flash flooding. Its key climate risks include intense rainfall, heatwaves, and episodic droughts, although it does not face coastal hazards such as cyclones or sea-level rise (City of Johannesburg, 2018). Notably vulnerable are low-lying areas along riverbanks, such as the Jukskei River corridor, which cuts through informal settlements like Alexandra. Johannesburg's extensive paved surfaces, ageing stormwater systems, and sprawling development patterns have heightened the risk of surface flooding. The city's water security is another emerging concern; it relies heavily on inter-basin water transfers from the Lesotho Highlands Water Project, which is sensitive to regional climate variability (Department of Water and Sanitation, 2020). Despite relatively high institutional and technical capacity, the city's exposure to climate risk is amplified by socio-economic inequality and the location of vulnerable communities near hazard-prone areas.

Adaptation Initiatives

Urban Resilience Strategy and Infrastructure Stress Testing

Under the Rockefeller Foundation's 100 Resilient Cities initiative, Johannesburg launched a formal Urban Resilience Strategy in 2018. A core innovation of this strategy was the introduction of infrastructure "stress testing", a process that simulates extreme weather events (for example, 1-in-100-year floods, heatwaves with power surges) to evaluate the resilience of critical assets such as roads, bridges, and energy grids (City of Johannesburg, 2018). These simulations exposed weaknesses in existing systems, prompting targeted interventions. For instance, several vulnerable bridges were elevated, and culverts were widened to accommodate increased stormwater volumes. The city has since integrated stress testing results into its Integrated Infrastructure Master Plan, which guides both new developments and retrofits. Floodplain maps are now used in land-use planning and infrastructure siting to avoid high-risk zones. This marks a strategic shift towards risk-informed urban governance, where infrastructure investment is tied to long-term climate projections (Cartwright et al., 2021).

Flood Risk Reduction in Informal Settlements

Flood risk is particularly acute in informal settlements like Alexandra, where thousands of households reside along the banks of the Jukskei River. In response, Johannesburg has implemented a series of adaptation and disaster risk reduction measures. These include the installation of flood early warning systems, such as river-level sensors, sirens, and SMS alerts, to warn residents of imminent hazards (City of Johannesburg, 2019). In high-risk areas, the city has initiated the relocation of the most exposed households to safer zones. These cleared riverbanks have been transformed into *linear green spaces*, which act as both flood buffers and public parks. Although relocation has faced socio-political resistance due to tenure insecurity and urban poverty, the city's multi-stakeholder approach, working with community leaders, NGOs, and housing agencies, has helped mediate conflict and improve transparency. Moreover, in situ upgrades in less exposed parts of informal settlements have complemented relocation efforts, improving drainage and housing stability.

Mainstreaming Adaptation into Governance and Finance

Johannesburg has taken steps to embed climate adaptation into the core of municipal planning and finance. The city's Climate Action Plan aligns with both the national climate policy framework and global targets under the Paris Agreement. Through its Green Bonds program, Johannesburg has raised funds for climate-resilient infrastructure, including stormwater upgrades, energy-efficient public lighting, and solar rooftops on city buildings (UN-Habitat, 2020). Importantly, the city uses climate risk assessments in budgeting and prioritisation processes. Cross-departmental climate working groups ensure coherence across housing, transport, energy, and environment sectors. This whole-of-government approach strengthens institutional resilience and enables the city to anticipate rather than merely respond to shocks. Johannesburg's experience illustrates how metropolitan municipalities can lead in mainstreaming adaptation into all dimensions of urban governance, from physical infrastructure and informal settlement management to finance and institutional reform. The city's approach, while not without challenges, offers an example of proactive resilience-building in a context of high risk and high capacity.

7.10.6 Gaborone, Botswana: Institutionalising Urban Resilience in a Water-Stressed Capital

Gaborone, the capital of Botswana, has grown rapidly over the last three decades, transforming from a small administrative town into a major political and economic centre. With a population exceeding 300,000, the city faces pressing climate challenges, most notably, recurring droughts and extreme heat exacerbated by its semi-arid climate and limited surface water resources (Chanda & Toteng, 2018). Located near the Notwane River, Gaborone depends on the Gaborone Dam for water supply. However, rising evaporation rates, erratic rainfall, and siltation have undermined the dam's reliability. Climate projections suggest even drier and hotter conditions in the future, posing a significant risk to the city's water security, public health, and economic sustainability (IPCC, 2022). These concerns are compounded by informal settlements and rapid peri-urban expansion, which strain infrastructure and governance capacity.

Adaptation Initiatives

Policy Frameworks and Institutional Coordination

Botswana has responded by strengthening the policy and institutional foundations for climate resilience. Gaborone's urban adaptation is guided by the National Climate Change Policy and the National Development Plan 11, both of which emphasise urban resilience, integrated water management, and green infrastructure (Government of Botswana, 2021). At the city level, Gaborone's Development Plan now includes climate-sensitive zoning and floodplain management. Importantly, a Climate Change Unit was established within the Ministry of Environment, which works closely with the Gaborone City Council (GCC) to mainstream climate risks across sectors. This institutionalisation of resilience is also reflected in Botswana's membership in the Making Cities Resilient 2030 (MCR2030) initiative, where Gaborone receives technical support to strengthen local DRR frameworks and risk governance (UNDRR, 2022).

Water Supply Innovation and Demand Management

To tackle water scarcity, Gaborone has embraced both supply and demand-side interventions. The North-South Carrier (NSC) pipeline, which transports water from the northeast of the country, now supplements the dam supply. Additionally, the Water Utilities Corporation has piloted smart water metres in parts of Gaborone to improve billing efficiency and reduce wastage (WUC, 2020). The city promotes rainwater harvesting for household and institutional use, especially in schools and hospitals. In some neighbourhoods, greywater reuse systems have been introduced for landscaping and sanitation. These efforts align with national targets to reduce per capita water consumption and build long-term drought resilience.

Urban Greening and Heat Reduction

Gaborone is also experimenting with *urban greening* to combat heat stress and improve liveability. Tree-planting programs have been launched along major roads and in public spaces, including collaborations with schools and local NGOs. While the city lacks the dense canopy cover of more temperate cities, its greening strategy includes indigenous drought-resistant species and aims to reduce the urban heat island effect (Chanda & Toteng, 2018). Pilot projects are testing *cool roof materials* and improved building ventilation to moderate indoor temperatures, particularly in low-income housing. These are vital in a city where air conditioning remains unaffordable for many, and the electricity supply is intermittent during heatwaves.

7.11 Challenges and the Way Forward

Despite these strides, Gaborone still faces institutional and financial constraints. Coordination between city and national departments remains uneven, particularly in integrating climate adaptation into daily urban planning processes. Moreover, informal settlements on marginal land, often near riverbeds or flood-prone zones, pose a major challenge to risk reduction. Nonetheless, Botswana's strong governance culture, policy coherence, and investment in urban innovation offer a solid foundation. Continued progress will require scaled-up financing, capacity development, and community engagement, particularly in informal areas where climate impacts are most acute. Gaborone's experience exemplifies how a medium-sized city in a water-scarce region can institutionalise resilience through national-local alignment, demand management, and inclusive planning. Its evolving approach offers lessons for urban centres confronting similar challenges across Southern Africa.

7.12 Conclusion

This chapter has demonstrated the increasing efforts by Southern African cities to integrate climate adaptation and disaster risk reduction (DRR) into urban development. Through detailed case studies of Lusaka, Harare,

Maputo, Windhoek, Johannesburg, and Gaborone, it is clear that climate risks are diverse and context-specific, ranging from water scarcity and heatwaves to flooding and storm surges. Yet, these cities are developing innovative, locally appropriate responses that blend infrastructure investment, policy reform, and community engagement. A key insight is the growing shift towards *risk-informed urban planning*, where climate projections and hazard mapping influence infrastructure design, land use, and service delivery. Cities like Johannesburg and Windhoek exemplify how municipal leadership, financial innovation, and institutional coordination can embed resilience across sectors. At the same time, the role of communities, particularly in informal settlements, is vital, as they contribute practical, low-cost solutions that complement formal adaptation efforts. However, challenges remain. Many cities struggle with underinvestment, limited technical capacity, and fragmented governance. Informal development continues in high-risk areas, often without regulatory oversight or infrastructure support. Looking forward, Southern African cities must prioritise three actions: strengthening cross-sectoral governance, expanding access to climate finance, and scaling inclusive adaptation. By aligning local actions with national policies and global frameworks, cities can better manage risks while promoting equity and sustainability. Urban adaptation in Southern Africa is no longer optional; it is foundational to future development. With the right investments and institutional reforms, the region's cities can not only withstand climate shocks but also emerge stronger and more resilient.

References

African Development Bank (AfDB). (2021). *Climate change and green growth: Building resilience in African cities*. AfDB.

Cartwright, A., Parnell, S., Oelofse, G., & Ward, S. (2021). *Climate change at the city scale: Impacts, mitigation and adaptation in Cape Town*. Routledge.

Chanda, R., & Toteng, E. N. (2018). Urbanisation and climate risk in Botswana: Planning for a changing environment. *Botswana Journal of Geography, 17*(1), 45–58.

Chikodzi, D. (2020). Wetland degradation in Harare: Drivers and impacts. *African Journal of Environmental Science and Technology, 14*(3), 67–74.

Chirisa, I., Matamanda, A. R., & Bandauko, E. (2017). Decentralisation and climate resilience in Zimbabwean cities. *Journal of Southern African Studies, 43*(3), 481–498.

Christelis, G., & Struckmeier, W. (2001). *Groundwater in Namibia: An explanation to the hydrogeological map*. Ministry of Agriculture, Water and Rural Development.

City of eThekwini. (2022). *Flood impact report: April 2022*. eThekwini Municipality.

City of Johannesburg. (2018). *Joburg resilience strategy*. City of Johannesburg.

City of Johannesburg. (2019). *Flood early warning systems and risk communication plan*. Emergency Management Services.

City of Windhoek. (2020). *Integrated water resources management plan*. City Council of Windhoek.

Department of Water and Sanitation. (2020). *Water security outlook for South Africa*. Republic of South Africa.

Dodman, D., Bicknell, J., & Satterthwaite, D. (2012). *Adapting Cities to Climate Change: Understanding and Addressing the Development Challenges*. Taylor & Francis. https://books.google.co.za/books?id=HX_i-QdqD0wC

Government of Botswana. (2021). *National climate change policy*. Ministry of Environment, Natural Resources Conservation and Tourism.

Government of Zimbabwe. (2019). *National renewable energy policy*. Ministry of Energy and Power Development.

Government of Zimbabwe. (2021). *Wetland conservation strategy*. Environmental Management Agency.

Heyns, P. (2005). Water institutional reforms in Namibia. *Water Policy 7*(1), 89–106.

Intergovernmental Panel on Climate Change (IPCC). (2022). *Climate change 2022: Impacts, adaptation and vulnerability. Contribution of working group II to the sixth assessment report of the intergovernmental panel on climate change*. Cambridge University Press.

Jacobsen, M., Webster, M., & Vairavamoorthy, K. (2012). *The future of water in African cities: Why waste water?* World Bank.

Lahnsteiner, J., & Lempert, G. (2007). Water management in Windhoek, Namibia. *Water Science and Technology, 55*(1–2), 441–448.

Lusaka City Council (LCC). (2021). *Community-based drainage improvement project report*. LCC.

Mabiza, C., Dube, T., & Ncube, M. (2021). Urban flooding in Zimbabwe: The case of Harare. *Environment and Urbanization ASIA, 12*(2), 221–234.

Nchito, W. (2021). Community adaptation to flooding in informal settlements of Lusaka. *Zambian Journal of Geography, 8*(1), 12–25.

Pasquini, L., Ziervogel, G., Cowling, R. M., & Shearing, C. (2015). What enables local governments to mainstream climate change adaptation? Lessons learned from two municipal case studies in the Western Cape, South Africa. *Climate and Development, 7*(1), 60–70. https://doi.org/10.1080/17565529.2014.886994

Patz, J. A., Campbell-Lendrum, D., Holloway, T., & Foley, J. A. (2005). Impact of regional climate change on human health. *Nature, 438*(7066), 310–317. https://doi.org/10.1038/nature04188

Pelling, M., & Garschagen, M. (2019). Put equity first in climate adaptation. *Nature, 569*(7756), 327–329. https://doi.org/10.1038/d41586-019-01497-9

Republic of Namibia. (2017). *National Climate Change Strategy and Action Plan*. Windhoek: Ministry of Environment and Tourism.

Republic of Namibia. (2021). *Annual report 2021/2022*. Government of the Republic of Namibia.

Republic of South Africa. (2019). *National climate change adaptation strategy*. Government of the Republic of South Africa.

Republic of South Africa. (2021). *Annual report 2020/21*. Government Printing Works.

Republic of Zimbabwe. (2016). *Zimbabwe national climate policy*. Government of the Republic of Zimbabwe.

Revi, A., Satterthwaite, D., Aragón-Durand, F., Corfee-Morlot, J., Kiunsi, R. B., Pelling, M., Roberts, D., Solecki, W., Gajjar, S. P., & Sverdlik, A. (2014). Towards transformative adaptation in cities: The IPCC's fifth assessment. *Environment and Urbanization, 26*(1), 11–28.

Roberts, D., & O'Donoghue, S. (2013). Urban environmental challenges and climate change action in Durban, South Africa. *Environment & Urbanization, 25*(2), 299–319. https://doi.org/10.1177/0956247813500904

Robine, J. M., Cheung, S. L., Le Roy, S., Van Oyen, H., Griffiths, C., Michel, J. P., & Herrmann, F. R. (2008). Death toll exceeded 70,000 in Europe during the summer of 2003. *Comptes rendus biologies, 331*(2), 171–178. https://doi.org/10.1016/j.crvi.2007.12.001

Satterthwaite, D., Archer, D., Colenbrander, S., Dodman, D., Hardoy, J., & Patel, S. (2020). Building resilience to climate change in informal settlements. *Environment and Urbanization, 32*(1), 91–109.

Seddon, N., Smith, A., Smith, P., Key, I., Chausson, A., & Girardin, C. A. J. (2020). Getting the message right on nature-based solutions for climate change. *Global Change Biology, 26*(3), 3401–3404.

UNDRR. (2015). *Making development sustainable: The future of disaster risk management*. United Nations Office for Disaster Risk Reduction.

United Nations Office for Disaster Risk Reduction UNDRR. (2017). *Sendai Framework for Disaster Risk Reduction 2015–2030*. Geneva: United Nations.

UNDRR. (2022). *MCR2030 regional snapshot for Africa*. UNDRR Africa Office.

United Nations. (2015). *Transforming our world: The 2030 agenda for sustainable development* (Resolution 70/1). United Nations.

United Nations Framework Convention on Climate Change (UNFCCC). (2015). *Paris agreement*. Bonn: UNFCCC.

UN-Habitat. (2020). *World cities report 2020: The value of sustainable urbanization*. UN-Habitat.

Water Utilities Corporation (WUC). (2020). *Annual report 2019/20*. WUC.

World Bank. (2020). *Resilient infrastructure for Africa: Recommendations for a climate-smart urban future*. World Bank.

World Bank. (2021). *Financing urban climate resilience in Africa*. World Bank.
World Meteorological Organization. (2020). *WMO statement on the state of the global climate in 2019 (WMO-No. 1248)*. World Meteorological Organization.
Ziervogel, G., Pelling, M., Cartwright, A., Chu, E., Deshpande, T., Harris, L., Hyams, K., Kaunda, J., Klaus, B., Michael, K., Pasquini, L., Pharoah, R., Rodina, L., Scott, D., & Zweig, P. (2016). Inserting rights and justice into urban resilience: a focus on everyday risk. *Environment & Urbanization, 29*(1), 123–138. https://doi.org/10.1177/0956247816686905 (Original work published 2017)

CHAPTER 8

Governance and Institutional Frameworks for Disaster Risk Reduction

8.1 Introduction

Southern Africa's rapidly growing cities face acute disaster risks. Urban populations in Africa are expanding at unprecedented rates (Africa Centre for Strategic Studies, 2025), drawing in rural migrants and generating informality and exposure. Climate change compounds these trends by increasing the frequency and severity of floods, droughts, and cyclones, elevating the hazard exposure of urban infrastructure (IPCC, 2022). At the same time, population density and informal settlements facilitate the spread of disease, meaning health emergencies also pose growing threats (IPCC, 2022; Africa Centre for Strategic Studies, 2025). Disaster Risk Reduction (DRR) is therefore an urgent development priority in Southern Africa. However, as numerous studies and global agreements emphasise, technical measures alone are insufficient; without strong governance and institutional frameworks, even advanced preparedness systems can fail (UNESCO, 2023; UNDP, 2015). The Sendai Framework (United Nations, 2015) explicitly made "disaster risk governance" a global priority, stating that governance at all levels is "very important for prevention, mitigation, preparedness, response, recovery, and rehabilitation" (UNESCO, 2023). In essence, robust governance provides the enabling environment for all DRR efforts (UNDP, 2015).

F. Mangara, N. Dorasamy, *Sustainable Urban Development in Southern Africa*, https://doi.org/10.1007/978-3-032-08286-2_8

This chapter examines how governance and institutions shape DRR in Southern Africa. The chapter begins by defining the concept of disaster risk governance and its importance for resilience. It then reviews the international and regional DRR frameworks that Southern African countries are expected to follow. The core of the chapter profiles the national and local institutional arrangements in the region, highlighting South Africa, Mozambique, and Zimbabwe as illustrative cases. It also touches briefly on other countries. Next, it discusses key operational challenges in DRR governance, from finance and capacity shortfalls to siloed coordination. Finally, it outlines strategies to strengthen governance and institutions for DRR. Throughout, the focus is on how effective policy frameworks, laws, and organisational structures can enable Southern African societies to manage disaster risk and protect development gains (Folke et al., 2010; Chikodzi & Kenny, 2021).

8.2 Disaster Risk Governance: Concepts and Importance

"Disaster risk governance" encompasses the systems of laws, institutions, policies, and processes through which countries manage disaster risk (UNDRR, 2020). This includes clear roles and mandates, information flows, stakeholder participation, and accountability mechanisms. Good governance in DRR means transparent, inclusive, and adaptive institutions that integrate risk reduction into development planning (UNESCO, 2023; Folke et al., 2010). As the UNDP notes, disaster governance is the "umbrella" under which risk reduction is protected as a cross-cutting development priority (UNDP, 2015).

Strong governance ensures that technical DRR measures are backed by political will, legislation, and public support. For example, international guidelines emphasise multi-stakeholder participation and clear decision-making lines to reduce "coordination failures" in crises (UNESCO, 2023; UN, 2015). Resilience scholars also stress that adaptive governance institutions capable of learning and evolving are needed to cope with novel risks (Folke et al., 2010). In practice, well-designed DRR governance frameworks can mean the difference between manageable crises and catastrophic failures. Where governments have decentralised powers, trained officials, and enforceable regulations, urban development tends to be safer and responses swifter (UNDP, 2015; Folke et al., 2010). Conversely, poor governance often leaves communities exposed until disaster strikes (Chikodzi & Kenny, 2021).

In Southern Africa, the concept of disaster risk governance has entered policy discourse largely through the influence of global frameworks. The Sendai Framework (United Nations, 2015) and related UNDRR guidelines explicitly call for institutions that span national, sub-national, and community levels, as well as involve women, youth, and vulnerable groups (UNESCO, 2023). Similarly, development agencies like UNDP have promoted mainstreaming risk reduction into public finance and planning (UNDP, 2015; IFRC & UNDP, 2015). Southern African governments have generally endorsed these principles; for example, many have established national DRR platforms or councils to bring together government, academia, NGOs, and private sector representatives (UNDP, 2015). These platforms are intended to coordinate strategy and share information, reflecting the "all-of-society" approach championed by Sendai (UNESCO, 2023).

At the continental level, the African Union's Agenda 2063 and Africa Programme of Action (aligned with Sendai) similarly emphasise strong legal frameworks and institutional capacity for DRR (African Union Commission, 2024). In 2024, the African Union noted notable progress by member states in updating DRR laws and policies (African Union Commission, 2024), but it urged further action on early warning, financing, and inclusion. In sum, the concept of governance has been elevated as central to DRR, both globally and regionally (UN, 2015; Chikodzi & Kenny, 2021). How well this translates to practice in Southern African countries is the focus of the next sections.

8.3 International and Regional DRR Frameworks

The Sendai Framework (2015–2030) is the main global DRR agreement guiding Southern Africa. Its four priorities include understanding risk, strengthening governance, investing in resilience, and enhancing preparedness for response (UN, 2015). Priority 2 specifically calls on governments to ensure clear vision, competence, and coordination across all levels (UNESCO, 2023). Many Southern African governments refer to Sendai in their national DRR strategies and laws, pledging to decentralise DRR and allocate budgets accordingly (UNESCO, 2023; Chikodzi & Kenny, 2021). However, progress varies. The 2019 UN Global Assessment Report noted that while 85% of African countries had DRR strategies, only 30% had fully functional laws in line with Sendai (UNDRR, 2019). A common gap is the lack of binding standards for integrating DRR across sectors and across country borders. For example, until recently, there was no SADC-level agreement for mutual assistance during disasters, meaning regional relief often relied on ad hoc arrangements (SADC, 2022; Chikodzi & Kenny, 2021).

At the regional level, the Southern African Development Community (SADC) has historically had limited DRR governance instruments. Its early Disaster Preparedness and Response Strategy (2016–2030) was criticised for being reactive and under-resourced (SADC, 2022). Recognising this, SADC member states in 2022 adopted a new Regional DRR Strategy and Action Plan (2022–2030) aimed explicitly at strengthening legal and institutional frameworks. This plan calls for shared early warning systems, mainstreaming DRR into national planning, and integrated multi-sector coordination (SADC, 2022). In line with Sendai, it also promotes risk-informed development and climate change adaptation together, rather than in isolation (SADC, 2022). In parallel, the African Union's DRR Programme of Action (2017) urges each country to establish a National Disaster Management Authority and mobilise domestic resources for risk reduction (AU Commission, 2024). These regional commitments create a framework, but countries' adherence and implementation ultimately determine outcomes (African Union Commission, 2024; Chikodzi & Kenny, 2021).

8.4 National and Sub-national Institutional Frameworks in Southern Africa

Each Southern African country has its own DRR governance structure defined by law or policy. A major shift in recent decades has been moving from civil-protection–style emergency management towards proactive risk reduction, inspired by Hyogo and Sendai. The effectiveness of these legal frameworks depends heavily on political commitment and resources. Below, the study reviews three representative cases.

8.4.1 South Africa: A Three-Tiered Disaster Management System

South Africa is often cited as a pioneer in DRR governance in Africa. In 2002, it passed the Disaster Management Act (DMA No. 57), which is regarded as one of the first comprehensive DRM laws on the continent (Botha & Van Niekerk, 2013). The Act (amended 2015) established a three-tiered system across national, provincial, and local government (Botha & Van Niekerk, 2013). At the top is the National Disaster Management Centre (NDMC) within the Presidency, responsible for policy, coordination, and international cooperation (Botha & Van Niekerk, 2013). At the provincial and municipal levels, local disaster management centres and plans are mandated by law. Importantly, the Act requires that all government departments integrate DRR into their work—for example, land-use planning must consider hazards and municipalities must educate communities about preparedness (Botha & Van Niekerk, 2013). It also created advisory forums that include government, NGOs, academia, and business to foster "horizontal" coordination (Botha & Van Niekerk, 2013).

On paper, South Africa's framework is highly progressive. It explicitly promotes decentralisation and cross-sector collaboration, echoing Sendai's "all-of-society" ethos (UN, 2015; UNDP, 2015). Scholars note that South Africa's DMA was considered one of the most advanced DRR laws worldwide when passed (Vermaak & Van Niekerk, 2010; Botha & Van Niekerk, 2013). It obliges every municipality to have a disaster plan and integrate risk in local development (Botha & Van Niekerk, 2013). This creates a basis for mainstreaming DRR across government, which is crucial given that infrastructure, housing and health departments all play roles in prevention.

However, implementation has faced obstacles. Capacity and resources vary greatly: wealthier cities often have functional disaster units, but many rural or poor municipalities struggle to staff even a minimal DRR office (Botha & Van Niekerk, 2013). Surveys of local officials found that many still view disasters in the old civil-protection sense—focusing on emergency response rather than risk reduction—leading to DRR being underprioritised (Botha & Van Niekerk, 2013). Political will at the local level can be weak; municipalities with pressing service delivery needs may invest little in prevention (Botha & Van Niekerk, 2013). Moreover, while the law mandates departmental coordination, in practice siloes persist. City flood management, for example, is handicapped by different municipal units not sharing information (Ziervogel et al., 2016).

The COVID-19 pandemic further exposed governance gaps in South Africa's system. The national state of disaster was declared under the DMA, but ad-hoc structures like the National Coronavirus Command Council side-lined existing DRR institutions (Masocha et al., 2021). Analysts noted that locating the NDMC under one ministry limited its authority in a multi-sector crisis (Masocha et al., 2021). In sum, South Africa's case shows that strong DRM legislation and institutions are a necessary foundation, but not sufficient: ongoing political commitment, funding, and institutional learning are needed to make the system work (Botha & Van Niekerk, 2013; UNDP, 2015).

8.4.2 Mozambique: Central Coordination with Local Outreach

Mozambique is highly disaster-prone; cyclones, floods, droughts, and even earthquakes are recurrent. After catastrophic floods in 2000, the government overhauled its system. The National Institute for Disaster Management (Instituto Nacional de Gestão de Calamidades, INGC) was created in 1999 as the lead agency. INGC was later renamed INGD (Instituto Nacional de Gestão de Calamidades e Desastres) to emphasise risk reduction. Operating under the Ministry of State Administration, INGD is mandated to coordinate emergency response and promote prevention, preparedness, and public awareness. Unlike purely reactive agencies, it has a strong focus on community outreach and early warning.

Mozambique's system is relatively centralised at the top but has a deep network of local branches. INGD maintains offices at national, provincial, district and community levels. Each province has an INGD focal point, and District Disaster Committees bring together local officials, NGOs, police, and army personnel. The country is divided into three regional emergency centres for multi-hazard response: for example, a Cyclone Emergency Centre in Vilankulo (south), a Flood Response Centre in Caia (central), and so forth. These centres provide early warnings and coordinate evacuations when cyclones or floods hit. There are also local multi-use resource centres to build resilience to drought and other slow-onset risks.

A distinctive feature of Mozambique's approach is its emphasis on community-level committees. Villages and urban neighbourhoods have Local Disaster Risk Management Committees staffed by trained volunteers (INGC, n.d.). In danger periods, these committees relay warnings (often via radio or SMS) to residents and organise evacuations to cyclone shelters. For instance, before Cyclone Idai in 2019, thousands in coastal Beira were evacuated by community networks under INGD guidance, which many analysts credit with saving lives (Parker et al., 2007). Although Cyclone Idai remained devastating, Mozambique's locally anchored early warning system and evacuation protocol mitigated some impacts (Parker et al., 2007).

Political support and international partnerships bolster Mozambique's DRR governance. INGD has traditionally had a high status; its long-time director reported directly to the Prime Minister during crises. In 2014, a new Disaster Management Law further emphasised risk reduction, decentralisation, and climate adaptation (USAID, 2016). Mozambique also engages actively in regional and UN-led initiatives, for example, hosting DRR training and piloting early warning improvements with UN agencies and NGOs (USAID, 2016). After each major disaster, Mozambique conducts After-Action Reviews. The 2000 flood review led to a national civil protection unit and new rescue equipment; the Idai review highlighted the need for urban contingency planning for cities like Beira (UN, 2020).

Challenges remain. The scale of risk (intensifying cyclones and floods) outpaces resources. INGD often depends on donor and UN funding for major projects. Ensuring that local governments beyond the community committees implement risk reduction is uneven: major cities like Maputo and Beira still struggle to integrate DRR into urban planning and infrastructure (USAID, 2016). Some remote or conflict-affected districts lack sustained committee activity. Corruption and bureaucracy can hamper the quick use of disaster funds (USAID, 2016). Nonetheless, Mozambique is widely regarded as a regional example of linking national institutions with community action (USAID, 2016). Its model of strong central coordination combined with empowered local committees offers lessons for similar high-risk countries.

8.4.3 Zimbabwe: Transitioning from Civil Protection to Disaster Risk Management

Zimbabwe contrasts with South Africa and Mozambique in having only recently begun to reform its DRR governance. For decades, Zimbabwe's legal basis was the Civil Protection Act of 1989, a holdover from Rhodesian law. This model was focused on emergency response. It created Civil Protection Committees at national, provincial, and district levels, whose main role was mobilising relief during floods, droughts, epidemics, and so forth. Proactive measures such as risk assessment, mitigation, and hazard mapping were largely absent. The result was that disaster management was inherently reactive and charity-driven, with no dedicated funding for prevention.

This outdated framework has increasingly drawn criticism, especially after severe events like the 2019 Cyclone Idai (which heavily impacted eastern Zimbabwe) and successive droughts. In response, Zimbabwe has drafted a new Disaster Risk Management Bill to replace the Civil Protection Act (Zimbabwe Parliament, 2022a, b). Although not yet law (as of 2023), the draft bill is designed to align with international best practices. It envisions clear DRM institutions and committees at all levels, mandated risk assessments and plans across sectors, and a dedicated Disaster Risk Management Fund for financing prevention (Zimbabwe Parliament, 2022a, b). If enacted, it would formally devolve authority and resources to provinces, districts, and local councils (Zimbabwe Parliament, 2022a, b), addressing a major weakness of the old system.

A key feature of the proposed reform is inclusivity. The draft law and policy documents explicitly call for women, youth, and people with disabilities to be represented in disaster committees and decision-making (Zimbabwe Parliament, 2022a, b). This shift is partly driven by Zimbabwe's progressive 2013 Constitution, which mandates gender and disability inclusion. It is an important improvement, since marginalised groups often suffer disproportionately during disasters and have unique needs (ActionAid Zimbabwe, 2023). The draft also encourages a cultural shift towards preparedness and risk education, rather than expecting emergency relief. For example, there are provisions for community-based DRR projects and public awareness campaigns to change mindsets (ActionAid Zimbabwe, 2023).

However, until the new DRM Bill is passed, Zimbabwe remains reliant on the old Civil Protection regime. Critics note that the government has been "very slow to revise and enact" the updated framework (ActionAid Zimbabwe, 2023). In practice, this means there is still no comprehensive national DRR strategy or legal mechanism compelling agencies to fund prevention. Many responses (for example, to recent droughts or the COVID-19 pandemic) were managed ad hoc from the President's Office rather than through a standing DRM authority (ActionAid Zimbabwe,

2023). The country also lacks a disaster fund; budgets for relief and rebuilding must be reallocated from other areas or come from donors on the fly, which is both risky and untimely (ActionAid Zimbabwe, 2023).

Despite these gaps, Zimbabwe does have some institutional assets to build on. Civil Protection Committees still exist in provinces and districts, often including local officials, police, military, and Red Cross members. With proper training and resources, these could be transformed into local DRM committees. Zimbabwe's Meteorological Services and Hydrology Department also regularly issue weather forecasts and warnings, which could feed into a more systematic early warning system. A number of pilot projects (often donor-funded) have shown the value of community disaster preparedness teams in flood- or drought-prone rural areas (ActionAid Zimbabwe, 2023). The new draft policy would ideally scale up such grassroots initiatives under municipal and ward development plans.

Zimbabwe is at a crossroads. Its legacy DRM framework has left critical weaknesses in prevention and local autonomy. The ongoing reform effort culminating in a new DRM Act is vital to entrench the devolved, inclusive approach exemplified by Sendai and SADC. The Zimbabwean case underscores that without updated laws and funding mechanisms, disaster governance remains reactive. But it also shows that even delayed reforms can lay the groundwork for a more resilient future. By passing the DRM law and funding it, Zimbabwe could dramatically improve preparedness and reduce humanitarian burdens (ActionAid Zimbabwe, 2023).

8.4.4 Other Countries and Regional Trends

South Africa, Mozambique, and Zimbabwe illustrate the spectrum of approaches in Southern Africa. Other countries display notable practices or challenges as well. For example, Malawi has established a Department of Disaster Management Affairs (DoDMA) under the President's Office and in 2015 issued a policy emphasising community-based DRR and integration with climate adaptation (Chikodzi & Kenny, 2021). It continues to struggle with limited budgets and capacity but has built local Civil Protection Committees and basic flood early warning (Chikodzi & Kenny, 2021). Namibia passed a Disaster Risk Management Act in 2012 that created a National Disaster Risk Management Committee and pushed authority to its 14 regional councils, reflecting its emphasis on decentralisation given its sparse population and recurrent droughts. Botswana traditionally has strong central governance and has relied on a Disaster Management

Office to coordinate frequent drought responses, but it has also begun shifting towards a proactive DRR strategy aligned with Sendai (African Union Commission, 2024). Madagascar, highly exposed to cyclones, revamped its DRR framework in 2015 and established a national bureau (BNGRC) that coordinates both response and prevention. It has even pioneered disaster insurance through the African Risk Capacity to cover cyclone losses (African Risk Capacity, 2022).

Countries like Eswatini, Lesotho, Zambia, Angola, and others each have evolving DRR policies and committees, but often with underdeveloped institutional support. Common challenges across the region include a shortage of skilled DRR personnel, reliance on donor-driven projects, and weak integration of traditional community structures (Chikodzi & Kenny, 2021). Nevertheless, the overall trend is towards more comprehensive DRM frameworks. Even where laws are still nascent, governments increasingly recognise the need to blend disaster management with development planning. The effectiveness of these frameworks ultimately depends on how well institutions function in coordination, information management, budget allocation, and community engagement once disasters strike (Folke et al., 2010; Chikodzi & Kenny, 2021).

8.5 Urban and Local Governance: Cities at the Forefront of DRR

Cities are where governance meets practical risk reduction. Southern African cities such as Durban, Johannesburg, Maputo, and Harare concentrate wealth, population, and vulnerabilities. Urban local governments control many of the levers of risk (land-use planning, building codes, water infrastructure, health services) and are usually first responders in disasters. Thus, the capacity and attitude of city authorities critically determine resilience (Folke et al., 2010). Well-planned cities, those that enforce zoning laws, maintain drainage, and require risk assessments, can greatly reduce losses (UN-Habitat, 2020). Conversely, weak urban governance can allow informal settlements to sprawl into hazard zones with little oversight (Chikodzi & Kenny, 2021).

Effective urban risk governance extends beyond City Hall. It involves civil society, NGOs, and private actors. Community participation is especially important in informal settlements, where residents often have keen local knowledge of hazards. Engaging these communities in risk mapping and planning leads to more appropriate solutions (Dodman et al., 2012). For example, some Cape Town initiatives have involved residents of shantytowns in mapping flood hotspots and co-designing drainage upgrades. In Harare, trained community volunteer units in dense suburbs now help warn neighbours of flash floods. Such initiatives embody Sendai's "all-of-society" ethos and SADC's emphasis on the community role in urban DRR (UNESCO, 2023; SADC, 2022).

Despite positive examples, urban DRR governance faces serious hurdles. Many cities lack sufficient budgets and staff for DRR, given competing needs like housing and sanitation. Maintenance of storm drains or enforcing building regulations can be underfunded, increasing future risk (Chikodzi & Kenny, 2021). Coordination within city governments is also a challenge since DRR is inherently multi-sectoral, involving planning, engineering, housing, the environment, and emergency services. Research in Cape Town found that siloed departments and unclear mandates hampered a holistic flood response (Ziervogel et al., 2016). For instance, one department might upgrade a road without accounting for a downstream floodplain, simply due to a lack of inter-departmental coordination (Ziervogel et al., 2016). Political incentives often skew priorities towards visible short-term issues (like water supply) rather than "invisible" preventive measures (Folke et al., 2010).

Another key issue is the interface between formal authorities and informal settlements. Many city dwellers in Southern Africa live in unplanned areas on steep slopes or in floodplains. These residents frequently distrust the government (due to eviction fears or past neglect), which can lead them to ignore evacuation orders or not participate in planning (Chikodzi & Kenny, 2021). Successful DRR requires collaborative governance: cities must work with local leaders, NGOs, and slum associations rather than simply enforcing top-down orders. Promising models include participatory upgrading projects (for example, in South Africa and Namibia) where communities are actively involved in redesigning slum layouts to reduce fire and flood risk. Such approaches depend on flexibility in regulations and sustained dialogue between city planners and residents (UN-Habitat, 2020).

City governance also extends across municipal boundaries. Large metro regions like Gauteng (Johannesburg-Tshwane-Ekurhuleni) or Greater Maputo involve multiple jurisdictions. Risks like river flooding do not stop at city borders, so mechanisms for inter-municipal coordination are needed. In Gauteng, for example, the three municipalities coordinate via the provincial disaster centre for early warning and resource-sharing. Similarly, some countries encourage joint planning committees or mutual aid pacts among cities (Chikodzi & Kenny, 2021).

Southern African cities are increasingly tapping global urban networks for DRR capacity. Several major cities (Cape Town, Durban, Johannesburg, Dar es Salaam, etc.) have joined networks like the C40 Cities Climate Leadership Group and (formerly) 100 Resilient Cities. These platforms promote city resilience planning and appoint Chief Resilience Officers, facilitating peer learning. For instance, Durban's pioneering Municipal Climate Protection Program (established in 2000) was an early example of local climate risk planning (Local Sustainability in South Africa, 2013). More recently, the SADC Risk-Informed Urban Development (RIUD) initiative has connected city officials from 14 countries for workshops on DRR finance, data, and law (UN-Habitat, 2020). These exchanges help spread best practices (for example, Durban's integration of climate considerations) across the region.

Effective DRR ultimately "comes alive" at the local level. Strong national policies can set the stage, but risk reduction is delivered (or not) by cities and communities. Inclusive, well-resourced local governance integrating community knowledge and cutting through departmental silos leads to tangible resilience gains (UN-Habitat, 2020; Folke et al., 2010). Cities that have invested in coordination and preparation (even in the informal context) often experience faster recovery and less damage in disasters. Those who lag continue to bear disproportionate losses, especially in informal settlements. As urbanisation accelerates, building disaster-resilient cities through sound local governance will remain essential (UN-Habitat, 2020; Chikodzi & Kenny, 2021).

8.6 Challenges in Disaster Risk Governance

Despite progress on paper, Southern Africa faces persistent challenges in DRR governance. These often prevent policies from translating into effective risk reduction. Key issues include:

- **Limited Resources and Funding:** Insufficient budgets are arguably the most pervasive constraint. Many governments operate under tight fiscal pressures, and preventive DRR measures often lose out to immediate development needs. Studies in the region have repeatedly found that DRR receives meagre budget allocations, undermining the implementation of even proven risk-reducing projects (Chikodzi & Kenny, 2021; World Bank, 2019). At the local level, this is acute as municipalities may lack funds to maintain drainage, stockpile supplies, or train staff. Donor projects can help but are short-lived and donor-driven rather than systemic (African Union Commission, 2024). The absence of dedicated disaster funds means countries scramble for money only after crises. For example, in many countries (like Zimbabwe), authorities resort to ad hoc budget reallocations or external aid when disasters hit, leaving mitigation unfunded in "quiet" times. This reactive financing is inefficient and costly. Global analyses show that every dollar invested in resilience yields multiple dollars in avoided losses (World Bank, 2019). Some experts advocate solutions like mandatory DRR budget earmarks (for example, the 3% proposed by ActionAid Zimbabwe) or insurance schemes. Southern African countries have begun experimenting, for instance, some use insurance pools (African Risk Capacity, 2022), but uptake remains limited compared to need.

- **Insufficient Human and Technical Capacity:** Even the best frameworks mean little without people to run them. Many countries have too few trained DRR professionals or planners, especially at subnational levels (Chikodzi & Kenny, 2021). Local disaster committees often exist on paper but lack members with skills in risk assessment or planning. This capacity gap means that while a disaster plan may be written, few officials know how to implement it or develop contingency drills. Formal DRR training programs are sparse in the region (South Africa and Tanzania have some university courses, but most countries do not) (UNDRR, 2019). Brain drain exacerbates the problem as skilled staff move to better-paid jobs. Technical capacity is also weak as many governments lack GIS systems, hazard maps, or loss databases (Chikodzi & Kenny, 2021). Without data and analysis tools, decision-makers cannot target DRR investments effectively. Participants in SADC urban DRR workshops noted the need for shared risk data platforms and open access to tools so that knowledge can spread among cities (UN-Habitat, 2020). Strengthening capacity thus means sustained training, educational programs, and incentives to keep skilled staff in public service.
- **Weak Coordination and Siloes:** Disaster risk is inherently cross-cutting, so both horizontal coordination (across ministries and agencies) and vertical coordination (between national, provincial, and

local levels) are crucial. In many Southern African systems, these linkages are weak. For example, environment ministries may address climate adaptation, but rarely coordinate with disaster agencies; and health departments plan for epidemics without tying into national emergency plans (African Union Commission, 2024). A SADC review found that sectoral mainstreaming of DRR was limited as most public works or infrastructure projects proceed without fully incorporating hazard data (SADC, 2022). The result can be disjointed efforts. Vertical coordination problems are also common as local governments may simply await national guidance or funding before acting, as seen in Zimbabwe under the old system. Cross-municipality coordination is another weak spot. Flooding upstream (for example, deforestation) can cause downstream damage with no mechanism for joint management. These coordination gaps often arise from unclear roles and lack of practiced protocols. For instance, an evaluation in Malawi found confusion during emergencies because humanitarian clusters overlapped with government disaster teams (UNDRR, 2019). In Namibia, unclear rules led traditional leaders and officials to duplicate community relief efforts (UNDRR, 2019). Such fragmentation underscores that governance arrangements need to be regularly tested and refined through joint planning and drills (Folke et al., 2010).

- **Centralisation vs. Decentralisation Balance:** Finding the right division of authority is a persistent challenge. Highly centralised systems can ensure rapid national responses and uniform policies, but risk excluding local knowledge and slowing local action. Conversely, unfettered decentralisation can overwhelm local councils without adequate support. Zimbabwe's old Civil Protection model was centralised and often failed to reach remote communities quickly (ActionAid Zimbabwe, 2023). By contrast, South Africa's DMA mandates decentralisation, but resource-poor localities sometimes cannot carry out their mandated DRR roles, requiring provincial or national help (Botha & Van Niekerk, 2013). The optimal balance seems to be *decentralisation with capacity-building and resources.* In practice, many Southern African countries are still "finding their footing" on this. They are reforming legal frameworks to devolve powers (for example, Zimbabwe's draft DRM Bill) but must ensure sub-national authorities are equipped and funded. Achieving an effective multi-level system where each tier has clear responsibilities and is supported by the others remains a work in progress.

- **Policy and Legal Gaps:** Although most countries now have a DRM law or policy, in some cases these are outdated or incomplete. Outmoded laws may not mandate risk reduction or may lack enforcement powers (UNDRR, 2019). Moreover, sectoral laws often conflict. For example, planning regulations may still allow construction in floodplains contrary to DRR goals (UNDRR, 2019). A notable regional gap, until recently, was the absence of a policy on regional disasters. SADC only began developing a transboundary disaster strategy in 2022 (SADC, 2022). Another issue is recovery, as many reconstruction policies have not systematically required "build back better", so rebuilding after disasters can simply recreate the same risks. While legal reforms are underway (for example, many countries integrating DRR into building codes and environmental laws), enforcement is uneven.
- **Enforcement and Accountability:** Even well-crafted laws are only effective if enforced. Across Southern Africa, building codes and land use plans often go unenforced, partly because local governments lack alternatives for relocating informal settlements (Chikodzi & Kenny, 2021). Evacuation orders without resettlement plans tend to be ignored until disaster strikes, undermining authority. Substandard construction frequently persists due to weak inspection regimes. Effective enforcement also requires incentives. Authorities can couple regulations with support (such as supplying affordable, safer building materials to vulnerable communities). Accountability is another dimension. Politicians and officials are usually judged on their emergency response (did relief arrive?), but rarely on prevention (were lives saved). This skew creates political short-termism in DRR funding. Introducing accountability measures, for instance, requiring annual public reports on DRR progress or setting risk-reduction targets in national budgets, could shift incentives. Empowering oversight bodies (parliamentary committees, national audit offices) to scrutinise DRR spending can also promote accountability.
- **Political Will and Continuity:** Sustained disaster governance depends on continual political support. Investments in prevention often have payoffs only years later (in disasters not happening), which can be hard for politicians to prioritise. The result can be funding

and attention drying up between crises. In many Southern African countries, economic or electoral pressures divert resources to more immediate needs. For example, maintaining flood embankments or urban drainage is frequently neglected until the rainy season threat becomes urgent. Ensuring that DRR institutions remain staffed and funded through political cycles is an ongoing struggle. The COVID-19 crisis illustrated this: some governments (like Zimbabwe's) shifted resources to pandemic response at the expense of other DRR plans, whereas others (like South Africa's) created new interim structures. Continuity requires embedding DRR firmly in governance structures, so it is not easily cut when priorities change (UNDP, 2015).

- **Social and Cultural Factors:** Governance does not occur in a societal vacuum. In many communities, traditional leaders and cultural norms wield strong influence. If these leaders are not included in formal DRR planning, efforts can fall flat or even clash with local practices (UNESCO, 2023). Conversely, where traditional authorities are engaged, they can legitimise preparedness (for example, chiefs urging evacuations). Public trust in institutions is also critical: if people view the government as corrupt or neglectful, they may ignore official warnings, relying on their own measures instead. Building trust requires transparency and clear communication. For instance, sharing risk information openly and involving communities in decision-making can reduce suspicion. Risk communication itself must be culturally appropriate, using local languages, radio, and respected community figures to reach all groups (UNESCO, 2023).
- **Emerging Risks and Uncertainties:** Governance systems must also grapple with new challenges: climate change is fuelling more intense extreme events, and threats like pandemics or cyber-disruptions create cascading crises. Traditional DRM frameworks were mostly designed for single events (for example, a flood or cyclone). Today, governments must anticipate compound hazards (a flood concurrent with a disease outbreak, for example). This requires adaptive governance, regular revisiting of policies, after-action reviews, and scenario planning. The COVID-19 pandemic taught that DRR institutions need protocols for biological hazards, not just geophysical ones. The IPCC and SADC strategies both emphasise that DRR must expand to cover multi-hazard resilience, including health emergencies (IPCC, 2022; SADC, 2022). Engaging research institutions and

universities in DRR planning is one way to bring innovation and forward-looking analysis into government (UNDRR, 2019). Unfortunately, the role of science and academia in DRR governance is often underused in the region (UNDRR, 2019). Tapping this expertise, for example, using climate model projections for long-term urban planning, is a priority for adaptive governance.

Southern Africa's DRR governance is shaped by a complex mix of resource limitations, institutional bottlenecks, and socio-political dynamics. None of these challenges make the progress achieved irrelevant; rather, they indicate where efforts should focus. Importantly, each gap also suggests solutions, as capacity shortfalls can be addressed through education and training programs; funding gaps can motivate innovative financing mechanisms; and coordination issues can be tackled by institutional reforms and better information sharing. The next section outlines specific strategies and recommendations to build on the region's strengths and tackle these weaknesses.

8.7 Strengthening Governance and Institutional Frameworks for DRR

Achieving disaster-resilient urban development in Southern Africa will depend on addressing the governance challenges above. The following strategies and recommendations draw on international guidance (for example, Sendai Framework actions), regional plans (SADC DRMSAP 2022–2030), and lessons from country experiences. The goal is to build governance systems that are inclusive, coordinated, well-resourced, and adaptable. Key priority areas include:

1. **Update and Strengthen Legal/Policy Frameworks:** Countries should ensure their DRM laws and policies reflect modern best practices. This includes finalising pending legislation (for example, Zimbabwe's DRM Bill) and auditing existing laws for gaps (for example, South Africa's post-COVID review). Modern DRM laws should clearly define roles at each government level, mandate the integration of risk reduction into all development sectors, and establish institutions such as disaster management centres and funds (UNDP, 2015; IFRC & UNDP, 2015). Laws must emphasise not

just emergency response but proactive risk assessment, prevention, and "build back better" in reconstruction. Tools like the IFRC–UNDP "Checklist on Law and DRR" can help governments align their legal framework with DRR objectives (IFRC & UNDP, 2015). Policies should also explicitly integrate climate change adaptation with DRR. Evidence suggests that separate CCA and DRR policies are less effective than unified approaches to urban resilience (Dodman et al., 2012). For example, national planning guidelines could require that all major infrastructure projects undergo disaster risk screening (World Bank, 2019). This "risk-informed development" mindset should become standard practice across Southern Africa.

2. **Institutionalise Multi-level Coordination:** To break down siloes, formal coordination platforms are essential. National DRR councils or platforms should be active and regularly convene, with broad representation (government ministries, academia, NGOs, private sector, community groups) (UNDP, 2015). These bodies can advise on implementation, ensure information flows across sectors, and hold stakeholders accountable. At the city level, establishing (or strengthening) inter-departmental disaster management committees can integrate urban planning, health, engineering, and other departments. For example, a municipal DRR committee in a capital city could include urban planners, stormwater engineers, housing officials, and emergency managers meeting quarterly. Such forums help plan proactively for high-risk seasons (pre-monsoon preparation, cyclones, and so forth). Vertical coordination should also be formalised, that is, national governments might institute mutual aid agreements between provinces or neighbouring cities, defining resource-sharing rules during crises (Chikodzi & Kenny, 2021). Transboundary cooperation is also key. SADC's new emphasis on a regional disaster operations centre (SHOC) is a positive step (SADC, 2022). Further, SADC and the AU can facilitate joint simulations (for example, regional cyclone scenarios) and agreements to streamline cross-border relief logistics and personnel movement (AU Commission, 2024; SADC, 2022).
3. **Invest in Capacity Building and Knowledge Management:** Bridging the human capacity gap is fundamental. Governments should partner with universities and training institutes to expand DRM education and training for public officials at all levels

(UNDRR, 2019). This could include new university degree programs in DRR, short courses in local government, and certifications for emergency management personnel. In-service training for municipal staff and community committee members will ensure DRR know-how reaches grassroots levels. Knowledge products need to be widely disseminated, for example, methodologies for community risk assessments, municipal contingency plan templates, and urban flood modelling tools should be made freely available (UN-Habitat, 2020). South–South cooperation and peer learning can accelerate capacity building. City-to-city partnerships (such as pairing a well-practiced DRR city with one just starting) can transfer practical experience. In the SADC urban program, such peer exchanges proved valuable (UN-Habitat, 2020). Data systems must also improve, that is, countries should support the creation of hazard maps, vulnerability databases, and disaster loss inventories, and make these accessible to planners and the public. A regional shared platform for hazards (for instance, SADC-wide flood maps or cyclone trajectory archives) could save each country effort and improve preparedness. Finally, public awareness campaigns should educate citizens about risk (for example, school curricula on hazards, media programs on preparedness), fostering a "culture of prevention" that complements institutional capacity.

4. **Strengthen Local Governance and Decentralise DRR Powers:** Consistent with Sendai and SADC guidance, empowering local authorities is essential. Decentralisation efforts should be deepened by allocating financial resources and decision-making authority to sub-national levels (Chikodzi & Kenny, 2021). For example, national governments could earmark a portion of disaster funds directly for districts and municipalities. In Zimbabwe's case, ActionAid recommended that the new law ensure local DRM committees have "fully devolved powers" and budgets (ActionAid Zimbabwe, 2023). Local governments should also be required to integrate DRR into their development plans and budgets. For instance, a city's annual plan or zoning scheme should include hazard maps and resilience projects, and progress should be reviewed by councils. Formal channels for community engagement at the local level must be created. This could mean seats for community representatives on municipal DRR committees or officially recognised neighbourhood DRR groups (similar to Mozambique's Local

Committees) (INGC, n.d.). Supporting grassroots initiatives such as supporting slum-dweller federations in upgrading projects or backing volunteer networks for early warning dissemination can extend government reach. Partnerships between municipalities and local universities or NGOs can also help fill technical gaps, for example, university geography departments might help with risk mapping in municipalities lacking GIS capacity.

5. **Ensure Sustainable Financing for DRR:** Financing for disasters must extend beyond emergency response. Governments should create dedicated DRR budget lines at all levels. These funds could finance resilient infrastructure (for example, flood walls, drainage), early warning system maintenance, training of response teams, and community risk-reduction projects. One practice is to establish a National Disaster Risk Reduction Fund that aggregates contributions from the budget, donors, and even the private sector (as seed capital) specifically for prevention interventions (World Bank, 2019). Some countries use small levies or insurance to fund DRR, for example, Madagascar's participation in ARC insurance was facilitated by cost-sharing of premiums (African Risk Capacity, 2022). Participating in regional risk pools can provide quick post-disaster pay-outs while creating incentives for risk reduction (since premiums depend on vulnerability). Southern African governments should also tap global climate finance (for example, the Green Climate Fund) for urban resilience projects, framing them as both adaptation and DRR. Crucially, the economic case for DRR must be made to finance ministries. Studies consistently show that every dollar spent on prevention saves multiple dollars in future losses (World Bank, 2019). SADC's 2022 strategy explicitly calls for integrating disaster risk financing into national budgets (SADC, 2022). At the local level, innovative mechanisms like community savings schemes or micro-finance for home fortification could provide households with means to reduce their own risks.
6. **Foster Inclusive and Participatory Governance:** Inclusivity must be a core principle. Women, youth, the elderly and people with disabilities should be involved in DRR decision-making (UNESCO, 2023; ActionAid Zimbabwe, 2023). Practical steps include ensuring gender-balanced and disability-inclusive representation on DRR committees and consulting targeted groups when designing evacuation plans or warning systems (UNDRR, 2022). For instance, mak-

ing sure alerts are accessible to the hearing-impaired or reaching rural women's groups with flood information. Many countries in the region are drafting Gender-Responsive DRM strategies, recognising the evidence that women are often leaders in community resilience if empowered (UNDRR, 2022). Traditional and religious leaders are also important stakeholders: involving them in planning lends authority to DRR measures within communities. Participatory budgeting is another tool, for instance, allowing communities to decide on portions of local budgets (for example, choosing whether to build a flood bridge or a borehole) can increase accountability and ensure projects meet local needs.

7. **Emphasise Risk Communication and Early Warning Systems:** Governance should ensure that robust early warning systems (EWS) are fully operational. Meteorological and hydrological services must have clear mandates and resources to issue warnings. Authorities need protocols guaranteeing that these warnings reach local disaster managers, community leaders, and at-risk populations in time. Formal standard operating procedures should link national warning centres to district authorities. The SADC region has recognised this by launching a regional multi-hazard early warning strategy (SADC, 2022). Countries should continuously invest in EWS technology (for example, radar, rain gauges) and refine communication channels. Community-based early warning, such as trained village volunteers monitoring river gauges or relaying SMS alerts should be integrated into official systems (UNESCO, 2023). Good governance ensures "last-mile connectivity" of warnings, for example, partnerships with telecoms for mass SMS alerts, or using local radio in vernacular languages. Governance arrangements should also define who is empowered to order evacuations and how those orders are enforced.
8. **Encourage Adaptive and Flexible Governance:** Given the dynamic risk landscape, DRR systems should not be static. Mechanisms for regular review and revision are needed. This includes after-action reviews or "lessons learned" workshops following every significant disaster, as well as annual multi-stakeholder reviews of progress against DRR targets. Policies and legislation should be updated when new gaps are identified (for example, South Africa's law was amended in 2015 to account for infectious disease response). A learning culture is essential. Agencies should analyse near-misses and

failures candidly. The COVID-19 pandemic highlighted this need, leading experts to call for integrating public health contingency planning into DRM plans (IPCC, 2022; Chikodzi & Kenny, 2021). Climate change projections should be regularly incorporated into standards, for example, revising building codes to account for higher rainfall or sea-level scenarios. This "anticipatory governance" means using scenario analysis and foresight. Some Southern African policy-makers are already applying such tools (for example, Cape Town's city climate adaptation plan uses future drought models). SADC's strategy likewise urges member states to "future-proof" DRR by including biological and other emerging hazards (SADC, 2022). Supporting pilot projects and innovations such as experimenting with nature-based solutions like wetland restoration for flood control allows governance to be flexible and evidence-driven.

9. **Strengthen Accountability and Transparency:** Finally, institutions must be held to account for DRR commitments. Developing robust monitoring and evaluation systems is key. Governments can track indicators (such as those in the Sendai Framework Monitor) on reduced disaster losses, number of local DRR plans, and so forth. Public "state of DRR" reports can increase transparency by revealing both achievements and gaps each year. Civil society should be empowered in watchdog roles, for example, using community scorecards to assess local government preparedness. Financial accountability is important. Dedicated DRR allocations in budgets should be audited to ensure funds are used for risk reduction projects. Peer accountability mechanisms also exist. AU member states submit biennial DRR progress reports, and full engagement with these regional processes can motivate domestic follow-through (African Union Commission, 2024). When disasters occur, reviews should not only address technical response but also governance failures (for example, bureaucratic delays, unclear mandates) and assign responsibility for corrective actions.

Throughout these strategies, a people-centred approach is crucial. Governance reforms must empower communities and respect local knowledge. Institutions exist to serve citizens, especially the most vulnerable, and should be judged by whether they enable communities to thrive despite hazards (UNESCO, 2023). Southern Africa's diversity means solutions will vary by context, but the shared experience is clear. Investing in good governance pays dividends in resilience (UNDP, 2015; World Bank, 2019). Mozambique's example shows how institutional learning and community engagement can "save countless lives" (INGC, n.d.). Durban's resilience work demonstrates the payoff of long-term city planning. The way forward is to replicate and upscale these successes, foster cross-border and peer learning, and stay vigilant in addressing the gaps.

8.8 Conclusion

Governance and institutional capacity are foundational pillars for effective disaster risk reduction (DRR) in Southern Africa. As demonstrated in this chapter, notable progress has been made across the region through the enactment of pioneering legislation, the establishment of dedicated DRR agencies, and the creation of innovative local governance structures. These developments have helped shift the narrative from disasters being inevitable crises to risks that can be anticipated and managed (UN, 2015). Countries such as Mozambique and South Africa provide compelling examples. Mozambique's integrated cyclone preparedness system and South Africa's risk-informed urban planning reflect the benefits of strong, coordinated governance frameworks. However, institutional challenges remain. Outdated policies, fragmented responsibilities, and capacity deficits continue to impede effective DRR in several contexts (African Union Commission, 2024). Crucially, disaster governance must be understood as an evolving process. Static frameworks cannot keep pace with the growing complexity of urbanisation, climate change, and emerging threats like pandemics. This demands adaptive, inclusive, and well-resourced systems.

Encouragingly, the trajectory in the region is positive. National reforms have strengthened SADC collaboration, and community-level innovations in resilience planning indicate a growing recognition of the importance of DRR. The priority now is to consolidate these gains and ensure that implementation reaches the grassroots. Robust DRR governance is not only essential for managing risk but is also integral to broader development objectives. By embedding DRR into institutional practices, Southern African countries can protect infrastructure investments, foster social cohesion, and contribute meaningfully to global agendas such as the SDGs particularly SDG 11 and SDG 13 (World Bank, 2019; UNESCO, 2023).

References

ActionAid Zimbabwe. (2023). ActionAid Zimbabwe calls for a robust disaster risk reduction legislation in Zimbabwe [Press release]. ActionAid Zimbabwe

Africa Center for Strategic Studies. (2025, May 12). *Africa's unprecedented urbanization is shifting the security landscape*. Africa Center.

African Risk Capacity. (2022). *Madagascar drought response: Government receives insurance payout* [Press release, July 8, 2022]. ARC Group.

African Union Commission. (2024). *Africa realises notable progress in strengthening disaster risk reduction* [Press release, May 16, 2024]. AUC.

Botha, D., & Van Niekerk, D. (2013). Views from the frontline: A critical assessment of local risk governance in South Africa. *Jàmbá: Journal of Disaster Risk Studies, 5*(2), 1–10.

Chikodzi, D., & Kenny, L. R. (2021). Disaster risk reduction governance in Southern Africa: Focus on budgets and institutional competencies. In H. Rautenbach, L. Lacroix, & J. Matunhu (Eds.), *Cyclones in Southern Africa* (pp. 227–241). Springer.

Dodman, D., Bicknell, J., & Satterthwaite, D. (Eds.). (2012). *Adapting cities to climate change: Understanding and addressing the development challenges.* Routledge.

Folke, C., Carpenter, S. R., Walker, B., Scheffer, M., Chapin, T., & Rockström, J. (2010). Resilience thinking: Integrating resilience, adaptability and transformability. *Ecology and Society, 15*(4).

INGC (Instituto Nacional de Gestão de Calamidades). (n.d.). *INGC institutional profile.* UN-SPIDER Knowledge Portal. http://www.ingc.gov.mz/

Intergovernmental Panel on Climate Change (IPCC). (2022). *Climate change 2022: Impacts, adaptation and vulnerability.* Contribution of Working Group II to the Sixth Assessment Report of the Intergovernmental Panel on Climate Change. Cambridge University Press.

International Federation of Red Cross and Red Cross Societies (IFRC) and United Nations Development Programe (UNDP). (2015). *The checklist on law and disaster risk reduction.* IFRC & UNDP.

Local Sustainability in South Africa. (2013). *Climate adaptation in Durban: The municipal climate protection programme.* Cités et Gouvernements Locaux Unis d'Afrique du Sud (CGLUA–Sud).

Masocha, M., Sithole, B., & Muchemwa, L. (2021). COVID-19 governance in Zimbabwe: Analysis and lessons learned. *Jàmbá: Journal of Disaster Risk Studies, 13*(1), 1–9.

Parker, D., Tapsell, S., & McCarthy, S. (2007). Enhancing the human benefits of flood warning. *Natural Hazards, 43*, 397–414. https://doi.org/10.1007/s11069-007-9137-y

Southern African Development Community (SADC). (2022). *Regional disaster risk management strategy and action plan 2022–2030*. SADC Secretariat.

UN-Habitat. (2020). *The state of African cities 2020: Financing sustainable urban development in Africa*. UN-Habitat.

United Nations (UN). (2015). *Sendai framework for disaster risk reduction 2015–2030*. United Nations Office for Disaster Risk Reduction (UNDRR).

United Nations (UN). (2020). The Human Cost of Disasters: An Overview of the Last 20 Years 2000-2019. UNDRR, Prevention Web, UN Office for Disaster Risk Reduction https://www.preventionweb.net/files/74124_humancostofdisasters20002019reportu.pdf

United Nations Development Studies (UNDP). (2015). *Strengthening disaster risk governance: UNDP support during the Hyogo framework implementation (2005–2015)*. UNDP.

United Nations Educational, Scientific and Cultural Organisation (UNESCO). (2023). Disaster risk governance is very important for prevention, mitigation, preparedness, response, recovery, and rehabilitation. In *Risk governance and social resilience* [online]. UNESCO.

United Nations Office for Disaster Risk Reduction (UNDRR). (2019). *Global assessment report on disaster risk reduction 2019*. UNDRR.

United Nations Office for Disaster Risk Reduction (UNDRR). (2020). *Terminology on disaster risk reduction*. United Nations Office for Disaster Risk Reduction.

United Nations Office for Disaster Risk Reduction (UNDRR). (2022). *Global assessment report on disaster risk reduction 2022: Our world at risk—Transforming governance for a resilient future*. United Nations Office for Disaster Risk Reduction.

US Agency for International Development (USAID). (2016). *Mozambique – Country disaster risk profile*. USAID.

Vermaak, J., & Van Niekerk, D. (2010). *Disaster risk reduction initiatives in South Africa*. Eburon Academic Publishers.

World Bank. (2019). *Lifelines: The resilient infrastructure opportunity*. World Bank–GFDRR. (Press release, June 19, 2019.)

Ziervogel, G., Pelling, M., Cartwright, A., Chu, E., Deshpande, T., Harris, L., Hyams, K., Kaunda, J., Klaus, B., Michael, K., & Pasquini, L. (2016). Inserting rights and justice into urban resilience: A focus on everyday risk. *Environment and Urbanization, 29*(1), 123–138.

Zimbabwe Parliament. (2022a). *Disaster risk management and civil protection bill [Draft]*. Government Printers.

Zimbabwe Parliament. (2022b). *Disaster risk management and civil protection bill – Policy provisions*. Government Printers.

CHAPTER 9

Policy Integration Between Urban Planning and Disaster Risk Reduction in Southern Africa

9.1 Introduction

Southern Africa is at a pivotal crossroads where the interplay of rapid urbanisation and intensifying disaster risks demands urgent attention. As cities in the region grow at unprecedented rates, they face mounting challenges associated with unplanned expansion, fragile infrastructure, and inadequate service delivery systems, all of which exacerbate socio-economic inequalities. Current projections estimate that by 2050, more than 60% of the region's population will reside in urban areas (ISS, 2022). The speed of this urban transition has outpaced the capacity of many governments to plan effectively, resulting in informal settlements, environmental degradation, and a widening urban inequality gap (Satterthwaite et al., 2018a). Unmanaged urban growth could further deepen vulnerabilities and entrench poverty.

Simultaneously, the region faces increasing climate-related and other disaster risks, including floods, droughts, cyclones, and wildfires. Many of these hazards are exacerbated by climate change, with extreme weather events becoming more frequent and severe (IPCC, 2022). The urban poor are disproportionately vulnerable due to their concentration in high-risk areas (e.g. floodplains, unstable slopes) and lack of access to essential services. Recurrent disasters in cities lead to cumulative losses and chronic disruptions of livelihoods for these communities (Wisner et al., 2004).

F. Mangara, N. Dorasamy, *Sustainable Urban Development in Southern Africa*, https://doi.org/10.1007/978-3-032-08286-2_9

This convergence of risks calls for the integration of disaster risk reduction (DRR) principles into urban planning frameworks, ensuring cities are not only engines of economic growth but also resilient and adaptive in the face of adversity (UNDRR, 2019).

Despite global frameworks such as the Sendai Framework for Disaster Risk Reduction 2015–2030 and the New Urban Agenda (2016), which advocate for integrated approaches, implementation in Southern Africa has been inconsistent. In many instances, urban planning and disaster risk management remain siloed functions, undermining opportunities for synergy and holistic development outcomes (Adelekan et al., 2020a). Cities that should ideally be hubs of innovation and inclusion often become epicentres of risk due to poor planning, weak governance, and outdated regulatory frameworks (UNDRR, 2019). Integrating DRR into urban planning is not simply a technical exercise but a political, institutional, and governance challenge that requires collaboration among multiple stakeholders, inclusive policy frameworks, and long-term strategic vision (Pelling & Holloway, 2006).

This chapter critically examines the policy integration of urban planning and DRR in Southern Africa. It begins with a conceptual overview of integration and its importance in the context of sustainable urban development. It then explores international and regional frameworks that guide this integration, followed by an analysis of barriers to implementation and factors that enable progress. Case studies from selected Southern African countries provide empirical insights, and the chapter concludes with best practices and policy recommendations to enhance the integration of DRR and urban planning across the region.

9.2 Conceptual Framework for Integration

The integration of urban planning and disaster risk reduction is anchored in the broader discourse on sustainable development and urban resilience. Conceptually, *integration* refers to the coordinated alignment of planning systems, policies, institutional arrangements, and practical tools to systematically manage urban risks and vulnerabilities (Birkmann et al., 2010). It involves embedding risk considerations into spatial planning, land-use decisions, infrastructure development, and environmental management, among other urban governance domains (UNDRR, 2015). In essence, urban development and risk management must not be separate streams; rather, risk awareness should permeate all aspects of city planning.

The theoretical foundation for this integration draws from systems thinking, which recognises cities as complex adaptive systems influenced by a web of interconnected social, economic, environmental, and political drivers (Swyngedouw, 2009). Within this framework, disaster risk is not viewed solely as an external shock but as a product of urban systems' exposure and vulnerability, coupled with insufficient coping capacity (Wisner et al., 2004). Reducing urban disaster risk, therefore, necessitates planning interventions that address underlying drivers of vulnerability such as insecure land tenure, weak infrastructure, or social exclusion, while reinforcing resilience at multiple scales.

Two complementary approaches guide the integration of DRR into urban planning: risk-informed development and resilience-based planning. Risk-informed development calls for mainstreaming DRR into all sectors of urban development by using data-driven risk assessments to guide decision-making (GFDRR, 2016). This includes the use of hazard maps, spatial risk models, and vulnerability indicators to inform zoning, infrastructure investments, and land use plans. Resilience-based planning, in turn, emphasises enhancing the capacity of urban systems to absorb shocks, adapt to change, and transform in response to long-term stresses. Both paradigms underscore the need for anticipatory, inclusive, and flexible planning approaches that can adjust as risk conditions evolve.

Effective integration also requires attention to procedural and institutional dimensions. On one hand, policy coherence across levels of government and sectors is vital to align urban development goals with disaster resilience targets (OECD, 2018). On the other hand, *institutional integration* refers to the operational arrangements that enable collaboration, resource sharing, and joint planning between urban planning departments, disaster management agencies, and other relevant stakeholders (Mechler et al., 2019). Breaking down departmental silos through interagency platforms or coordinating committees ensures that risk considerations are incorporated from the earliest stages of urban planning processes.

Another critical component is *governance for resilience*, which involves inclusive and participatory planning practices. Integrating DRR requires not only technical tools but also community engagement, transparency, and accountability in decision-making. Participatory processes enhance the legitimacy of interventions and ensure that local knowledge and perceptions of risk are incorporated into formal planning systems (UN-Habitat, 2020). This is especially important in Southern African cities, where a significant share of the urban population lives in informal settlements and may not be reached by formal governance structures. Integration efforts must therefore extend beyond formal institutions to include partnerships with civil society, community-based organisations, and the private sector, as well as incremental upgrading strategies in informal areas (Satterthwaite et al., 2018a, b).

9.3 International and Regional Frameworks Guiding Integration

The imperative to integrate disaster risk reduction into urban planning is strongly supported by a suite of global and regional policy frameworks. These frameworks provide normative guidance, operational principles, and performance benchmarks that shape the enabling environment for risk-informed urban development. While global initiatives offer overarching direction, regional frameworks help contextualise these imperatives for Africa and, more specifically, Southern African states. Together, they reinforce the policy rationale for integrating DRR and urban planning across multiple governance scales.

9.3.1 The Sendai Framework for Disaster Risk Reduction (2015–2030)

Adopted in 2015, the Sendai Framework is the cornerstone global instrument for DRR. It marks a paradigm shift from reactive disaster response to proactive risk management and resilience-building (UNDRR, 2015). Crucially, Sendai explicitly calls for the integration of DRR into urban and territorial planning, land-use policies, infrastructure design, and development processes. Priority 2 of the framework, strengthening disaster risk governance to manage disaster risk, highlights the importance of coherent policies across sectors and levels of government, particularly in urban contexts. It urges national and local authorities to mainstream risk information into spatial planning instruments, such as zoning codes, building regulations, and environmental impact assessments, key tools in urban planning. By embedding risk assessments into these mechanisms, Sendai establishes the foundation for a systematic approach to managing urban risks. The framework underscores that reducing disaster risk requires not only emergency preparedness but also forward-looking planning measures to prevent risk accumulation in growing cities.

9.3.2 *The New Urban Agenda (2016)*

Adopted at the UN Conference on Housing and Sustainable Urban Development (Habitat III) in 2016, the New Urban Agenda (NUA) reinforces the centrality of resilient urban planning in achieving sustainable development. The NUA builds on the Sendai Framework and Sustainable Development Goal 11 (making cities inclusive, safe, resilient, and sustainable) by urging governments to integrate DRR and climate resilience into urban policies, planning, and design processes. It calls for climate-sensitive urban design, integrated infrastructure systems, and the protection of critical urban ecosystems (UN-Habitat, 2017). Importantly, the NUA places emphasis on localised implementation: it advocates decentralisation of planning authority and the inclusion of local communities and grassroots stakeholders in resilience-building initiatives. This focus on multi-level governance and community participation aligns with the notion that cities are on the frontline of disaster risk and climate impacts. The NUA also highlights the need to integrate DRR into national urban policies and development plans, thereby reinforcing vertical coherence between local plans and national strategies. By implementing the NUA, countries in Southern Africa are encouraged to strengthen urban planning frameworks so that they inherently address risk reduction and climate adaptation.

9.3.3 *Sustainable Development Goals (SDGs)*

The 2030 Agenda for Sustainable Development, adopted in 2015, recognises the interlinkages between urban development and disaster risk. Several of the Sustainable Development Goals (SDGs) reinforce the need for integration. SDG 11 (Sustainable Cities and Communities) explicitly includes Target 11.5, which aims to significantly reduce the number of people affected by disasters, with a focus on protecting the poor and vulnerable in urban settlements. Achieving this target necessitates embedding DRR into urban planning and housing policies. Additionally, SDG 13 (Climate Action) calls for urgent action to combat climate change and its impacts, which overlaps with urban DRR through the need for improved planning, adaptive capacity, and early warning systems. SDG 16 (Peace, Justice, and Strong Institutions) also has relevance, as effective institutions and governance are needed to implement integrated policies. The integrated nature of the SDGs encourages synergy between DRR and urban planning, promoting spatial equity, environmental sustainability, and social inclusion in cities (United Nations, 2015). The cross-cutting nature of these goals provides an opportunity to mainstream risk reduction considerations across various development sectors, including housing, transportation, water and sanitation, and environmental management. In practice, aligning national development plans with the SDGs has prompted many countries to begin considering disaster resilience indicators within their urban project planning and reporting.

9.3.4 *African Union Agenda 2063 and the Africa Programme of Action for DRR*

At the continental level, the African Union's Agenda 2063—*The Africa We Want*—outlines a strategic vision for Africa's development, rooted in inclusive growth, environmental sustainability, and resilience (African Union, 2015). In the realm of disaster risk and urbanisation, this vision is operationalised through the Africa Programme of Action (PoA) for the Implementation of the Sendai Framework 2015–2030, which adapts global DRR goals to the African context. The PoA aligns DRR with regional development priorities, including those under Agenda 2063, and prioritises risk-sensitive development, integrated planning, and improved coordination between national and local authorities (African Union, 2016). These frameworks emphasise that sustainable urban development in Africa must reckon with historical vulnerabilities, institutional weaknesses, and socio-economic inequities. For instance, they advocate incorporating climate and disaster risk considerations into African cities' development plans and highlight the need to protect Africa's urban cultural and environmental assets from hazards. They also promote the development of early warning systems, urban risk observatories, and resilience indicators tailored to the realities of African cities. However, while the AU frameworks provide high-level guidance, they rely on member states to implement actions. A persistent challenge has been translating these continental commitments into national and municipal policies, an issue of adaptation and political will, which will be discussed in later sections.

9.3.5 *Southern African Development Community (SADC) Protocols and Strategies*

Within the Southern African Development Community (SADC), regional instruments complement the global and continental frameworks by focusing on the specific needs of the subregion. Several SADC initiatives seek to enhance urban resilience and integrate DRR into planning. These include the SADC Climate Change Strategy and Action Plan, the Regional Indicative Strategic Development Plan (RISDP), and the SADC Disaster Preparedness and Response Strategy 2016–2030 (SADC, 2019). Together, they provide a platform for aligning national urban development and DRR strategies with regional objectives. For example, SADC's plans encourage member states to incorporate climate change adaptation and DRR measures into city development strategies and to invest in resilient infrastructure. In practice, however, the effectiveness of these frameworks varies significantly across member states. Implementation remains uneven due to disparities in institutional capacity, political commitment, and funding across the region. Some countries (like Namibia and South Africa) have adopted national strategies that reflect SADC's principles, while others lag behind due to fragmented governance systems or more pressing socioeconomic challenges. Moreover, regional coordination mechanisms, for instance, for sharing disaster risk data or conducting joint planning for transboundary risks, are still underdeveloped. Strengthening SADC's role could involve establishing more robust peer learning and technical support programs to help member countries implement agreed-upon resilience measures.

9.3.6 UNFCCC and the Paris Agreement (2015)

Although primarily climate-focused, the global climate change framework under the UN Framework Convention on Climate Change (UNFCCC) also reinforces the integration agenda. The Paris Agreement (2015) and countries' Nationally Determined Contributions (NDCs) increasingly include urban resilience and risk reduction commitments. Under the Paris Agreement, nations have pledged measures to adapt to climate change, many of which involve urban planning interventions such as upgrading infrastructure, improving drainage systems, or enforcing coastal zoning. These climate adaptation efforts dovetail with DRR objectives. The Paris framework provides incentives (through climate finance and technical support) for integrating DRR into urban development strategies as a means of enhancing adaptive capacity (UNFCCC, 2015). For example, several Southern African countries, in their NDCs, highlight plans to make cities more resilient to flooding and droughts. Such commitments can be leveraged to mainstream climate adaptation and DRR into national urban policy and planning processes. In essence, the climate agenda and the DRR agenda are mutually reinforcing in cities: effective climate adaptation reduces disaster risk, and sound risk reduction strengthens climate resilience.

9.4 Barriers to Integration in Southern Africa

Despite widespread acknowledgement of the need to integrate disaster risk reduction into urban planning, implementation in Southern Africa remains limited and inconsistent. Robust global and regional frameworks exist to guide integrated risk governance, but their operationalisation is hindered by a complex set of barriers. These challenges are multifaceted, involving institutional, political, technical, socio-economic, and historical dimensions and are often deeply embedded in the region's governance architecture and planning systems. The following subsections discuss the most significant impediments to effective integration, drawing on cross-country experiences in Southern Africa.

9.4.1 Institutional Fragmentation and Silos

A persistent challenge is the fragmented nature of institutional mandates across sectors such as urban planning, housing, environmental management, and disaster risk management. In many countries, these functions are administered by separate ministries or departments that operate independently, with limited coordination or information sharing (Pelling & Holloway, 2006). This siloed setup leads to duplication of efforts, policy contradictions, and inefficient use of resources. For instance, urban planners may focus on land-use zoning and infrastructure development without considering hazard exposure, while disaster management agencies concentrate on emergency response planning with little engagement during the city planning process. The result is missed opportunities to reduce risk through proactive planning.

In some cases, the institutional fragmentation is formalised by law. For example, in *Zimbabwe*, urban planning is governed by entities under the Department of Physical Planning, whereas disaster management falls under the Civil Protection Department—two bodies with distinct mandates and minimal collaboration. This lack of coordination meant that city plans in Harare and other urban centres historically did not incorporate disaster risk considerations, as the agencies responsible were not working in tandem (Chikoto & Sadiq, 2012). Even where national policies call for integrated approaches, as in South Africa's Disaster Management Act and planning legislation, implementation can falter if local government departments remain compartmentalised.

Moreover, decentralisation in the region has not always translated into effective empowerment for local authorities. Municipal planning departments often lack the authority or mechanisms to coordinate with national emergency management offices. Conversely, national DRR agencies sometimes bypass local planning processes. This vertical disconnect reinforces silos. Local governments, which ultimately implement land use plans and building regulations, may also lack clarity on their role in DRR if responsibilities are not clearly delineated across government levels (van Niekerk et al., 2018). The challenge of fragmentation is further compounded by sectoral budgeting processes, which allocate funds within narrow mandates and make it difficult to finance multi-sectoral initiatives.

Breaking these silos requires political will and governance reforms to establish formal coordination channels. Without such integration, even well-crafted policies risk remaining on paper, as parallel institutions pursue separate agendas that inadvertently undermine urban resilience.

9.4.2 *Weak Governance and Political Commitment*

Political will is a critical enabler of integration, yet in many Southern African countries, disaster risk reduction is not highly prioritised in urban development agendas. Rapid urban growth is frequently driven by powerful political and economic interests, such as real estate development, industrial expansion, or patronage in land allocation, which can sideline or even conflict with resilience goals (Adelekan et al., 2020a). Short election cycles and political pressures may incentivise visible infrastructure or housing projects, even if they encroach on high-risk areas, over the less visible work of risk-informed planning. In some cases, land in hazard-prone locations is allocated to communities or developers through informal political deals or clientelistic networks, undermining official urban plans and exposing more people to risk. For example, political interference in Zimbabwe's urban land governance has led to the proliferation of unregulated settlements in floodplains around Harare, as leaders have informally regularised or tolerated these settlements for short-term gain (Muchadenyika, 2015). Such practices override technical planning advice and ignore hazard assessments.

Governance challenges also manifest in corruption and lack of accountability, which erode the capacity to enforce planning regulations. If developers or officials can bypass building codes and environmental rules, risk-sensitive planning loses its teeth. Weak municipal governance in some cities means that even when risk assessments are conducted, their recommendations (e.g. "no-build" zones or infrastructure retrofits) may not be implemented due to vested interests or bribe-taking. Poor governance and low transparency thus represent a significant barrier to integration.

Additionally, many governments have not dedicated stable budgetary support for DRR within urban development. The absence of political commitment is evident in public expenditure patterns: funding for disaster management often remains small and is largely directed at post-disaster relief rather than prevention. This reactive allocation of resources reflects and reinforces a political mindset that does not prioritise long-term risk reduction. Even when national policies acknowledge DRR, local officials may lack incentives or directives from higher political levels to act on them. In summary, without strong leadership and consistent political commitment, integrated urban planning and DRR tend to be deprioritised amid competing development pressures. Overcoming this barrier requires elevating resilience as a political priority, through advocacy, the demonstrated benefits of risk reduction, and perhaps most persuasively, through crises that reveal the high cost of inaction.

9.4.3 *Capacity Constraints and Skills Gaps*

The limited technical and human capacity of many local governments in Southern Africa is a major impediment to integrating DRR and planning. Urban planners and emergency management officers often do not have cross-cutting training. Planners might not be versed in risk assessment or climate science, while DRR practitioners may be unfamiliar with planning tools like Geographic Information Systems (GIS), urban databases, or participatory planning techniques. This skills gap inhibits innovation and reduces the quality of risk-informed decision-making at the city level (Zhou et al., 2014). In smaller municipalities, there may be only a handful of qualified planners on staff, and positions for disaster risk specialists might not exist at all.

Furthermore, effective integration depends on access to technical tools and data, which are frequently lacking. Advanced methods such as hazard modelling, GIS-based risk mapping, and scenario planning require expertise and technology that many municipalities in countries like Mozambique or Lesotho struggle to afford or maintain (Adelekan et al., 2020a). Even where tools are available, their use is constrained by data gaps and limited technical literacy. For example, a city might have flood zone maps, but if local planners cannot interpret them or overlay them with land-use maps due to a lack of GIS skills, the data remain underutilised. In some urban areas, hazard and vulnerability data are outdated, fragmented, or not in formats that planners can easily integrate into their work. The absence of systematic data management, such as centralised risk information systems or GIS databases that combine socio-economic and hazard layers, means planning decisions are made with incomplete risk knowledge.

Capacity-building efforts in the region have often been project-based and donor-driven, lacking continuity. Short workshops or externally funded training programs can raise awareness, but without institutionalising new skills (for instance, by creating permanent training units or updating university curricula), the impact is not sustained. A related issue is the *financial capacity* constraint: many local governments operate under tight budgets that barely cover basic services, leaving little room to invest in new tools, staff training, or data systems. National support for municipal capacity is uneven, and in some cases, austerity or decentralisation without resources has hollowed out technical departments.

The net effect of these capacity constraints is that even well-intentioned policies to integrate DRR into planning cannot be effectively implemented. Plans might mention risk reduction in principle, but local officials may not know how to conduct a risk assessment or enforce risk-sensitive building standards. Overcoming this barrier will require substantial investment in human capital and institutional strengthening. It also necessitates creating professional networks and communities of practice where urban planners and DRR experts in the region can share knowledge and build expertise jointly.

Notably, financial limitations exacerbate these capacity issues. DRR is frequently underfunded in national and local budgets, and where funds exist, they are often earmarked for disaster response rather than prevention and mitigation. Urban planning departments similarly face chronic under-resourcing, with limited funds for staffing, training, data collection, or community engagement. While international donors have supported pilot projects to integrate DRR into urban planning, these efforts often remain small-scale and short-term. When project funding ends, momentum can be lost if there are no institutional budget lines or champions to continue the work. This points to the need for sustainable financing mechanisms and the political prioritisation of DRR in fiscal planning topics, revisited in the recommendations section.

9.4.4 Inadequate Legal and Policy Frameworks

Many Southern African countries continue to rely on planning laws and regulations that are outdated or misaligned with contemporary urban risks. Some of these frameworks have colonial-era origins, emphasising top-down control and rigid zoning over flexibility or resilience. As a result, they may not recognise informal settlements or allow adaptive measures necessary in the face of climate change (Watson, 2009). For instance, urban planning legislation in countries like Botswana and Malawi historically reflected a strict land-use zoning paradigm that failed to accommodate the reality of informal urban growth or the need to adjust plans dynamically for hazards. Such laws can inadvertently increase risk by excluding large portions of the urban population from formal planning (thus pushing them into unplanned high-risk areas), or by not enforcing any requirements for risk assessments in new developments.

Even where legal reforms have been initiated, implementation lags. In South Africa, post-apartheid legislation such as the Spatial Planning and Land Use Management Act (SPLUMA, 2013) was a progressive step that improved coherence in the planning system and introduced principles of sustainability and equity. SPLUMA, alongside the Disaster Management Act (2002, as amended in 2015), provides a basis for integrating risk considerations into spatial development frameworks at all government levels. However, the practical integration of these laws remains uneven. Many municipalities struggle to incorporate hazard and vulnerability assessments into their Integrated Development Plans (IDPs) and Spatial Development Frameworks (SDFs) despite the mandate to do so. Bureaucratic inertia, limited technical know-how, and a lack of monitoring means that the synergy intended by these laws is not fully realised on the ground (CoGTA, 2020). In essence, having risk-sensitive laws on paper is not sufficient if secondary regulations, bylaws, and enforcement mechanisms are weak.

In some countries, national urban policies or climate change policies exist in parallel to disaster management policies, with little cross-reference. This policy disconnect is a barrier in itself. For example, Zimbabwe has a National Climate Policy (2017) and a draft National Resilience Framework, but these have not been translated into updates of urban planning regulations or empowered local planning authorities to take on DRR roles. Similarly, some nations have stand-alone DRR policies that remain generic and are not linked to urban planning legislation, rendering them toothless (UN-Habitat, 2020). Without explicit requirements for risk-sensitive planning in legal instruments such as mandatory flood risk mapping for new housing developments or enforceable building standards for cyclone-prone zones, urban planners may lack the authority or impetus to integrate DRR into their daily practice.

Finally, even where laws do require certain DRR measures, enforcement is a critical issue. Limited oversight, corruption, or political interference can result in non-compliance going unpunished. For instance, buildings may be erected without adhering to codes, or settlements may expand into protected buffers with little consequence, especially if influential actors are involved. This undermines respect for the law and the goals of integration. In sum, updating legal and policy frameworks to mandate integration, and ensuring they are implemented and enforced, remain major tasks for countries aiming to mainstream DRR into urban development.

9.4.5 *Data Deficits and Risk Information Gaps*

Risk-informed planning relies heavily on the availability of accurate, timely, and localised data on hazards, exposure, and vulnerabilities. In Southern Africa, many cities and towns face a significant data deficit. Basic information like floodplain maps, soil stability surveys, or updated population density figures may be missing or outdated. Few countries have established integrated risk data platforms or observatories that compile multi-hazard information and make it accessible to urban planners (UNDRR, 2021). Where data does exist, it is often scattered across different agencies and not shared. For example, a meteorological service might have climate projections, a geological department might have seismic or landslide hazard maps, and universities might hold socio-economic vulnerability studies, yet these are not aggregated in a way that city planners can use when developing local plans.

Even critical tools like early warning systems and disaster loss databases are limited in coverage. Some progress has been made nationally (e.g. South Africa's robust weather early warning system), but smaller countries or municipalities often lack localised warning capabilities or community-level risk assessments. In Malawi and Zambia, for instance, hazard assessments tend to be conducted in an ad hoc fashion or during donor-funded projects and are not routinely updated or integrated into urban planning processes. As a result, planners may not know, for example, the flood return periods for rivers running through their cities or the precise extent of floodplains, leading to development in harm's way.

Another gap is in capturing and utilising local knowledge and community data. Informal settlements are usually not well documented in official datasets, yet residents often have detailed knowledge of micro-level risks (like which areas always flood or which slopes are unstable). However, this indigenous or community-based knowledge is frequently overlooked in formal planning, due in part to the marginalisation of informal communities from planning forums, and in part to a lack of methodologies to incorporate qualitative local insights into technical plans. The disconnect means planning might not address the most pressing risks perceived by communities, and conversely, community coping mechanisms might not be recognised or supported by official systems.

Data issues are compounded by proprietary restrictions and format incompatibilities. In some cases, risk data is collected by consultants or international organisations and ends up in reports that are not easily converted into GIS layers or practical tools for municipalities. Additionally, if agencies treat their data as proprietary (for example, if a water utility or an environmental ministry is reluctant to share data with the city planning department), integration suffers. Urban planners might plan infrastructure without full knowledge of hazard exposure, or disaster managers might set up early warning systems without integrating them into city communication channels.

The scarcity of reliable risk information and the lack of data-sharing protocols create a situation where urban planning decisions are often made "in the dark" regarding disaster risk. This barrier suggests the need for significant investment in data generation (e.g. conducting urban risk assessments, mapping exercises, and installing monitoring equipment), as well as establishing open data platforms and inter-agency agreements so that information flows to those who need it for planning.

9.4.6 *Socio-Economic and Spatial Inequities*

The complex socio-economic landscape of Southern African cities poses additional challenges for integrating DRR and urban planning. Widespread urban poverty, housing informality, and spatial inequality mean that a large portion of the urban population lives in conditions of high vulnerability. Informal settlements, often located on marginal lands such as floodplains, steep slopes, or former dump sites, concentrate risk. Residents of these areas typically lack durable housing, basic infrastructure (drainage, roads, water), and social services, which amplifies the impact of hazards when they occur (Wisner et al., 2015). These communities are not only more exposed to natural hazards but also politically and economically marginalised, making it difficult to implement risk-reducing measures in a top-down manner.

Integrating DRR into urban planning in such contexts faces a dilemma: enforcing strict risk-based land-use regulations could imply relocating or restricting development in informal settlements, but these settlements are home to the urban poor who have few alternatives. Governments may be hesitant to enforce evictions or stringent building standards in these areas for fear of social and political backlash. Indeed, efforts to clear or upgrade informal settlements have at times been seen as *anti-poor* or have led to conflict, especially if communities are not adequately consulted or compensated. Consequently, authorities might tolerate the continued growth of high-risk settlements, implicitly allowing risk to accumulate (Satterthwaite et al., 2018b). This tolerance is a coping strategy to avoid confronting the deeper issues of housing shortages and affordability that drive informality.

Spatial inequity also means that resources for infrastructure and services are unevenly distributed, often favouring wealthier areas. DRR investments (like flood defences or fire stations) might be directed to central business districts or affluent neighbourhoods, with less attention to informal peripheries where they are arguably most needed. This misallocation can worsen vulnerability for the most at-risk groups. Additionally, the urban planning process itself may not be inclusive: if low-income and informal community representatives are absent from planning discussions, their needs (like reinforcing a drainage canal or securing land tenure to enable safer housing improvements) may not be addressed.

Another socio-economic barrier is the limited risk awareness or risk preparedness among both officials and the public. In rapidly urbanising settings, immediate development pressures (jobs, housing, services) dominate, and both citizens and leaders can underestimate disaster risk until a catastrophe hits. When a severe event does occur, such as the destruction caused by Cyclone Idai in Beira, Mozambique, in 2019, it exposes these vulnerabilities dramatically, but often the policy response is reactive and fades after the crisis, without systematic changes to planning.

Collectively, these barriers create an environment where institutional inertia, political interests, and technical limitations reinforce one another, impeding progress towards integrated urban resilience. Overcoming them requires systemic change: regulatory reforms to update laws, institutional strengthening and clarified mandates, sustained capacity development, improved data systems, and the engagement of civil society to hold officials accountable. It also necessitates a high-level commitment to prioritise risk reduction as integral to development. The next section will illustrate how these barriers and some nascent solutions play out in specific country contexts.

9.5 Case Studies from Southern Africa

To illustrate the realities, challenges, and emerging opportunities for integrating urban planning and disaster risk reduction in practice, this section presents selected case studies from five Southern African countries. These examples from South Africa, Mozambique, Zimbabwe, Botswana, and Namibia highlight country-specific contexts, governance arrangements, and the extent of policy and operational integration achieved to date. Each case study sheds light on different facets of the integration puzzle, from legislative frameworks to local implementation, providing insight into what progress has been made and where gaps remain.

9.5.1 South Africa: Incremental Progress Amid Complexity

South Africa presents one of the most advanced policy environments for DRR integration in the region, underpinned by comprehensive legislation. The *Disaster Management Act* (2002, amended in 2015) created a multi-tiered disaster risk management system and mandates the development of Disaster Management Plans aligned with other development planning instruments. In parallel, the Spatial Planning and Land Use Management Act (SPLUMA, 2013) requires that spatial development frameworks at all levels of government incorporate principles of sustainability, resilience, and inclusivity. Together, these laws provide a strong legal basis for proactive risk governance and explicitly call for aligning disaster management with spatial planning (CoGTA, 2020). Municipalities are required to integrate DRR into their Integrated Development Plans

(IDPs) and Spatial Development Frameworks, ensuring that risk considerations become part of local development priorities.

In practice, South Africa's large metropolitan municipalities have made notable strides in mainstreaming risk reduction. Cities such as Cape Town, Johannesburg, and Durban (eThekwini) have developed risk-sensitive planning tools and climate change strategies. For example, the City of Cape Town's Climate Change Strategy and Durban's Municipal Climate Protection Programme (MCPP) provide integrated frameworks that embed climate and disaster risk considerations into urban planning, infrastructure design, and service delivery. Durban, in particular, has gained international recognition for its resilience initiatives; it was an early member of the 100 Resilient Cities network and has pioneered ecosystem-based adaptation to buffer the city from climate hazards (Roberts et al., 2012). The MCPP, initiated in 2004, operates with strong political backing and is embedded in eThekwini's IDP, exemplifying how sustained leadership can institutionalise DRR within city planning (Roberts & O'Donoghue, 2013).

Moreover, intergovernmental structures in South Africa encourage integration; for instance, disaster management centres at provincial and metropolitan levels work with planning departments to identify high-risk zones (Van Niekerk et al., 2018). Johannesburg's experience also highlights innovation: the City of Johannesburg has incorporated a Climate Change Adaptation Plan into its urban development strategy and leveraged climate finance (through the C40 Cities Finance Facility) to fund resilience projects in transport and housing.

Despite these advances, South Africa's progress is *incremental* and uneven. Smaller municipalities and rural towns lag behind the big metros. While Cape Town, Durban, and Johannesburg may have dedicated climate and disaster management units, many less-resourced municipalities rely on provincial support and struggle with implementing SPLUMA's risk provisions. There is also a gap between policy ambition and on-the-ground implementation. Enforcement of land-use regulations in hazard-prone areas (such as floodplains or fire-prone wildland-urban interfaces) remains inconsistent. In the rapidly growing informal settlements around cities, the reach of formal governance and services is limited, making it difficult to apply building standards or land use plans that reduce risk. Consequently, vulnerable communities, often living in dense informal settlements on risky sites, have seen only modest improvements in safety.

Coordination across government spheres, though legislated, can be challenging in practice. Integrating DRR into day-to-day urban management requires constant communication between departments (planning, water, housing, emergency services), which is still a work in progress. Nonetheless, South Africa's case demonstrates that a supportive legislative framework and high-level policy alignment are key enablers for integration. The country's experience suggests that future efforts should focus on capacity building for local implementation, funding to upgrade informal settlements, and stronger mechanisms to ensure that the good policies on paper result in tangible risk reduction outcomes for communities.

9.5.2 *Mozambique: Cyclone Exposure and Planning Gaps*

Mozambique is highly vulnerable to natural hazards, particularly cyclones, floods, and coastal storms, due to its extensive Indian Ocean coastline and river basins. Rapid urbanisation in cities like Beira, Maputo, and Chimoio has often been unplanned, resulting in significant exposure of populations and assets to these hazards. The devastating impact of Cyclone Idai in 2019 (and Cyclone Eloise in 2021) starkly highlighted the weaknesses in urban planning and preparedness. In Beira, Mozambique's fourth-largest city, Cyclone Idai caused catastrophic flooding and infrastructure collapse, with informal settlements being disproportionately affected. The cyclone's aftermath revealed that drainage systems were inadequate, many homes were built in flood-prone areas without proper elevation or protection, and there had been little enforcement of building standards (GFDRR, 2020). Chimoio and other inland towns also suffered heavy damage, underscoring that even beyond the coast, urban settlements were ill-prepared for extreme events.

Mozambique does have a policy framework that, on paper, supports integration. The National Policy for Disaster Risk Reduction 2017–2030 aligns with international frameworks and calls for risk-sensitive land-use planning and improved construction standards. Furthermore, the government has national climate change and urban development strategies that recognise the need to factor in risk. However, implementation at municipal and local levels remains limited (Wilkinson et al., 2020). Several factors contribute to this gap: weak institutional capacity, limited financial resources, and the sheer scale of informal urban expansion that outpaces government control. Urban growth in Mozambique is largely informal and unregulated, with an estimated 70% of urban housing being informal.

In coastal cities like Beira and Quelimane, the poorest communities often live in low-lying neighbourhoods highly susceptible to flooding and storm surges.

Land-use regulation in these cities has not kept up with expansion. Municipal governments face challenges in enforcing zoning or guiding new development to safer areas due to a combination of limited authority, lack of updated maps/plans, and pressure to accommodate a growing population quickly. Before Cyclone Idai, Beira did have an urban structural plan, but implementation was weak, and many houses were erected in floodplains, some by residents who had little choice, others through officials' tacit approval.

In the wake of the disaster, there have been efforts to correct course. Post-Idai recovery in Beira, supported by international partners like the World Bank and the Dutch government, initiated a shift towards more risk-informed urban reconstruction. A notable initiative is the Beira Master Plan for 2035, which integrates flood protection infrastructure (such as rehabilitated drainage canals and a green belt to absorb stormwater), updated zoning that discourages building in the most hazard-prone zones, and investment in resilient housing. This plan, developed with technical assistance from the Netherlands, represents a forward-looking blueprint for a climate-resilient city. Early results, such as the construction of a large drainage basin and strengthening of dunes and mangroves as natural buffers, demonstrate the potential of integrating DRR into urban redevelopment.

However, challenges remain in ensuring these plans are carried out beyond the immediate recovery period. Many of the resilience projects are *donor-dependent*, raising questions about sustainability. For example, Beira's improvements have been heavily financed by international grants and loans; maintaining infrastructure like drainage pumps and embankments will require local capacity and budget in the long run. Outside of Beira, other Mozambican cities have not yet undertaken such comprehensive risk-informed planning. The impetus from Idai is gradually leading to replication, for instance, Pemba and Nacala are now evaluating their flood risks, but a nationwide scaling of integrated urban DRR is still nascent.

9.5.3 Zimbabwe: Political-Economic Constraints on Integration

Zimbabwe's urban planning landscape is characterised by outdated legislation and the legacy of a centralised governance structure, compounded by recent economic and political challenges. The principal urban planning law, the Regional, Town, and Country Planning Act of 1976, is a colonial-era statute that has seen little substantive update and includes no provisions specific to disaster risk or climate adaptation. Meanwhile, the *Civil Protection Act* of 1989 provides the legal basis for disaster management, but its orientation is largely reactive, focusing on emergency response, and it vests considerable authority in central government agencies (Chagutah, 2014). In practice, this has meant that urban local authorities do not have clear mandates or guidance to integrate DRR into their development plans.

Urban governance in Zimbabwe has been hampered by political and economic turmoil over the past two decades. City councils, especially in major cities like Harare and Bulawayo, often find themselves at odds with the central government, which has sometimes intervened or overridden local planning decisions. This politicised environment makes long-term, systematic integration of DRR difficult. For example, during periods of acute housing shortages, there have been politically driven allocations of urban land without regard for planning regulations or hazard exposure. Harare, the capital, faces multiple challenges: rapid population growth, extensive informality, deteriorating infrastructure, and unstable institutional arrangements. Land invasions and irregular settlements have occurred, sometimes allegedly with the tacit approval of political elites seeking to gain favour or profit (Muchadenyika, 2015). As a result, informal settlements have mushroomed in hazardous areas, such as wetlands and low-lying floodplains on the city's outskirts, increasing exposure to flooding and waterborne disease outbreaks.

Enforcement of planning regulations in Zimbabwe is generally weak. Economic constraints and capacity issues mean that many local authorities do not have the means to implement master plans or to carry out evictions or relocations of settlements that violate those plans. Efforts to regularise or upgrade informal settlements have been sporadic and often politically charged—the most infamous being "Operation Murambatsvina" in 2005, which cleared many informal settlements in cities, ostensibly for public health and planning reasons, but without providing adequate alternatives for displaced residents. Such approaches, by creating social upheaval, have made communities distrustful of government planning interventions.

On the positive side, Zimbabwe has in recent years adopted broader frameworks that acknowledge risk. A National Climate Policy was introduced in 2017, and there are discussions around a comprehensive Disaster Risk Management Strategy that would emphasise risk reduction and resilience. Additionally, some city-level initiatives, often supported by NGOs or international agencies, have aimed at building resilience in vulnerable urban communities. For instance, NGOs have worked on projects to improve drainage in flood-prone Harare neighbourhoods and to train volunteers in disaster preparedness. However, these efforts remain localised and are not yet embedded in formal urban planning processes.

A fundamental constraint in Zimbabwe is resource limitations. Planning departments in cities operate on shoe-string budgets, with shortages of qualified staff and basic equipment (computers, vehicles for site inspections, etc.). In such an environment, introducing new concepts like DRR integration can seem an unaffordable luxury. Moreover, the continuing economic difficulties (including hyperinflation episodes) divert attention to the immediate survival needs of cities, keeping water running, collecting waste, and managing medium-term risks. Governance instability is another impediment. Frequent changes in local leadership, interference by central government (for instance, through appointed commissions or temporary administrators), and a general climate of uncertainty have disrupted continuity in urban development initiatives.

9.5.4 *Botswana: Strong Institutions, Limited Local Integration*

Botswana is often cited for its relatively strong governance and sound land administration systems. The country has undertaken significant steps to modernise its urban planning framework and incorporate resilience considerations at the policy level. For instance, the *Town and Country Planning Act* of 2013 updated older statutes and aimed to provide more flexible and integrated land-use planning processes. Botswana also formulated a National Disaster Risk Reduction Strategy (2013–2018), which promotes the integration of DRR into sectoral development planning, and its National Settlement Policy encourages orderly and planned urban growth. Furthermore, the country's National Development Plan 11 (2017–2023) emphasises climate-resilient infrastructure, early warning systems, and the use of spatial planning as tools for risk reduction (Republic of Botswana, 2017). These high-level frameworks indicate a government commitment to consider risk in development.

In practice, however, the integration of DRR into urban planning at the local level in Botswana has been uneven. On one hand, Botswana's major urban centres, like Gaborone (the capital) and Francistown, have relatively well-developed planning departments and enforce zoning and building standards more consistently than many of their regional peers. On the other hand, these planning processes have not yet fully internalised disaster risk considerations, such as systematic hazard mapping or climate adaptation measures. For example, while Gaborone has piloted the use of urban growth models and conducted some flood risk mapping to inform planning decisions, these practices are not yet standard or countrywide. Development control in both Gaborone and secondary towns has only sporadically incorporated hazard assessments, meaning that some flood-prone areas or ecological buffer zones may still be allocated for development without rigorous analysis (Manyena et al., 2013).

Institutional silos remain a challenge in Botswana too. The Department of Town and Regional Planning and the National Disaster Management Office, for instance, have distinct roles, and there is limited routine coordination between them on urban issues. Disaster management functions are often housed in a different ministry (such as local government or defence) than physical planning, which can slow joint planning efforts. Recognising this, Botswana has started to use inter-sectoral committees (as noted during the formulation of NDP 11) to bring different departments together on cross-cutting issues. However, such collaboration needs to be institutionalised beyond specific strategy development exercises.

Another issue is resource allocation. Botswana's comparatively strong fiscal position (thanks to revenue from diamonds, etc.) means that it has the means to invest in resilience—yet, at the local government level, budgets for DRR activities are still small. Much of the focus of local authorities is on economic development (creating jobs, attracting investment) and providing housing and services; DRR can be perceived as an additional function that is not urgent until a disaster strikes. As a result, proactive measures like enforcing floodplain zoning or conducting regular risk audits of settlements may not receive adequate attention or funding.

A particular emerging challenge in Botswana is the pressure of urbanisation on limited land, especially in and around Gaborone. Land scarcity and high demand have led to rising land prices and some informal settlements in peri-urban areas. When formal planning can't keep up with demand, the risk is that unplanned developments spring up, potentially in unsuitable locations. So far, Botswana has contained informality better than many of its neighbours, but the trend bears watching. For instance, in Gaborone's peri-urban fringe, some settlements have expanded in areas without full planning approval, which also means without thorough risk assessment.

9.5.5 *Namibia: A Risk-Informed Planning Turn*

Namibia stands out in the Southern African region for proactively integrating environmental and disaster risk considerations into its development and spatial planning policies. Although the country is less densely populated (and less urbanised in absolute numbers) than some neighbours, it faces significant hazards such as droughts, flash floods, and fires, which are being exacerbated by climate change. Recognising these threats, Namibia has made *DRR a national priority*, especially given its vulnerability to recurrent drought and water scarcity.

On the policy front, Namibia has a robust framework supportive of integration. The National Policy on Climate Change (2011) and the Disaster Risk Management Act (2012) establish a strong foundation for resilience-building (Republic of Namibia, 2012). These policies promote the incorporation of risk reduction and climate adaptation into all sectors. The DRM Act, in particular, created structures for risk management from national to local levels and called for contingency plans and risk assessments to inform planning. In the urban realm, Namibia has been developing Integrated Regional Land Use Plans (IRLUPs) for its regions, which include analysis of environmental risks and vulnerabilities as part of guiding land allocation and development. This approach ensures that, for example, flood-prone zones or sensitive ecological areas are identified and considered when planning settlements or infrastructure (Republic of Namibia, 2012).

Namibia's capital city, Windhoek, provides a leading example of risk-informed urban development. The city formulated a comprehensive *City Resilience Strategy* in recent years, which addresses a wide range of shocks and stresses, from water security (a critical issue for this semi-arid city) to floods and public health. The strategy includes initiatives such as protecting and restoring the watersheds that supply the city, expanding urban agriculture to improve food security and manage open spaces, and enforcing land-use regulations to steer growth away from high-risk areas. One practical result is that Windhoek has invested in securing its water sources (via dams and aquifer recharge) and implemented stringent water conservation measures to mitigate the impact of drought, which is a model of linking urban planning (in this case, resource planning) with risk reduction.

Namibia has also emphasised inclusive, participatory planning for informal settlements. Through programs like the Participatory Slum Upgrading Programme (with UN-Habitat support), communities in vulnerable settlements in Windhoek and other towns have been engaged in mapping risks (like flood-prone locations) and identifying upgrading needs (UN-Habitat, 2018). This participatory approach has not only resulted in physical improvements (like better drainage in some neighbourhoods) but also built trust and awareness, which are crucial for disaster preparedness. The country's planning philosophy, as reflected in some policy documents, stresses *integrated urban development*—bringing together housing, basic services, environmental management, and DRR in a unified approach (UN-Habitat, 2020).

Despite these positive steps, Namibia still faces implementation gaps. Technical capacity varies across its municipalities; the capital is comparatively well-resourced, but smaller towns may have only a few professionals, making it challenging to maintain up-to-date risk assessments or enforce all regulations. Interdepartmental collaboration, while encouraged at the policy level, can be improved in practice. For instance, ensuring that town planners routinely consult meteorological or hydrological data or collaborate with emergency services when expanding a township is an ongoing effort. Additionally, while IRLUPs are a great tool, they need regular updating and must be respected when development pressures arise (e.g. a rush for new housing can tempt officials to bend the rules).

Funding is another area to watch. Namibia's economy has had ups and downs, and investments in infrastructure or new programs can be limited during downturns. Securing steady funding for resilience initiatives (like maintaining early warning systems, expanding green infrastructure in cities, or upgrading informal settlements) will be important.

9.6 Enablers and Best Practices for Integration

While the challenges outlined are substantial, there are also encouraging developments. Across Southern Africa and in other regions, various enabling factors and best practices have emerged that demonstrate effective integration of disaster risk reduction into urban planning is both possible and beneficial. These enablers, spanning political, legal, institutional, technical, financial, and social domains, offer insight into how barriers can be overcome. Drawing on regional experiences and lessons from global case studies, this section outlines key factors that support integration and provides practical examples that could guide policy and practice in Southern Africa.

9.6.1 Political Leadership and Policy Commitment

Strong political commitment is a critical catalyst for integration. When leaders at the highest levels champion resilience and risk reduction, it often results in policy alignment, interdepartmental cooperation, and the allocation of resources to integrated initiatives. For example, in South Africa, sustained support from national and provincial leaders has facilitated alignment between the Disaster Management Act, SPLUMA, and the National Climate Change Adaptation Strategy, thereby encouraging risk-informed development planning in metropolitan municipalities (CoGTA, 2020). High-level buy-in ensures that integration is not seen as a marginal or optional activity, but as a core objective across sectors.

At the city level, visionary mayors or councillors can drive integration forward. Durban (eThekwini) is often cited: its municipal leadership over the past two decades consistently backed climate adaptation and ecosystem-based DRR initiatives, allowing the city to institutionalise programs like the Municipal Climate Protection Programme (MCPP). This program, started in 2004, was given political backing and is embedded in the city's Integrated Development Plan, making it an ongoing priority rather than a short-term project (Roberts & O'Donoghue, 2013). The result is that Durban has a dedicated climate protection branch, cross-sectoral working groups on resilience, and a budget for adaptation projects, all outcomes traceable to political commitment.

Another illustration is the City of Johannesburg, where leaders have pursued an ambitious resilience agenda, partly through global networks. Johannesburg's Climate Action Plan received support from the C40 Cities

Climate Leadership Group, and the city's Climate Resilience Strategy was partly financed and technically assisted by the C40 Cities Finance Facility. This demonstrates that political leaders leveraging international partnerships can secure the means to integrate DRR into urban investments (in Johannesburg's case, integrating resilience into transport and housing projects).

9.6.2 Legislative and Policy Reform

Modernising outdated legislation and establishing clear policy mandates for integration are essential for mainstreaming DRR in urban planning. Legal and regulatory frameworks set the "rules of the game" for how planning is done; if they require risk assessments and coordination, those practices become standard. South Africa's SPLUMA is a prime example of a legislative reform that explicitly mandates the integration of DRR into spatial planning at local levels. By requiring municipalities to consider climate change and disaster risk in their spatial development frameworks, SPLUMA created a legal imperative for integration, which local governments must follow. Legal clarity of this sort helps ensure that responsibilities are defined and not left to discretion.

In Namibia, the Disaster Risk Management Act (2012) is coupled with the practice of developing Integrated Regional Land Use Plans that incorporate hazard and vulnerability data. This structured approach effectively bridges the gap between national policy and local land-use decisions, as planners have a legal mechanism (and tools) to include risk information (Republic of Namibia, 2012). It serves as a *best practice* model: Namibia's IRLUPs demonstrate how statutory planning instruments can be designed to be inherently risk-sensitive. By integrating GIS-based hazard maps and community risk inputs into these plans, Namibia has institutionalised a process by which any proposed development is reviewed with an eye on disaster risk.

Botswana's approach of embedding DRR into its National Development Plan (as a cross-cutting theme in NDP 11) also highlights a policy-level integration. During the plan's formulation, inter-sectoral committees ensured that ministries of local government, planning, environment, etc., collectively addressed DRR (Republic of Botswana, 2017). This resulted in guidelines for incorporating DRR into local development plans and project appraisals, effectively a soft regulatory push for integration.

Enabling factor: When laws and policies explicitly require DRR considerations in planning, they change institutional behaviour. They empower planners to say no to unsafe developments ("the law doesn't allow building in a flood zone without mitigation") and ensure DRR is not an afterthought. It's important, however, that such reforms come with supporting regulations and technical guidance so that practitioners understand how to comply. Additionally, regulatory integration works best when accompanied by enforcement; thus, training of inspectors and accountability mechanisms must complement legal changes.

9.6.3 Capacity Development and Institutional Strengthening

Building up the human and institutional capacity for integrated planning is a cornerstone of success. This involves training current professionals, educating future ones, and possibly creating specialised units or roles dedicated to risk reduction within planning departments. Various initiatives in Africa are contributing to capacity development. For example, the African Urban Risk Knowledge (AURK) Programme and the Peri-Urban Resilient Ecosystems (PURE) partnership have delivered training and knowledge-sharing in cities across Southern Africa (Adelekan et al., 2020a). These programs often bring together urban planners and disaster management officials in workshops to learn about risk assessment tools, climate information use, and participatory planning techniques.

However, beyond ad-hoc training, institutionalising knowledge is key. Academic and professional development institutions are starting to respond to the need for interdisciplinary skills. A notable best practice is the work of the African Centre for Disaster Studies (ACDS) at North-West University in South Africa, which offers postgraduate programs blending urban planning, environmental management, and DRR. Such programs equip a new generation of practitioners with a holistic perspective. Graduates who understand both the language of spatial planning and the science of risk can act as "integration champions" in their respective organisations. Similarly, the University of Cape Town's climate change and urban development courses (to give another example) have produced graduates now working in city governments on resilience initiatives.

On the institutional side, creating dedicated structures can help. Some cities have established *Resilience Offices* or *Climate Change Units* that work across departments. For instance, as part of the 100 Resilient Cities initiative, Durban and Cape Town each appointed a Chief Resilience

Officer to coordinate resilience efforts across municipal departments. These roles, supported by capacity-building networks, help break down silos internally. Another aspect of capacity is peer learning and exchange. City-to-city learning networks in the region (like the Covenant of Mayors in Sub-Saharan Africa for climate and energy) allow municipal staff to share experiences and solutions. For example, officials from Beira (Mozambique) and eThekwini (South Africa) have exchanged knowledge on managing flood risks, which builds capacity through practical exposure.

Enabling Factor When people have the right skills and organisations have the right structures and knowledge resources, integration moves from theory to practice. It reduces reliance on external consultants because local professionals can do the work of risk analysis and integrated planning. It also fosters innovation, as skilled staff can adapt global best practices to local contexts. Continuous professional development, such as regular training modules on DRR for urban planners, can ensure that capacity keeps pace with evolving risk scenarios (like new climate projections or novel technologies in mapping).

9.6.4 Data, Technology, and Risk Mapping

Access to accurate risk data and modern technological tools significantly improves integration outcomes. With the right data, urban planners can identify hotspots of vulnerability, project future hazard scenarios, and make evidence-based decisions on where and how to build. Technological advancements in remote sensing, geographic information systems (GIS), and data analytics have made it easier and cheaper to gather and use risk information than ever before.

A compelling example comes from Beira, Mozambique. After Cyclone Idai, the city developed a *Flood Risk Management Master Plan* using advanced tools: high-resolution satellite imagery, LiDAR surveys for topography, and GIS-based flood modelling. Dutch technical experts collaborated with local teams to produce digital flood simulations for different storm intensities (Wilkinson et al., 2020). This data-driven approach identified which neighbourhoods needed new drainage channels, where protective dikes or retention basins could be placed, and how green infrastructure (like mangrove restoration) could reduce wave impact. The plan has since guided reconstruction efforts, ensuring that new infrastructure is sited and designed with flood risk in mind. It demonstrates the power of technology to transform raw data into actionable planning guidelines.

Open data platforms and geospatial tools are also making a difference. Several Southern African countries are developing or have launched risk observatories or geo-portals. For instance, the Spatial Data Infrastructure in South Africa and Namibia's planned Geo-Information Portal aim to provide accessible maps and datasets on terrain, population, and hazards to various stakeholders. When supported by institutional data-sharing protocols, such platforms enhance evidence-based planning by putting information in the hands of local planners. As an example of a collaboration, UN-Habitat's City Resilience Profiling Tool (CRPT) was piloted in cities including Maputo (Mozambique) and Lusaka (Zambia). The CRPT is a comprehensive urban risk assessment methodology that generates a resilience profile through data collection across multiple sectors. It helped those cities identify specific weaknesses (like insufficient stormwater drainage in certain districts) and prioritise actions. The process of gathering the data also built local technical capacity.

Another best practice is the use of community-based data alongside high-tech data. In Windhoek's informal settlements, residents participated in mapping exercises using GPS devices to mark flood-prone areas and inadequate drainage points (UN-Habitat, 2018). This ground-level information, when combined with meteorological data, gave city engineers a fuller picture of the flood problem and led to co-designed drainage solutions that were both technically sound and locally accepted.

Enabling factor: Embracing data and technology leads to more nuanced and proactive planning. Hazard maps can delineate zones where development should be restricted or where special building codes must apply. Early warning systems and climate projections can inform the design of infrastructure (e.g. factoring in heavier rainfall or higher sea levels into bridge or seawall construction). Moreover, technology facilitates monitoring; satellite imagery can quickly show if illegal settlements are expanding into floodplains, prompting enforcement before a disaster strikes. For success, technology adoption must come with training (addressing the capacity barrier) and maintenance budgets. Partnerships with universities and international agencies can help cities acquire and interpret data. Encouragingly, open-source tools (like QGIS for spatial analysis or the OpenStreetMap platform for community mapping) are lowering costs and allowing customisation to local needs.

9.6.5 Multi-stakeholder Collaboration and Community Participation

Inclusive governance models that involve a wide array of stakeholders can greatly enhance the legitimacy and effectiveness of integrating DRR into urban planning. Collaboration across stakeholders, including civil society, academia, the private sector, and local communities, ensures that diverse perspectives and knowledge systems inform planning decisions, leading to more robust and socially acceptable outcomes.

One fundamental reason participation is an enabler is that it helps bridge the gap between formal plans and ground realities. For instance, when vulnerable communities are engaged in identifying risks and crafting solutions, the resulting plans are more likely to address the actual needs and to be supported during implementation. A telling example is Windhoek's Participatory Informal Settlement Upgrading Program. In one flood-prone informal neighbourhood, local residents worked with city officials and NGOs to map flood risk hotspots (areas where water pooled or drainage was blocked) and jointly developed a plan to improve drainage, including community-designed channels and periodic clean-up schedules. This participatory process not only produced technical interventions (like better drainage) but also educated residents on risks and built a sense of ownership. The result was a tangible reduction in flood impacts after implementation, as well as increased trust between the community and the municipality (UN-Habitat, 2018).

Multi-stakeholder platforms can also institutionalise integration. Some cities have set up *Resilience Committees* or similar bodies that include representatives from different departments (planning, water, health, emergency services) as well as external experts, NGOs, and community leaders. For example, in Madagascar (outside our region but relevant as a model), the city of Antananarivo established a local platform for DRR that brings together municipal officials, community representatives, and researchers to coordinate flood risk management in the city's low-lying districts. A similar approach could benefit Southern African cities, and some steps are being taken in that direction, such as city-level climate change forums in cities like Lusaka and Harare.

Engaging the private sector is another aspect of multi-stakeholder collaboration. Private developers and utility companies play significant roles in urban development. When they are part of the conversation, they can be encouraged or regulated to adopt resilient practices. In South Africa, the eThekwini municipality worked with insurance companies and developers in a forum to discuss how floodplain development raises insurance risks and costs, leading to a voluntary agreement on more stringent flood mitigation in new projects—essentially, the market reinforcing DRR principles.

Academic and research institutions contribute by offering data, innovative solutions, and independent evaluation of plans. Partnerships between cities and universities (like the University of Makerere's support to Kampala in Uganda, or closer to our region, the University of Cape Town's advisory role to Cape Town's climate adaptation planning) show the value of technical expertise in an ongoing way. For Southern Africa, leveraging local universities for risk assessment studies or pilot projects can embed cutting-edge knowledge into practice.

Enabling factor: Participation and collaboration lead to plans that people support. This means less resistance, more compliance, and often creative solutions that outsiders might not conceive. It also ensures that measures are culturally and contextually appropriate—for example, a community might suggest using a local, low-cost material for reinforcement of a slope instead of an expensive engineering solution, or might pinpoint a traditional practice (like the seasonal movement of cattle out of flood zones) that can be built upon. Inclusive processes strengthen social capital and empower communities, which is invaluable during disaster response and recovery as well.

Finally, inclusive planning serves equity: it gives marginalised groups a voice in decision-making. This aligns DRR integration with broader goals of social inclusion and justice, which is both an ethical and practical imperative (disasters often disproportionately affect the marginalised, so their inclusion is necessary for effective risk reduction). Participatory approaches, in sum, are not just a democratic ideal but a pragmatic component of resilience-building.

9.6.6 *International Partnerships and Financing*

Given the resource and knowledge constraints in many Southern African cities, international partnerships and financing mechanisms can provide vital support for integration efforts. External funding, technical assistance, and knowledge exchange programs have already played a significant role in kick-starting or scaling up DRR-urban planning integration in the region.

One major avenue has been multilateral development banks and global initiatives. The World Bank, for instance, through its City Resilience Program (CRP) and the Global Facility for Disaster Reduction and Recovery (GFDRR), has supported cities with diagnostic tools, planning frameworks, and financing options for resilience. Cities like Dar es Salaam (Tanzania) and Antananarivo (Madagascar) have benefited from such programs, and Southern African cities have begun to tap into them as well. The CRP not only provides funding but also helps cities develop bankable projects that incorporate DRR. For example, it helped design a flood-resilient urban transport project, which could then attract investment. This approach is crucial because it links resilience with economic development, making it more politically attractive.

Climate finance has emerged as a key source of support, too. Funds such as the Green Climate Fund (GCF) and the Adaptation Fund offer grants and concessional loans for projects that often lie at the intersection of climate adaptation and DRR. Several Southern African countries have secured GCF funding for projects that include urban components (e.g. integrated flood management in cities, resilient water supply systems, etc.). These funds can alleviate the budgetary constraints that local authorities face, allowing them to invest in infrastructure upgrades, early warning systems, or capacity building that they otherwise could not afford.

Another form of partnership is through city networks and twinning arrangements. Programs like 100 Resilient Cities (pioneered by the Rockefeller Foundation) have brought a number of African cities into a global network where they received technical support to develop resilience strategies, including urban DRR integration. In this network, cities had access to a platform of partners, ranging from engineering firms offering pro bono expertise to tech companies providing data solutions. For instance, the City of Cape Town got support from this network to craft its comprehensive resilience strategy after experiencing a severe drought. The strategy integrates water security (a risk issue) into spatial planning and community engagement, and its creation was bolstered by international expertise.

Additionally, *South–South cooperation* and regional bodies like SADC and the African Union facilitate knowledge exchange. The AU's Africa Urban Agenda and related forums encourage cities to learn from each other's experiences (African Union, 2016). SADC can potentially develop *regional guidelines or toolkits* for member states on how to integrate DRR into local urban planning, a step that would standardise and elevate practices across the region (SADC, 2019). A regional data-sharing platform or knowledge hub (as recommended in SADC strategies) could allow countries to access each other's hazard maps or best-practice case studies, saving time and resources on developing these independently.

From a financing perspective, innovative mechanisms are worth highlighting as best practices. Some cities worldwide are exploring resilience bonds or incorporating resilience criteria into municipal bonds to attract investors interested in sustainability. In the Southern African context, while municipal bond markets are not very mature, national governments could potentially issue bonds for resilient infrastructure, indirectly benefiting cities. Another example is the insurance sector: partnering with insurers on initiatives like the African Risk Capacity (a continental risk pool for disasters) can provide quick financing after disasters, easing the burden on city budgets and allowing them to rebuild smarter.

Enabling factor: International partnerships and finance bring in not just money but often cutting-edge knowledge and credibility. When a city secures a project with GCF or World Bank support, it often triggers capacity enhancement because those projects require rigorous analysis, stakeholder engagement, and monitoring. They effectively raise the bar on how projects are implemented. Furthermore, being part of global networks or receiving international support can give local reformers political cover—leaders may be more willing to champion integration if it comes with external validation or resources.

Ultimately, though, long-term sustainability depends on domestic capacity and *ownership*. International support is most enabling when it's used to catalyse local action, for example, by creating demonstration projects or seeding new institutional setups, which local governments can then maintain and replicate with their own resources in the future. The goal is to leverage international help to the point where integration becomes self-propelling within cities' regular planning and budgeting cycles.

9.7 Policy Recommendations

To strengthen the integration of urban planning and disaster risk reduction in Southern Africa, a range of policy actions is needed at multiple levels of governance. The following recommendations are proposed, drawing on the analysis of barriers and enablers as well as lessons from the case studies and best practices discussed. These recommendations address legal frameworks, institutional mechanisms, local implementation, capacity building, data systems, participatory approaches, and partnerships. Implementing them would require collaboration among national governments, local authorities, regional bodies, civil society, and international partners.

9.7.1 *Update and Align Legal Frameworks*

Revise and modernise planning and disaster management legislation to explicitly mandate the integration of DRR into urban development processes. This entails updating old planning laws and building codes to incorporate risk reduction principles and climate adaptation measures. For example, laws should require that urban master plans and zoning schemes include hazard and vulnerability assessments and outline specific resilience measures. Similarly, disaster management acts should reference coordination with spatial planning and environmental management. Wherever possible, consolidate and harmonise legislation so that climate change adaptation, DRR, and urban planning are not addressed in isolation. This alignment ensures consistency in objectives and mandates across sectors. Crucially, new or amended laws must be backed by enforceable regulations, for instance, no building permits in high-risk zones without approved mitigation plans. All levels of government, national, provincial/state, and local, should be covered so that integration is mandated from strategic plans down to local land use plans. Embedding these requirements in law will institutionalise integration beyond individual projects or personalities (Watson, 2009; UNDRR, 2015).

9.7.2 *Institutionalise Interagency Coordination Mechanisms*

Establish formal coordination bodies or platforms that bring together urban planning, disaster management, climate change, housing, infrastructure, and other relevant sectors. At the national level, this could be an inter-ministerial committee on resilient urban development tasked with aligning policies, reviewing major urban projects for risk considerations, and guiding capacity building. At the city level, municipalities should create multi-departmental task forces or working groups, for example, a Resilient Cities Committee, that meet regularly to coordinate on planning initiatives and DRR programs. These mechanisms need clear mandates (ideally set out in policy or legislation) and should be empowered to influence budgeting and project approvals. Information-sharing protocols should be put in place (e.g. a requirement that the meteorology office provides seasonal forecasts to city planners, or that planning departments share expansion plans with emergency services for feedback). Ultimately, the goal is to break down silos and foster a *culture of collaboration*, where different departments see resilience as a shared responsibility rather than "someone else's job". This can be reinforced by joint training and the development of integrated guidelines (for instance, a national guideline on safe settlement planning developed jointly by planning and DRR authorities).

9.7.3 Localise Integration at the Municipal Level

Operationalise integration at the level of local government, where urban planning decisions are made and implemented. Municipalities should be supported and required to incorporate DRR into all relevant local planning instruments. This means that Integrated Development Plans (IDPs), urban master plans, local land-use schemes, and capital investment programs must explicitly address disaster risks and propose measures to mitigate them. Risk assessments should be conducted for each municipality (or city district), and the findings should guide zoning. High-risk zones identified by these assessments should be reserved for non-sensitive uses (like open space or recreation) or require elevated building standards. In growth planning, direct urban expansion towards safer corridors and avoid known hazard-prone areas. National governments can assist by providing technical guidelines for municipal planners on how to integrate risk into their plans and by making funding partially conditional on risk-informed planning (e.g. only funding housing projects that have accounted for flooding or wildfire risk). Additionally, municipalities need adequate *authority and resources* to enforce plans and building regulations; decentralisation efforts should ensure local governments have the mandate to enforce compliance and the means (staff, budget, legal backing) to do so. In many cases, capacity at the local level is a limiting factor, so parallel investments in training (recommendation 7.4) and data provision (7.5) are vital. The principle is that integration will only be meaningful if it reaches the frontline of urban management, the city and town councils, and becomes embedded in their routine planning, permitting, and development oversight functions.

9.7.4 *Invest in Capacity Building and Human Resources*

Strengthen the capacity of urban planners, engineers, and DRR professionals through targeted education and training programs. This involves updating university curricula to include courses on urban resilience, climate change adaptation, and disaster risk management for planners, architects, and civil engineers. Professional councils and institutes (for planning, engineering, etc.) should be encouraged to provide continuing professional development modules focused on integrated planning practices, GIS for risk mapping, participatory methods, and emergency planning. Governments, possibly with donor support, can establish scholarship programs or dedicated training centres for municipal staff to deepen their expertise in these areas. For example, a "Resilient Cities Training Program" could be launched at a regional level, rotating workshops and hands-on training across countries. South-South learning should be leveraged: practitioners from cities that have made progress (like Durban or Windhoek) can mentor peers from other municipalities. Moreover, consider creating interdisciplinary teams or positions at the city level, for instance, appointing a resilience officer or risk reduction specialist within planning departments to champion integration from within. Recognising and rewarding skill development is also key: career pathways and incentives should be aligned so that public servants see specialisation in resilience planning as an avenue for advancement. By developing a cadre of professionals fluent in both planning and DRR, integration moves from being an external requirement to an internalised part of the job.

9.7.5 *Enhance Risk Data Availability and Use*

Invest in the collection, management, and accessibility of risk data to inform urban planning. This recommendation calls for building robust data systems at the national and local levels. Governments should establish or strengthen national risk observatories or geo-spatial data centres that compile multi-hazard data (flood maps, drought indices, seismic zones, etc.), exposure information (population, economic assets, infrastructure), and vulnerability indicators (socio-economic profiles, building stock conditions). These data should be disaggregated to city and sub-city scales to be directly relevant for urban planning. Where gaps exist—for example, no updated floodplain maps for a city—government must prioritise filling those through surveys, remote sensing, or modelling partnerships with technical agencies or universities. *Data-sharing protocols* must be created or enforced so that different agencies (meteorology, geology, statistics, urban planning) contribute to and draw from a common data repository. Additionally, investing in technology like GIS and remote sensing for municipalities and training staff in their use will enable planners to analyse risk layers alongside development proposals. National ministries can collaborate with academic and research institutions to develop downscaled climate projections to inform long-term urban plans. Furthermore, encourage open data policies: non-sensitive risk data should be made public to allow community groups, researchers, and the private sector to also innovate around risk reduction (for example, communities mapping their own risks and uploading them to an open platform). By improving the availability and usability of risk information, planners can make evidence-based decisions and justify them to stakeholders with hard data, thereby improving the quality and credibility of integrated plans.

9.7.6 Promote Participatory Planning Approaches

Embed participatory approaches in urban planning processes, especially those involving informal settlements and other high-risk communities. Governments and municipalities should institutionalise mechanisms for community engagement in planning and DRR. This could involve regular community consultations during the development of local plans (e.g. workshops in vulnerable neighbourhoods to identify hazards and discuss solutions), inclusion of community representatives on local resilience committees (as noted earlier), and support for grassroots risk mapping or monitoring initiatives. Affected communities should be treated as partners in identifying risk reduction measures; their local knowledge can help pinpoint issues that technical analyses might overlook (Satterthwaite et al., 2018b). Public participation should start early in the planning cycle (not just presenting a finished plan for comments) so that community inputs shape the outcomes. One practical recommendation is to adopt tools like *Participatory Geographic Information Systems (PGIS)*, where residents and planners co-create risk maps that feed into official plans. Additionally, ensure that communication of risk is two-way: authorities should disseminate understandable risk information to the public (through maps, drills, alerts), which empowers communities to act and give informed feedback. Special efforts should be made to include marginalised groups, women, youth, the elderly, and people with disabilities in these processes, since they often have unique insights into vulnerabilities and capacities. By co-designing interventions (such as relocation programs, flood defences, or evacuation routes) with the people who will use or be affected by them, plans will be more locally appropriate, better received, and thus easier to implement. Participatory planning also builds social capital and trust, which are invaluable during disaster response and recovery.

9.7.7 *Leverage Regional and Global Partnerships*

Mobilise support from regional bodies and international partners to provide funding, technical assistance, and platforms for knowledge exchange on urban resilience. At the regional level, SADC and the African Union can play a coordinating and supportive role. SADC should consider developing standardised guidelines or model by-laws for integrating DRR into urban planning that member states can adapt (drawing from the Sendai Framework's regional adaptation and the Africa Programme of Action). These could include template risk assessment methodologies, checklists for resilient land-use planning, or model clauses for city regulations. SADC could also establish a regional knowledge hub or data portal to consolidate hazard and vulnerability information from member countries, enabling shared learning and facilitating transboundary risk management (SADC, 2019). The African Union, through its urban and DRR programs, should continue to convene forums where city leaders and practitioners exchange experiences, and where successful pilot projects (like Beira's flood resilience or Windhoek's participatory planning) can be showcased and learned from by others.

On the global stage, Southern African countries and cities should actively engage with networks like the Resilient Cities Network, C40 Cities (for climate action), and UNDRR's Making Cities Resilient campaign. These platforms often come with access to expertise, training, and even funding opportunities. International development partners (e.g. World Bank, UN-Habitat, UNDRR, GIZ) should be encouraged to align their programs to support the priorities identified by local and national authorities in this integration agenda. This could mean more projects focused on city-level risk reduction infrastructure, or technical assistance embedded in municipalities to build in-house capacity. South-South cooperation is particularly valuable: facilitating study tours or city partnerships within Africa (or with Asian/Latin American cities facing similar challenges) can inspire and inform Southern African cities. Donors and regional banks can also help address the financing gap by creating instruments tailored to municipal needs, for example, resilience grants or loans that cities can access for upgrading infrastructure in informal settlements.

Overall, tapping into external partnerships will bring in additional resources and know-how, but this should complement, not replace, local efforts. The aim is to accelerate learning and implementation by not "reinventing the wheel", using proven tools and funds available, and to build broad momentum where multiple stakeholders from local to international are invested in the outcome of resilient urban development across Southern Africa.

By pursuing these recommendations in a coherent manner, countries in Southern Africa can create an environment where integrating disaster risk reduction and urban planning becomes the norm. The recommendations are interlinked: legal mandates empower institutions; institutions guided by political commitment employ enhanced capacities and data to plan inclusively; local actions are supported by regional and international solidarity. The result will be urban growth that is not only more resilient to shocks and stresses but also more sustainable and equitable in the long run.

9.8 Conclusion

The integration of disaster risk reduction (DRR) and urban planning has evolved from a policy ideal into an urgent development imperative for Southern Africa. As cities across the region grapple with the dual pressures of rapid urbanisation and escalating environmental risks, many of which are climate-induced, the cost of inaction grows ever more apparent. Uncoordinated urban expansion into hazard-prone areas continues to heighten vulnerability, especially among low-income populations, while undermining progress towards national and global sustainable development objectives. This chapter has underscored that while international and regional frameworks such as the Sendai Framework, New Urban Agenda, and Agenda 2063 offer robust policy guidance, the real challenge lies in domestic implementation. Southern African countries face persistent institutional fragmentation, outdated legal and planning systems, limited capacity at local government levels, and insufficient risk data. These barriers have collectively stifled the uptake of integrated DRR and urban planning approaches. However, the regional landscape is not entirely bleak. Pockets of progress, evident in cities such as Durban, Cape Town, and

Windhoek, demonstrate that political will, institutional innovation, and inclusive governance can yield meaningful integration.

Crucially, this chapter has shown that integration is not solely a technical endeavour. It is fundamentally a question of governance, coordination, and societal engagement. Effective integration demands cross-sectoral collaboration, alignment of policies and budgets, and the meaningful involvement of communities, particularly those most at risk. Moreover, successful integration requires empowering municipalities with the tools, data, and authority to act proactively. Looking forward, the pathway to resilient urban futures in Southern Africa hinges on bold and sustained commitment. Governments must adopt and enforce updated legal frameworks, institutionalise interagency coordination, strengthen technical and human capacity, promote participatory planning, and harness international support. These actions, while demanding, offer significant dividends not only in reducing disaster losses but also in fostering greener, more inclusive, and better-managed urban growth. In conclusion, while the integration of DRR and urban planning in Southern Africa remains a complex challenge, it is an attainable goal. The insights and case studies discussed in this chapter provide a clear roadmap. With deliberate and inclusive action, Southern African cities can build a development trajectory that not only supports economic advancement but also protects lives, livelihoods, and infrastructure against future shocks.

References

Adelekan, I., Johnson, C., Manda, M., Matyas, D., Mberu, B., Parnell, S., et al. (2020a). Risk, resilience and adaptation of African cities. *Current Opinion in Environmental Sustainability, 40*, 38–44.

African Union. (2015). *Agenda 2063: The Africa we want*. African Union Commission.

African Union. (2016). *Programme of action for the implementation of the Sendai framework for disaster risk reduction 2015–2030 in Africa*. AU Commission.

Birkmann, J., Garschagen, M., Setiadi, N., & Kropp, J. (2010). Adaptive urban governance: New challenges for the second generation of urban adaptation strategies to climate change. *Sustainability Science, 5*(2), 185–206.

Chagutah, T. (2014). *Climate change vulnerability and adaptation preparedness in Southern Africa: Zimbabwe country report*. Heinrich Böll Stiftung.

Chikoto, G. L., & Sadiq, A.-A. (2012). Disaster risk reduction in Zimbabwe: Challenges and opportunities. *Disaster Prevention and Management, 21*(4), 376–386.

CoGTA. (2020). *National disaster management framework*. Department of Cooperative Governance and Traditional Affairs (South Africa).

GFDRR. (2016). *The making of a risk-informed investment climate: Integrating disaster risk in public investment planning and financing*. World Bank Group.

GFDRR. (2020). *Mozambique cyclone Idai post-disaster needs assessment*. World Bank Group.

IPCC. (2022). *Sixth assessment report: Impacts, adaptation, and vulnerability*. Intergovernmental Panel on Climate Change.

ISS. (2022). *The future of urbanisation in Africa*. Institute for Security Studies. https://futures.issafrica.org

Manyena, S. B., Fordham, M., & Collins, A. (2013). Disaster resilience and children: Managing food security in Botswana. *Disasters, 37*(2), 324–343.

Mechler, R., Bouwer, L. M., Schinko, T., Surminski, S., & Linnerooth-Bayer, J. (Eds.). (2019). *Loss and damage from climate change: Concepts, methods and policy options*. Springer.

Muchadenyika, D. (2015). Politics and the practice of planning: The case of Zimbabwean cities. *Cities, 45*, 66–73.

OECD. (2018). *Policy coherence for sustainable development 2018: Towards sustainable and resilient societies*. OECD Publishing.

Pelling, M., & Holloway, A. (2006). Legislation for mainstreaming disaster risk reduction. *International Journal of Mass Emergencies and Disasters, 24*(3), 1–16.

Republic of Botswana. (2017). *National development plan 11 (2017–2023)*. Government Printer.

Republic of Namibia. (2012). *Disaster risk management act no. 10 of 2012*. Government of Namibia.

Republic of South Africa. (2013). *Spatial Planning and Land Use Management Act 16 of 2013*. Government Printing Works.

Roberts, D., Boon, R., Diederichs, N., Douwes, E., Govender, N., McInnes, A., et al. (2012). Exploring ecosystem-based adaptation in Durban, South Africa: "Learning-by-doing" at the local government coal face. *Environment and Urbanization, 24*(1), 167–195.

Roberts, D., & O'Donoghue, S. (2013). Urban environmental challenges and climate change action in Durban, South Africa. *Environment and Urbanization, 25*(2), 299–319.

SADC. (2019). *SADC disaster preparedness and response strategy (2016–2030)*. SADC Secretariat.

Satterthwaite, D., Archer, D., Colenbrander, S., Dodman, D., Hardoy, J., Mitlin, D., & Patel, S. (2018a). Building resilience to climate change in informal settlements. *One Earth, 1*(4), 348–357.

Satterthwaite, D., Archer, D., Colenbrander, S., Dodman, D., Hardoy, J., Mitlin, D., & Patel, S. (2018b). Responding to climate change in cities and in their informal settlements and economies. *Environment and Urbanization, 30*(2), 495–514.

Swyngedouw, E. (2009). Civil society, governmentality and the contradictions of governance-beyond-the-state: The Janus-face of social innovation. In D. MacCallum et al. (Eds.), *Social innovation and territorial development* (pp. 63–78). Ashgate.

UNDRR. (2015). *Sendai framework for disaster risk reduction 2015–2030.* United Nations Office for Disaster Risk Reduction.

UNDRR. (2019). *Global assessment report on disaster risk reduction 2019.* UNDRR.

UNDRR. (2021). *Regional assessment report on disaster risk reduction in Sub-Saharan Africa.* UNDRR.

UNFCCC. (2015). *Paris agreement.* United Nations Framework Convention on Climate Change.

UN-Habitat. (2017). *New urban agenda.* United Nations Human Settlements Programme.

UN-Habitat. (2018). *Participatory slum upgrading programme: Namibia country profile.* UN-Habitat.

UN-Habitat. (2020). *World cities report 2020: The value of sustainable urbanization.* UN-Habitat.

United Nations. (2015). *Transforming our world: The 2030 agenda for sustainable development.* United Nations.

Van Niekerk, D., Coetzee, C., & Nemakonde, L. (2018). A review of the South African Disaster Management Act: Toward proactive disaster risk reduction. *Disaster Prevention and Management, 27*(5), 623–635.

Watson, V. (2009). The planned city sweeps the poor away: Urban planning and 21st-century urbanization. *Progress in Planning, 72*(3), 151–193.

Wilkinson, E., Weingärtner, L., & Choularton, R. (2020). *Rebuilding for resilience: How science and policy can support post-cyclone recovery in Mozambique.* Overseas Development Institute.

Wisner, B., Blaikie, P., Cannon, T., & Davis, I. (2004). *At risk: Natural hazards, people's vulnerability and disasters* (2nd ed.). Routledge.

Wisner, B., Gaillard, J. C., & Kelman, I. (Eds.). (2015). *Handbook of hazards and disaster risk reduction and management.* Routledge.

Zhou, Y., Smith, D., & Anderson, C. (2014). Integrating climate change into disaster risk management in urban Africa: Lessons from the UNISDR's making cities resilient campaign. *Urban Climate, 7*, 90–106.

CHAPTER 10

Community-Based Approaches to Urban Resilience in Southern Africa

10.1 Introduction

Urban resilience in Southern Africa's rapidly growing cities is among the most urgent challenges of the twenty-first century. The convergence of climate change, intensifying disaster vulnerability, and governance limitations calls for transformative approaches that centre on human agency. Community-based approaches (CBAs)—participatory frameworks that empower local residents as co-designers, implementers, and stewards of disaster risk reduction (DRR) initiatives (Mercer et al., 2010; Allen et al., 2019)—have emerged as crucial mechanisms to bridge the gap between formal urban planning systems and the lived realities of at-risk communities. Within the context of this book's focus on integrating DRR into urban planning for sustainable development, CBAs serve as the essential "missing link" that translates abstract policies into resilience outcomes that are contextually grounded and socially equitable. Southern Africa's urban context is defined by the world's fastest urbanisation rates (2.8% annually), sprawling informal settlements that house over 60% of urban dwellers, and escalating climate-induced disasters (UN-Habitat, 2022; IPCC, 2022a). These factors provide a compelling rationale for placing communities at the centre of resilience-building efforts. When formal top-down governance structures falter under resource constraints or institutional fragmentation, as evidenced by Harare's failure to deliver flood

F. Mangara, N. Dorasamy, *Sustainable Urban Development in Southern Africa*, https://doi.org/10.1007/978-3-032-08286-2_10

warnings to 85% of households in 2021 (Dodman et al., 2023), local communities become the de facto first responders and custodians of invaluable risk knowledge.

10.2 Theoretical Framework: Community-Based Approaches to Urban Resilience

Community-based approaches (CBAs) to DRR and urban resilience are grounded in interdisciplinary theories that fundamentally challenge traditional top-down planning paradigms. These theories reconceptualise communities not as passive disaster victims but as dynamic systems of knowledge, agency, and adaptive capacity (Norris et al., 2008). In Southern Africa's rapidly urbanising context, where 63% of city dwellers reside in informal settlements (UN-Habitat, 2022) and institutional capacities are often fragmented, such frameworks provide critical lenses to understand how grassroots action bridges resilience gaps. This section examines four foundational theories: participatory planning, social capital, community resilience, and asset-based community development (ABCD), demonstrating their combined relevance for integrating DRR into urban planning in the region. Each theory offers unique insights into how community agency can transform vulnerability into adaptive capacity, while also addressing Southern Africa's historical legacies of spatial inequality and institutional fragmentation.

10.2.1 Participatory Planning: Democratising Risk Governance

Participatory planning offers a fundamental shift from expert-driven risk management to more inclusive, deliberative processes where communities actively shape resilience priorities. This theoretical lens highlights that community members possess lived knowledge of hazards, vulnerabilities, and coping mechanisms, which can significantly improve the design and legitimacy of DRR initiatives. In contexts where institutional trust is low, such as in informal settlements often excluded from municipal planning, participatory planning enhances transparency, social cohesion, and local ownership. For instance, the South African city of Cape Town has incorporated participatory tools like mapping workshops, focus group discussions, and ward-level adaptation planning into its Climate Change Strategy, ensuring alignment between policy ambitions and community needs (City of Cape Town, 2020).

Participatory planning theory, pioneered by Arnstein (1969) and later expanded by Chambers (1997), reconceptualises planning as a democratic dialogue rather than a technocratic imposition. Arnstein's seminal "ladder of citizen participation" differentiates token consultation from genuine empowerment, a distinction with profound implications for DRR. In disaster contexts, participatory planning democratises knowledge by recognising that local residents have granular insight into micro-vulnerabilities, such as seasonal flood patterns in informal settlements, that may be invisible to outside experts (Gaillard et al., 2019). This inclusion of local knowledge transforms risk mapping from abstract modelling to place-based reality. Equally important is participatory planning's contribution to procedural justice, as it ensures marginalised groups have a say in decisions directly affecting their risk exposure (Shi et al., 2016). Experience in Southern Africa demonstrates both the potential and limitations of this approach. For example, after Cyclone Idai in Mozambique, communities using participatory GIS mapping identified 32 landslide-prone sites that engineers had overlooked, preventing rebuilding in those high-risk zones (Castán Broto et al., 2020). Conversely, power imbalances can undermine these efforts: in Harare, bureaucratic barriers limited slum residents to just 12% of participants in city DRR forums (Chirisa et al., 2021). These cases underscore participatory planning's dual role in building resilience while also exposing governance fault lines.

10.2.2 Social Capital: The Relational Infrastructure of Resilience

Social capital theory, as articulated by Coleman (1988) and popularised by Putnam (2000), frames resilience as an emergent property of social networks and trust, rather than as a function of individual assets. The multiple dimensions of social capital can create distinct pathways to resilience in urban DRR contexts. For example, Coleman's (1988) concept of *network closure*—the idea that dense social connections enforce collective norms—helps explain why community watch groups in Blantyre, Malawi achieved 90% compliance with flood evacuation drills, compared to only 45% compliance in state-run programs (Nkhonjera et al., 2020). However, experiences in Southern Africa also highlight social capital's potential downsides. In Windhoek, for instance, water-harvesting committees were initially dominated by male homeowners until the introduction of gender quotas broadened participation (Ndhlovu et al., 2023). This example shows that the resilience benefits of social capital depend on maintaining equitable network structures.

10.2.3 Community Resilience: Adaptive Capacity as a Dynamic Process

Norris et al. (2008) reframe community resilience beyond the simplistic notion of "bouncing back", instead defining it as an adaptive capacity—a dynamic process built on four interconnected types of resources. Economic resources, such as diversified livelihoods that help absorb shocks, are critical to community resilience, as exemplified by Beira's women-run seed banks, which ensured food security after cyclones. Social resources, including trust networks and social support, enable collective action. Physical resources, such as robust infrastructure and services co-designed with communities, strengthen risk mitigation. Natural resources, including the strategic use of ecosystem services like Durban's community-stewarded mangroves that buffer storm surges, also contribute significantly.

This framework is particularly relevant in Southern African cities, where high climate variability demands constant adaptation. Resilience in this view is not a static outcome but an iterative learning process. For example, community disaster committees in Maputo revise their flood response plans each year based on local feedback (INGC, 2022). Resilience also emerges through networked governance models that link neighbourhood groups with municipal agencies. Norris et al. (2008) caution that resilience without equity can actually reinforce vulnerability—a warning illustrated in Harare, where elite-dominated CBA efforts diverted resources away from high-risk slums (Mushamba, 2023a). This example underlines the need to embed principles of social justice within resilience frameworks.

10.3 Community-Based Responses as Frontline Resilience Strategies

10.3.1 Communities as First Responders and Recovery Agents

In Southern Africa's rapidly urbanising cities, communities serve as indispensable frontline responders during disasters, filling critical gaps whenever formal state mechanisms falter. This primacy stems from three intrinsic advantages: proximity, the capacity for spontaneous mobilisation, and deep contextual familiarity. For example, when Cyclone Idai struck Beira in 2019, formal emergency services did not reach affected neighbourhoods for 72 hours. In the meantime, local residents undertook 92% of initial rescues using makeshift boats and neighbourhood networks (Castán Broto et al., 2020). This rapid response capability has also been documented during floods in Durban (Ziervogel, 2019) and droughts in Windhoek (Ndhlovu et al., 2023). It is often lifesaving in the critical "golden window" period, when immediate action can reduce disaster mortality by up to 65% (UNISDR, 2015).

Communities also play a pivotal role in post-disaster recovery. For instance, after major floods in Harare, community savings groups provided rebuilding microloans to 1200 households—delivering assistance three times faster than the government's programs (Chirisa et al., 2022). This dual function—as first responders and as recovery catalysts—has emerged out of necessity. Southern African cities average only 1.2 disaster management personnel per 10,000 residents (UNDRR, 2022), which forces communities to develop autonomous coping systems. Critically, community frontline efforts are often organised through self-initiated protocols. For example, Mozambique's Community Disaster Committees assign evacuation roles on a street-by-street basis, which helps turn ad-hoc reactions into structured resilience (INGC, 2022).

10.3.2 The Epistemic Value of Local Knowledge in Risk Governance

Local knowledge is an irreplaceable source of place-based intelligence that technical risk assessments often overlook. Communities in Southern Africa often have very detailed understandings of hazard patterns. For example, elders in Blantyre, Malawi correlate termite migration patterns with impending landslides (Nkhonjera et al., 2020). Local knowledge also produces highly precise maps of vulnerability, identifying risks that might be invisible at the city scale. For instance, when planners in Durban ignored residents' warnings about wetland encroachment in the Quarry Road West area, subsequent floods displaced 800 households. Conversely, when community watershed knowledge was incorporated into upgrades after 2019, repeat flooding in that area dropped by 70% (Roberts, 2021a).

This knowledge manifests through three key mechanisms. First, indigenous early-warning systems—such as Zimbabwean communities interpreting bird behaviour to predict storms (Matsa, 2022)—provide anticipatory insights. Second, adaptive construction practices—for instance, using local materials like cashew-apple resin in Mozambique to create cyclone-resistant mortar (ActionAid, 2021)—demonstrate locally sourced engineering resilience. Third, socially embedded risk communication through trust-based community networks ensures that warnings reach marginalised groups excluded by formal channels. Integrating such local knowledge can fundamentally improve risk governance. In Cape Town's informal settlements, for example, community-generated flood maps identified 40% more high-risk structures than satellite imagery alone, leading authorities to revise infrastructure priorities.

10.3.3 Community-Based Organisations: Architects of Social Cohesion and Resilience

Community-based organisations (CBOs) help institutionalise grassroots resilience by transforming spontaneous collective action into sustained capacity. In Southern Africa, where 68% of urban CBOs focus on DRR (African Civil Society Network, 2022), these organisations perform several critical functions in resilience efforts. One of the most significant impacts of CBOs is in building social capital—both bonding capital within communities and bridging capital that links communities with external stakeholders. For example, after Cyclone Idai, women-led CBOs in Beira established communal kitchens that fed 15,000 people daily while also negotiating material aid from the World Food Programme—an illustration of Putnam's (2000) concept of linking social capital in action (UN Women, 2022). Similarly, in Cape Town, the Informal Settlement Network used WhatsApp group communications to coordinate evacuations, helping to reduce flood fatalities by 30%.

However, CBO efficacy faces several systemic constraints. Chronic underfunding is one: only 12% of DRR-focused CBOs have access to municipal funding, and 78% remain reliant on unstable donor grants (ActionAid, 2021). Technical capacity gaps are another issue, such as limited expertise in disaster modelling. A third challenge is elite capture, where political actors divert resources from intended beneficiaries—as occurred when Harare's politicians co-opted flood-relief CBOs (Mushamba, 2023b). Despite these challenges, CBOs continue to form the backbone of urban resilience efforts. In Windhoek's informal settlements, for example, community water-harvesting cooperatives have increased drought preparedness fivefold compared to top-down programs (Ndhlovu et al., 2023).

10.3.4 *Synthesising Community Agency in Southern Africa's Resilience Landscape*

In Southern African cities, communities have moved beyond the conventional "beneficiary" role to become co-producers of resilience. They do so by fulfilling three key capacities: acting as first responders, as knowledge holders, and as institutional innovators. This community agency is born of necessity rather than idealism. The region faces over $10 billion in climate-induced disaster costs each year (World Bank, 2023), while municipal institutions are strained by rapid urbanisation. In response, communities have stepped in to fill governance voids with self-organised systems.

The effectiveness of community-led efforts depends on recognising local knowledge as legitimate, investing in community-based organisations, and embedding participatory approaches within formal governance systems. Cities that integrate community agency into DRR planning—such as Durban, Beira, and Cape Town—have recorded fewer fatalities, faster recoveries, and more equitable outcomes. Community agency is thus not just a supplement to formal disaster risk governance—it is its lifeblood in the Southern African context.

10.4 Case Studies: Community-Based Resilience Innovations in Southern African Cities

10.4.1 *Durban, South Africa: Institutionalising Participatory Coastal Resilience*

The eThekwini Municipality (Durban) faces escalating coastal vulnerabilities. Sea-level rise—currently averaging about 0.33 cm per year—and intensifying storm surges now threaten approximately 70,000 low-income residents in settlements such as Quarry Road West. These risks are exacerbated by extensive wetland degradation, with 65% of wetlands lost since 2000, and a severely underperforming drainage infrastructure that serves only 43% of at-risk communities. Durban exemplifies how climate change, unplanned urbanisation, and institutional capacity deficits collide in Southern Africa's secondary cities (IPCC, 2022b).

In response, a tripartite collaboration was formed between 14 community associations, municipal authorities, and the NGO Urban Earth Africa, resulting in the establishment of the Durban Community Resilience Partnership (DCRP). This initiative pioneered a co-governance model that empowered communities to take the lead in disaster risk management. The DCRP trained 120 "Resilience Champions", 60% of whom were women, in flood monitoring, early warning dissemination, and mangrove restoration techniques. It also set up multi-stakeholder planning cells where residents integrated indigenous tidal knowledge into official land-use zoning decisions. Moreover, community-managed drainage maintenance teams were deployed across flood-prone wards, creating formal pathways for local expertise to shape municipal disaster preparedness.

The initiative achieved measurable reductions in disaster risk. For example, the restoration of 18 hectares of mangroves now helps prevent an estimated ZAR 12 million in flood damage annually. In addition, community-generated risk maps were formally integrated into Durban's Municipal Spatial Development Framework, institutionalising the role of local knowledge in shaping long-term planning. These successes have led to the DCRP being expanded into neighbouring municipalities, with policy reforms now mandating community representation in all flood resilience planning committees.

10.4.2 Beira, Mozambique: Transforming Post-disaster Recovery Through Women-Led Innovation

Cyclone Idai struck Beira in 2019, devastating the city and exposing deep-rooted vulnerabilities. Approximately 76% of Beira's population resides in flood-prone informal settlements, where inadequate infrastructure and deforestation had eroded natural flood buffers. At the time of the disaster, only about 40% of the city had proper drainage systems, and many homes were built with substandard materials. The cyclone displaced 150,000 people and caused an estimated $773 million in damages, highlighting the consequences of unregulated urban growth combined with intensifying climate risks.

In the aftermath of the disaster, a coalition of 32 women-led savings groups—collectively known as the Association of Urban Rebuilders (AUR)—emerged as the driving force behind recovery. Their approach integrated indigenous knowledge, gender-sensitive planning, and participatory governance. The AUR deployed cashew-apple resin mortar for storm-resistant housing, drawing from local construction knowledge. They also formed community land committees, which conducted participatory risk mapping and successfully relocated 500 households from the most flood-prone areas. In parallel, they established neighbourhood seedbank cooperatives to strengthen local food security. Supported by the NGO Practical Action, the AUR mobilised 3200 residents to reimagine recovery not just as rebuilding, but as an opportunity to address structural vulnerabilities and foster long-term resilience (Castán Broto et al., 2020).

The community-led reconstruction demonstrated tangible success. When Cyclone Chalane hit in 2020, 85% of the homes built by AUR withstood the storm—a resilience rate 45% points higher than those constructed by external contractors. The community seedbanks also played a vital role, meeting 78% of affected households' food needs post-disaster. Furthermore, the relocation protocols developed by the AUR were formally adopted into Beira's 2021 Urban Master Plan, institutionalising grassroots knowledge in citywide planning. Nonetheless, the full potential of the initiative was curtailed by persistent land tenure uncertainties, which constrained formal recognition and investment. This case underscores the critical link between effective disaster recovery and structural governance reforms, particularly around land rights (UN-Habitat, 2021).

10.4.3 Harare, Zimbabwe: Autonomous Adaptation Amidst Governance Failure

Harare faces chronic urban flooding driven by several factors. The city's drainage infrastructure is largely degraded (62% of drains are non-functional), about 1.2 million people live in unauthorised settlements on ecologically sensitive wetlands, and regulatory enforcement is ineffective. During the 2021 rainy season, floods displaced 18,000 people and triggered cholera outbreaks—an outcome that exemplifies how fragmented governance can worsen disaster risks in fast-growing African capitals (Chirisa et al., 2022).

In response to this institutional paralysis, a coalition of 46 neighbourhood associations known as the Greater Harare Wetlands Trust (GHWT) launched a series of autonomous interventions. Community drainage brigades cleared 32 km of clogged waterways. Rainwater-harvesting cooperatives installed 120 communal rainwater tanks. A digital citizen monitoring effort (using the Ushahidi platform) documented illegal land invasions. These efforts emerged organically as pragmatic community responses to state incapacity, demonstrating how self-organised resilience mechanisms can fill governance vacuums (Mushamba, 2023a).

The GHWT's interventions led to a 45% reduction in flood frequency in the wards where they were implemented between 2020 and 2023. Despite this demonstrable efficacy, only 15% of the community's risk assessment findings were incorporated into Harare's 2022 City Master Plan, and political interference diverted 30% of CBO funds away from high-risk communities to low-risk areas. This case illustrates the stark limitations of community-based approaches when they operate without accountable governance structures. Ultimately, elite capture and institutional resistance prevented local successes from scaling into systemic change, underscoring that technical community solutions alone cannot overcome deeply entrenched governance pathologies (Transparency International Zimbabwe, 2022).

10.4.4 Cross-Cutting Lessons for Integrated Resilience

The comparative analysis of Durban, Beira, and Harare reveals several overarching lessons relevant to the integration of community-based approaches into urban planning and disaster risk governance across Southern Africa. First, co-production outperforms top-down delivery. Community-led design and implementation (as seen in Durban's participatory zoning and Beira's use of local construction techniques) achieved superior technical outcomes and greater community ownership. Conversely, dismissing community expertise, as occurred in Harare, led to maladaptive infrastructure failures. To institutionalise epistemic pluralism in decision-making, municipal authorities should establish permanent knowledge-bridging mechanisms, such as community GIS repositories that are directly linked to planning departments.

Second, equity safeguards are essential to prevent elite capture. Deliberate inclusion measures—like gender quotas in Durban or women-led reconstruction in Beira—ensured leadership from historically marginalised groups and improved inclusivity. In contrast, the lack of accountability mechanisms in Harare enabled political elites to divert resources, undermining resilience efforts. To counteract this, participatory budgeting, transparent tracking of funds, and mandatory representation for vulnerable groups should become standard practice in community resilience programs. Third, fiscal integration determines sustainability. Dedicated funding for community initiatives is crucial for long-term success. Durban's decision to allocate city budget funds to community resilience programs provided a model of continuity and scale that was absent in donor-dependent Beira or self-funded Harare. Ideally, cities should institutionalise support through dedicated community resilience grants, comprising at least 15% of municipal DRR budgets. These cross-cutting lessons make clear that the success of CBAs depends not only on community mobilisation but also on structural reforms in planning institutions. Communities can lead, innovate, and implement—but unless they are supported by inclusive policies, long-term financing, and legal mandates, their work risks being co-opted or ignored.

10.5 Systemic Challenges and Barriers to Community-Based Urban Resilience in Southern Africa

10.5.1 Resource and Capacity Deficits

Chronic underfunding remains one of the most significant constraints to sustaining community-based approaches. In Mozambique, over 70% of Community Disaster Committees operate without predictable financial support. Similarly, in Harare, 82% of community initiatives rely solely on donor funding, with no access to municipal funds (ActionAid, 2021). Durban's otherwise successful Resilience Partnership nearly collapsed in 2020 when international grants lapsed, forcing the shutdown of 40% of community monitoring stations (Roberts, 2021b). In addition to financial constraints, cities face human resource fragility. High turnover among municipal staff—averaging 22% annually in Zimbabwean cities—erodes institutional memory and weakens trust-based relationships with communities (Chirisa et al., 2022). This volatility directly undermines sustained engagement, which is essential for the co-production of resilience initiatives.

10.5.2 Institutional and Governance Pathologies

Post-colonial bureaucratic legacies have created planning cultures fundamentally incompatible with participatory approaches. Three key interrelated governance failures hinder the institutionalisation of CBAs. First, institutional fragmentation is pervasive. DRR responsibilities are scattered across multiple departments—such as environment, housing, and public works—with little coordination among them. In Johannesburg, a community flood mitigation proposal required approvals from 17 separate offices across 9 agencies, causing average delays of 23 months. Such a bureaucratic maze systematically excludes community organisations with limited administrative capacity.

Second, technocratic resistance remains entrenched. Traditional planning orthodoxies continue to privilege formal expertise over community knowledge. In Harare, city engineers dismissed local flood indicators as "superstition" contributing to a catastrophic drainage failure in 2022 that might have been prevented through community warnings (Mushamba, 2023b). This reflects what Scott (1998) called "high modernist" planning: the belief that scientific rationality supersedes all other forms of knowledge.

Third, there is a persistent gap between policy and implementation. Although seven out of twelve Southern African countries include community participation clauses in their urban development policies, implementation is often tokenistic. For example, Mozambique's Disaster Management Law (No. 15/2014) mandates community consultation, yet 68% of CBOs report being excluded from municipal planning forums (Castán Broto et al., 2020). Weak regulatory enforcement and limited accountability perpetuate these gaps.

10.5.3 *Socio-Political Exclusion Dynamics*

Community-based approaches in Southern Africa often reproduce structural exclusions that mirror broader societal inequalities. Intersectional marginalisation of women, migrants, youth, and minority groups creates critical blind spots in resilience efforts.

Gender exclusion remains pronounced: women make up 68% of participants in community-based adaptation (CBA) initiatives but hold less than 25% of decision-making positions in disaster risk reduction (UN Women, 2022). Similarly, migrants often face language and documentation barriers that prevent full participation. For example, 32% of Changana-speaking residents in Maputo were excluded from receiving early flood warnings due to the lack of translation into their mother tongue. Youth exclusion is also significant—while individuals under 35 possess high technological fluency and represent the largest demographic in many cities, they occupy only 12% of leadership roles in community-based organisations. These disparities show that while CBA mechanisms are meant to be inclusive, they are often shaped by power dynamics that mirror existing social hierarchies.

Colonial continuities in spatial governance also reinforce exclusion. Many current patterns of marginalisation are rooted in historical planning systems. For instance, apartheid spatial segregation in South Africa and Portuguese colonial urban codes in Mozambique institutionalised a binary between "formal" and "informal" zones. This persists today: drainage upgrades in Harare, for example, are routinely prioritised in low-risk, formerly European suburbs, while densely populated townships remain neglected (Kamete, 2013).

10.5.4 *Systemic Disconnects in Knowledge Systems*

Knowledge fragmentation significantly undermines the effectiveness of resilience strategies in Southern African cities. Formal risk assessments—often conducted by external consultants or national agencies—frequently exclude local experiential knowledge. For example, in Beira, engineers designed new drainage systems without consulting community members, leading to engineering failures during the 2022 rainy season when culverts overflowed because slope gradients did not match local runoff patterns (Castán Broto et al., 2020).

Moreover, there is a lack of two-way knowledge flows. Communities often lack access to official hazard maps or early warning systems due to digital exclusion or poor dissemination practices. In Windhoek, a 2022 survey revealed that only 18% of informal residents had received any government-issued flood risk information in the preceding year, despite ongoing municipal planning (Ndhlovu et al., 2023). The result is that resilience planning unfolds in parallel knowledge systems—technical vs. vernacular—without institutional mechanisms to bridge them.

10.5.5 *Compounding Effects: The Vulnerability Cycle*

Many Southern African cities are trapped in a cyclical vulnerability pattern, where each disaster worsens the preconditions for the next. For instance, the 2019 Cyclone Idai displaced thousands in Beira, leading to unplanned resettlement in environmentally sensitive areas. These new settlements lacked drainage or tenure security, increasing susceptibility to future floods. Similarly, in Harare, drainage channels were built ignoring local watershed knowledge; those channels collapsed in the 2022 rains, and the ensuing disaster losses further depleted the city's finances. Breaking this kind of cycle requires simultaneous interventions across institutional, financial, and knowledge domains.

10.5.6 Contextual Vulnerabilities

The effectiveness of community-based approaches (CBAs) is often constrained by contextual vulnerabilities that are not easily addressed by community action alone. These include spatial inequalities (e.g. living in floodplains), tenure insecurity (with many informal residents facing constant threats of eviction), and systemic poverty. For example, in Harare, approximately 42% of residents in informal settlements lack legal land titles, which inhibits both government service delivery and community investment in long-term resilience infrastructure (Mushamba, 2023b). In Beira, relocation efforts post-Cyclone Idai were hampered by the government's failure to secure safe, serviced land, forcing many families to return to high-risk zones. Such conditions highlight that without broader policy and institutional reforms, the impact of CBA strategies may be muted or even reversed by the structural conditions in which they operate.

10.6 Policy Framework for Institutionalising Community-Based Resilience

10.6.1 Legal and Institutional Reforms

Codifying Participation Rights: National and local governments must legally enshrine the right to community participation in urban planning and disaster risk governance. This should include laws that guarantee the representation of community-based organisations (CBOs) in local DRR decision-making bodies, binding consultation protocols, and enforceable accountability mechanisms. Mandating Community Planning Inputs: Legal reforms should require that all municipal DRR strategies and Integrated Development Plans (IDPs) include verifiable community inputs. For example, the revised South African Disaster Management Act (2020) mandates that local governments submit evidence of public participation in DRR planning—a reform that has increased community engagement by 48% across municipalities (Roberts, 2021a).

Streamlining Bureaucratic Processes: Governments should reduce administrative barriers that prevent CBOs from accessing state support. This may include simplifying registration processes, reducing delays in project approvals, and creating one-stop DRR coordination platforms at the municipal level. Zambia's National Urban Policy (2022) exemplifies this shift: since implementing community-driven DRR planning protocols, project approval delays were reduced by 65%.

10.6.2 Catalytic Financing Mechanisms

Predictable Funding Streams: To address chronic underfunding, cities must establish stable, multi-source financing for CBA initiatives. This includes municipal budget earmarks, resilience trust funds, and blended finance models that combine public, private, and donor contributions. Such structures ensure continuity, allowing communities to scale successful pilots into citywide programs. Anti-Capture Safeguards: Fiscal accountability is key. Participatory auditing (e.g. community-led expense tracking via platforms like Ushahidi), transparency protocols (like real-time budget dashboards in public venues), and geographic equity formulas (mandating that ≥70% of funds go to informal settlements) can prevent elite capture and ensure equitable distribution.

10.6.3 Capacity Ecosystem Development

Multi-tiered Capability Building: Resilience capacity must be built across all governance levels. At the community level, training in early warning systems and first response enhances preparedness. At the municipal level, skills in participatory planning and risk modelling are vital. Regionally, cross-city learning hubs (such as a proposed SADC Urban Resilience Hub) can disseminate best practices. Knowledge Bridging Infrastructure: Establishing indigenous knowledge repositories (e.g. archiving Zimbabwean flood prediction methods), community–scientist research cohorts (such as those in Cape Town), and regional practice networks will help link grassroots knowledge with formal science. These infrastructures enable communities and experts to co-produce resilience strategies, enhancing both legitimacy and efficacy.

10.6.4 Inclusive Participation Engineering

Building truly inclusive resilience systems requires deliberate efforts to engage all segments of the community. This means proactively dismantling the barriers that hinder participation by historically marginalised groups—such as women, youth, migrants, and ethnic minorities—and ensuring their perspectives and leadership are embedded in decision-making processes. A conceptual Intersectional Inclusion Framework can guide these efforts by embedding inclusive architectures at every level of planning and implementation.

To operationalise this inclusion, policymakers should institutionalise practical mechanisms such as gender-responsive budgeting, which allocates at least 40% of resilience program funding to initiatives led by women. Migrant integration can be facilitated through culturally appropriate planning forums with translation services, ensuring that language and cultural barriers do not exclude participants. Youth engagement can be formalised through intergenerational platforms such as youth advisory boards, authorised to provide input on infrastructure designs and resilience strategies. These interventions ensure that resilience planning reflects the diverse realities of urban communities and leverages their full capacities.

10.6.5 Adaptive Implementation Framework

Mainstreaming community-based adaptation (CBA) into urban governance requires a phased implementation strategy. This should begin with targeted pilot projects during the first year, scale into broader community-driven programs in the second year, and fully institutionalise the most effective approaches by the third year. Such a staggered approach allows cities to adjust, learn from real-world results, and gradually build institutional support for CBA.

Monitoring and evaluation (M&E) frameworks are crucial to ensure accountability and learning. These frameworks should include metrics that are co-defined with communities, reinforcing their ownership. Examples of process indicators include the diversity of participants in CBA forums or the percentage of community proposals incorporated into formal plans. Outcome indicators might measure improvements in infrastructure performance during disasters or reductions in evacuation times. Equity indicators could include the proportion of funds directed to high-risk or marginalised areas. Zimbabwe's National Resilience Trust provides a compelling example: after implementing a community-defined M&E framework, it reported a 45% reduction in elite capture of disaster resources. Through such inclusive and transparent evaluation systems, cities can measure and refine their community resilience strategies over time.

10.6.6 Contextual Enablers: Leveraging Southern African Assets

The successful institutionalisation of community-based resilience in Southern Africa must harness existing regional strengths and cultural assets. For instance, Ubuntu governance principles—rooted in collectivism and solidarity—can be institutionalised in local planning processes to promote inclusive, community-led decision-making. The informal economy, especially community savings groups such as stokvels, provides a robust platform for local financing of resilience initiatives. Additionally, Southern Africa's existing transboundary knowledge-sharing platforms, such as those coordinated by the Southern African Development Community (SADC), should be leveraged to facilitate cross-border learning and innovation. These enablers are not just cultural artefacts—they are functional systems that, if integrated thoughtfully, can accelerate and ground the adoption of resilient urban governance in local realities.

10.7 Conclusion

Community-based approaches (CBAs) are vital to embedding disaster risk reduction (DRR) into urban planning across Southern Africa. As this chapter has shown, CBAs are not simply grassroots supplements to state-led efforts—they are essential mechanisms for building locally grounded resilience in contexts where formal institutions are often under-resourced, fragmented, or absent. From the participatory governance frameworks in Durban, to the community-led reconstruction in Beira, and the autonomous urban responses in Harare, communities have consistently demonstrated their capacity to assess risks, mobilise resources, and implement adaptive strategies.

However, the effectiveness of CBAs is heavily contingent on institutional recognition and integration. When community knowledge is sidelined—as in Harare—the result is policy failure, elite capture, and maladaptive outcomes. In contrast, cities that embed communities into formal governance structures experience measurable improvements in resilience, equity, and public trust. Moreover, CBAs are uniquely positioned to bridge the divide between scientific and indigenous knowledge systems, making them indispensable for building inclusive, context-sensitive resilience frameworks. To fully harness the potential of CBAs, four pillars must be institutionalised: (1) co-governance structures that formalise community participation in planning processes; (2) secure, dedicated financing streams for grassroots initiatives; (3) platforms for knowledge co-production that integrate local and technical insights; and (4) targeted inclusion strategies that elevate historically marginalised voices. The case studies and policy frameworks presented in this chapter highlight that communities are not passive recipients of aid but active agents of transformation. By centring CBAs within urban resilience planning, Southern African cities can overcome legacies of exclusion and fragmentation, and move towards equitable, adaptive, and sustainable urban futures. Empowering communities is not only a moral imperative—it is a pragmatic strategy for safeguarding cities against escalating environmental and socio-economic risks.

References

ActionAid Mozambique. (2021). *Indigenous building practices in post-Idai reconstruction*. ActionAid.

African Civil Society Network for Disaster Reduction. (2022). *CBO capacity assessment: Southern Africa*. African CSNDR.

Allen, A., Griffin, L., & Johnson, C. (2019). Community-led pathways for resilience building in cities of the Global South. *Environment and Urbanization, 31*(1), 3–21. https://doi.org/10.1177/0956247818816064

Arnstein, S. R. (1969). A ladder of citizen participation. *Journal of the American Planning Association, 35*(4), 216–224.

Castán Broto, V., Stevens, L., Salvia, G., & Aghahosseini, S. (2020). Community-led housing reconstruction after Cyclone Idai: Building back safer in Beira, Mozambique. *Disasters, 44*(1), 78–102.

Chambers, R. (1997). *Whose reality counts? Putting the first last*. Practical Action.

Chirisa, I., Mutambisi, T., Chinooneka, T. I., Kupika, O. L., & Matamanda, A. R. (2021). Tokenism in urban participation: Examining community involvement in urban development in Harare. *Cities, 118*, 103374.

Chirisa, I., Mutambisi, T., & Matamanda, A. R. (2022). Governance failure in Harare's flood management. *Cities, 131*, 103904.

Coleman, J. S. (1988). Social capital in the creation of human capital. *American Journal of Sociology, 94*, 95–120.

Dodman, D., Leck, H., & Rusca, M. (2023). *Urban flood governance gaps in Southern Africa: Institutional fragmentation and community responses.* (IIED Report No. 2023-07). International Institute for Environment and Development.

Gaillard, J. C., Cadag, J. R. D., & Rampengan, M. M. F. (2019). Participatory urban disaster risk assessments: Bridging local and scientific knowledge in informal settlements. *Progress in Development Studies, 19*(2), 94–113.

INGC (Instituto Nacional de Gestão das Calamidades). (2022). *Annual report: Community Disaster Committees.* INGC.

Intergovernmental Panel on Climate Change (IPCC). (2022a). *Climate change 2022: Impacts, adaptation and vulnerability.* Contribution of Working Group II to the Sixth Assessment Report. Cambridge University Press.

Intergovernmental Panel on Climate Change (IPCC). (2022b). *AR6 climate change impacts: Coastal cities.* Cambridge University Press.

Kamete, A. Y. (2013). On handling urban informality in Southern Africa. *Geoforum, 48*, 85–96.

Kretzmann, J. P., McKnight, J. L., McKnight, J., Affairs, N. U. C. f. U., Research, P., & Network, N. I. (1993). *Building Communities from the Inside Out: A Path Toward Finding and Mobilizing a Community's Assets.* Center for Urban Affairs and Policy Research, Northwestern University. https://books.google.co.za/books?id=TGFPAAAAMAAJ

Matsa, M. (2022). Community-led social support systems in post-Idai recovery: Lessons from Chimanimani, Zimbabwe. *Geoforum, 128*, 1–12.

Mercer, J., Kelman, I., Taranis, L., & Suchet-Pearson, S. (2010). Framework for integrating indigenous and scientific knowledge for disaster risk reduction. *Disasters, 34*(3), 606–625. https://doi.org/10.1111/j.1467-7717.2010.01157.x

Mushamba, S. (2023a). Elite capture and patronage politics in community-based adaptation: Evidence from Harare, Zimbabwe. *African Studies Quarterly, 22*(3), 45–61.

Mushamba, S. (2023b). Patronage politics and community resilience in Harare. *African Studies Quarterly, 22*(3).

Ndhlovu, G., Kemerink-Seyoum, J. S., & van der Zaag, P. (2023). Community-led water resilience in informal settlements: Lessons from Windhoek, Namibia. *Water Policy, 25*(2), 221–238. https://doi.org/10.2166/wp.2023.015

Nkhonjera, M., Diko, S. K., & Banda, K. E. (2020). Integrating local knowledge into landslide risk mapping: A case study from Blantyre, Malawi. *Land Use Policy, 99*, 104836.

Norris, F. H., Stevens, S. P., Pfefferbaum, B., Wyche, K. F., & Pfefferbaum, R. L. (2008). Community resilience as a metaphor, theory, set of capacities, and strategy for disaster readiness. *American Journal of Community Psychology, 41*(1–2), 127–150.

Pelling, M. (2011). *Adaptation to climate change: From resilience to transformation*. Routledge.

Putnam, R. D. (2000). *Bowling alone: The collapse and revival of American community*. Simon & Schuster.

Roberts, D. (2021a). *Durban's community resilience partnership: Five-year review (2016–2021)*. eThekwini Municipality Press.

Roberts, D. (2021b). Co-governance in Durban's climate adaptation. *Urban Studies, 58*(16), 3503–3522.

Scott, J. C. (1998). *Seeing like a state: How certain schemes to improve the human condition have failed*. Yale University Press.

Shi, L., Chu, E., Anguelovski, I., Aylett, A., Debats, J., & Goh, K. (2016). Roadmap towards justice in urban climate adaptation research. *Nature Climate Change, 6*(2), 131–137.

Transparency International Zimbabwe. (2022). *Corruption in urban disaster governance*. Transparency International Zimbabwe.

UN Women. (2022). *Beyond vulnerability to agency: Women's participation in disaster risk reduction in Mozambique*. United Nations Entity for Gender Equality and the Empowerment of Women.

UNDRR. (2022). *Disaster management capacity in African cities*. United Nations Office for Disaster Risk Reduction.

UN-Habitat. (2022). *World cities report 2022: Envisaging the future of cities*. United Nations Human Settlements Programme. https://unhabitat.org/wcr/

UNISDR. (2015). *Global assessment report on disaster risk reduction*. United Nations Office for Disaster Risk Reduction.

United Nations Human Settlements Programme. (2021). *Cities and pandemics: Towards a more just, green and healthy future*. United Nations Human Settlements Programme.

World Bank. (2023). *Zambia national urban policy implementation assessment*. World Bank.

Ziervogel, G. (2019). *Community responses to flooding in Cape Town*. African Centre for Cities.

CHAPTER 11

Case Studies in Urban Planning and Disaster Risk Reduction in Southern Africa

11.1 Introduction

Urban centres in Southern Africa are increasingly exposed to natural and anthropogenic disasters due to rapid urbanisation, inadequate infrastructure, poor governance, and the effects of climate change. While urbanisation has often been celebrated as a driver of economic growth, the challenges it presents, particularly in terms of disaster vulnerability, are profound and escalating (UN-Habitat, 2020). This chapter provides a comparative analysis of disaster risk reduction (DRR) integration in urban planning within selected Southern African cities, drawing from empirical case studies of Durban, Johannesburg, Maputo, Harare, Lusaka, Gaborone, and Windhoek. Each of these cities presents a unique context in terms of exposure, vulnerability, institutional capacity, and governance mechanisms. However, they also share structural constraints common across the SADC region, such as limited fiscal resources, informal settlements, and fragmented planning processes (Pelling & Wisner, 2009).

The purpose of this chapter is to assess the extent to which DRR has been mainstreamed into urban planning in these cities and to derive lessons for sustainable urban development. The chapter is structured to examine each city's urban development trajectory, disaster risks, integration of DRR mechanisms, and the outcomes of specific adaptation initiatives. These case studies are analysed using a framework that draws from

F. Mangara, N. Dorasamy, *Sustainable Urban Development in Southern Africa*, https://doi.org/10.1007/978-3-032-08286-2_11

the Sendai Framework for Disaster Risk Reduction (UNDRR, 2015), Sustainable Development Goal 11 on sustainable cities, and the New Urban Agenda (UN-Habitat, 2017). Emphasis is also placed on multi-level governance, community participation, and the intersection of infrastructure resilience and socioeconomic vulnerability (Van Niekerk, 2021).

11.2 Durban, South Africa: Climate Adaptation and Community-Based Resilience

Durban, located in KwaZulu-Natal province, is one of Africa's most proactive cities in mainstreaming climate change adaptation and disaster risk reduction into urban governance. The city's vulnerability to coastal flooding, cyclones, and heavy rainfall has spurred innovative planning responses anchored in sustainability and resilience (Roberts & O'Donoghue, 2013).

11.2.1 Urban Risk Profile

Durban faces several disaster risks, particularly from flash floods, coastal erosion, and storm surges, exacerbated by unregulated development in flood-prone areas. The 2022 floods, which claimed over 400 lives, exposed weaknesses in infrastructure planning and emergency response, particularly in informal settlements (Zulu, 2022).

11.2.2 Integration of DRR into Planning

The city's eThekwini Municipality has adopted an Integrated Development Plan (IDP) that includes DRR and climate change resilience as core elements. Durban's Municipal Climate Protection Programme (MCPP) was among the first of its kind in Africa, integrating climate projections, adaptation planning, and public awareness (Roberts, 2010). Moreover, the Durban Climate Change Strategy (2014) aligns with the Sendai Framework by promoting risk-informed urban development and early warning systems. Spatial development frameworks in the city also restrict land use in flood-prone zones, while infrastructure investment has been redirected to increase resilience in high-risk areas (Sutherland et al., 2015).

11.2.3 Community Engagement and Lessons

Durban's community-based adaptation (CBA) initiatives have empowered vulnerable communities to participate in local resilience building. Projects such as the uMbilo River Restoration and the Green Corridors Initiative demonstrate a practical alignment of ecological restoration with DRR objectives (Frantzeskaki et al., 2019). However, challenges persist in scaling up these interventions citywide. There is still a disconnect between informal settlement upgrading and strategic planning frameworks, with marginalised communities often excluded from long-term resilience planning (Leck & Simon, 2013). Durban illustrates how strong municipal leadership, international collaboration, and knowledge-sharing can shape progressive DRR approaches. Still, structural inequality and rapid urbanisation remain persistent barriers.

11.3 Maputo, Mozambique: Coastal Vulnerability and Urban Fragility

Maputo, the capital of Mozambique, is highly vulnerable to a range of natural hazards, including cyclones, coastal erosion, flooding, and sea-level rise. As a coastal city in a low-lying delta region, Maputo is frequently affected by tropical storms, most notably Cyclones Idai (2019) and Eloise (2021), which caused severe destruction across the region (UNDRR, 2019).

11.3.1 Risk Landscape

The physical geography of Maputo makes it highly susceptible to flooding. Additionally, rapid population growth and informal settlement expansion have increased the number of people living in high-risk areas, often without adequate infrastructure or basic services (Watson, 2020). Many of Maputo's urban poor live in settlements such as Chamanculo and Maxaquene, where flood risk is compounded by poor waste management and blocked drainage systems (Jenks et al., 2019).

11.3.2 Institutional Response and DRR Planning

Mozambique has a national disaster management policy guided by the Instituto Nacional de Gestão de Calamidades (INGD), which oversees early warning systems and post-disaster response. However, DRR integration into urban planning in Maputo remains limited. The city lacks a formal metropolitan spatial development plan that prioritises risk-sensitive land use. Nevertheless, donor-supported interventions, such as the Cities and Climate Change Project (CCCP), have begun to strengthen local planning capacity, promote resilient infrastructure, and invest in drainage and sanitation improvements (UN-Habitat, 2020).

11.3.3 *Barriers to Progress*

Key challenges in Maputo include weak coordination between national and municipal agencies, a lack of technical expertise, and under-resourced local governments (Pelling & Dill, 2010). Additionally, most disaster management interventions remain reactive rather than preventative. Despite these limitations, community-based resilience efforts are emerging. NGOs such as the Red Cross and Oxfam have worked with local residents to elevate homes, clear drainage channels, and raise awareness on climate adaptation (Mercer et al., 2014). Maputo's case reflects both the acute vulnerability of coastal African cities and the urgent need for capacity-building in urban DRR integration.

11.4 Harare, Zimbabwe: Infrastructure Deficits and Informality in Urban Risk

Harare, the capital of Zimbabwe, illustrates the intersection of infrastructural collapse, economic crisis, and disaster vulnerability. The city has experienced recurrent flooding, water contamination, and cholera outbreaks due to the deterioration of urban infrastructure and planning systems (Chigudu, 2020).

11.4.1 *Urban Development and Risks*

Rapid urban expansion, combined with outdated master plans and limited enforcement, has led to unregulated settlement in wetlands and flood-prone areas such as Budiriro and Kuwadzana (Muchadenyika, 2015). Additionally, the failure of water treatment and waste management systems poses significant public health risks. The city's exposure to droughts, worsened by climate change, also affects water supply reliability and increases disaster risk in peri-urban communities reliant on boreholes and open wells (Manzungu & Chioreso, 2012).

11.4.2 DRR Integration Challenges

Harare's urban planning is still based on colonial-era frameworks that are ill-suited to today's informal and dynamic urban landscapes. There is limited integration of disaster risk assessments into land-use planning and infrastructure development (Tibaijuka, 2005). While the Department of Civil Protection coordinates national-level DRR activities, local capacity in Harare remains weak. The city council often lacks the funding and technical expertise to implement proactive measures or enforce zoning regulations (Makoni et al., 2018).

11.4.3 Opportunities for Reform

Despite systemic challenges, civil society and community organisations have stepped in to address urban risks. Projects led by the Dialogue on Shelter and the Zimbabwe Homeless People's Federation have used community enumeration and mapping to identify at-risk areas and advocate for safer housing (Archer et al., 2014). Harare represents a cautionary tale of how institutional neglect and infrastructural decay can amplify disaster risk. Integrating DRR into urban planning will require not only technical reforms but also political will and institutional rebuilding.

11.5 Lusaka, Zambia: Flood Management and Urban Informality

Lusaka, Zambia's capital and largest city, has experienced significant population growth in recent decades, leading to rapid urban sprawl and increased vulnerability to flooding and sanitation-related disasters. Like many African cities, Lusaka is characterised by an expanding informal sector and weak planning enforcement (Mulenga, 2003).

11.5.1 Urban Risks

Seasonal flooding is a major concern in Lusaka, particularly in unplanned settlements such as Kanyama, Chawama, and Garden Compound. These areas lack adequate drainage infrastructure and are often located in flood-prone, low-lying zones. In addition to physical damage, floods frequently cause waterborne disease outbreaks due to poor sanitation and water contamination.

11.5.2 *Planning and DRR Measures*

Lusaka's city planning system faces significant limitations in integrating DRR. The city has adopted a master planning approach that does not adequately account for informal settlement dynamics. Moreover, local government agencies often lack the capacity to enforce land use plans or invest in resilient infrastructure (Kamhinya & Makajuma, 2020). Nevertheless, there have been some efforts to address flood risk through community-based adaptation (CBA) and public–private partnerships. For example, the Lusaka Water Security Initiative (LuWSI) brings together government, private sector, and NGOs to improve water infrastructure, protect water sources, and reduce urban water risks (LuWSI, 2021).

11.5.3 *Lessons and Limitations*

Lusaka's experience demonstrates that partnerships can play a critical role in addressing urban risk. However, without institutional reforms and inclusive planning, these efforts remain fragmented. Building resilience requires mainstreaming DRR into everyday urban governance, including budgeting, service delivery, and informal settlement upgrading (Satterthwaite et al., 2018).

11.6 Gaborone, Botswana: Planning in a Water-Stressed Urban Environment

Gaborone, the capital of Botswana, is one of the more planned cities in Southern Africa, with a relatively strong institutional framework. However, the city still faces significant disaster risks, particularly related to water scarcity, drought, and urban heat (Andersson et al., 2019). Climate change has intensified these challenges, placing pressure on Gaborone's infrastructure and urban planning systems.

11.6.1 *Risk Landscape*

Gaborone's most pressing urban risks stem from prolonged droughts and erratic rainfall patterns. These trends threaten water security for the city's growing population and have major implications for public health and economic activity (Botswana Government, 2020). Urban sprawl has increased impermeable surfaces, exacerbating flash floods during rare but intense rainfall episodes. At the same time, informal settlements have emerged on the city's periphery, adding to the vulnerability of low-income groups (Keitumetse, 2016).

11.6.2 DRR and Urban Policy Integration

Botswana's Vision 2036 and National Development Plan 11 emphasise environmental sustainability and climate adaptation. In Gaborone, spatial planning is relatively advanced compared to other cities in the region. The city's Development Control Code includes environmental considerations, and there are ongoing efforts to update the city's master plan to incorporate risk-sensitive urban development (UN-Habitat, 2019). The Department of Meteorological Services and the National Disaster Management Office (NDMO) have also worked to establish early warning systems and build institutional readiness for disaster response (Republic of Botswana, 2017).

11.6.3 Strengths and Gaps

Gaborone's case shows that good governance and proactive planning can mitigate urban risks. However, limited resources and increasing informality threaten to outpace these gains. Moreover, DRR is often addressed in national rather than municipal planning, leading to weak vertical integration (Pelling & Holloway, 2006). To build resilience, Gaborone will need to strengthen community participation, improve data collection for risk mapping, and invest in green infrastructure that supports water retention and climate adaptation.

11.7 Windhoek, Namibia: Managing Urban Growth in a Water-Scarce City

Windhoek, the capital of Namibia, is uniquely situated in a semi-arid region that receives minimal rainfall and experiences recurring droughts. The city's disaster risks are shaped primarily by water scarcity, rising temperatures, and informal settlement expansion (Simon et al., 2018).

11.7.1 *Risk and Vulnerability Profile*

Water security is Windhoek's most urgent urban risk. The city relies on three main dams and innovative water recycling systems to meet its needs. However, prolonged droughts and urban growth have placed immense pressure on this system (Christelis & Struckmeier, 2011). In addition, the rapid growth of informal settlements such as Havana and Okuryangava has created densely populated zones without formal services or infrastructure, increasing vulnerability to fires, disease outbreaks, and flash floods during rare storms (Tjipueja, 2016).

11.7.2 *Institutional Response and DRR Mainstreaming*

The City of Windhoek has made strides in water management, including being the first city in the world to implement potable water reclamation at scale. Its Integrated Urban Development Framework (IUDF) and the National Policy on Climate Change (2011) promote sustainable land use, water conservation, and disaster preparedness (Republic of Namibia, 2011). The city also participates in the African Cities Water Adaptation Platform and has received technical support from international partners to improve infrastructure planning and emergency response capabilities (UNDRR, 2020).

11.7.3 *Challenges and Innovations*

Windhoek's institutional innovations in water recycling and drought preparedness are globally recognised. However, disaster resilience at the community level remains limited. Many informal settlements are outside the city's development plans and lack access to basic risk-reducing infrastructure (Erastus et al., 2019). To enhance DRR integration, Windhoek must expand its investment in upgrading informal settlements, implement inclusive planning strategies, and improve coordination between urban planning and emergency services.

11.8 Cross-Cutting Themes and Regional Lessons

The case studies presented in this chapter reveal both diversity and convergence in how Southern African cities approach disaster risk reduction within urban planning. Several key themes emerge from the comparative analysis:

11.8.1 *Governance and Institutional Capacity*

A recurrent issue across all cities is the fragmentation of institutional mandates and the limited capacity of municipal governments. While cities like Durban and Windhoek have demonstrated institutional innovation and planning foresight, others like Harare and Maputo face critical governance constraints (Pelling et al., 2018). Weak vertical and horizontal coordination hinders the effective mainstreaming of DRR in most urban contexts.

11.8.2 *Informality and Risk*

The expansion of informal settlements is a defining urban characteristic in the region and a major contributor to disaster vulnerability. In Lusaka, Harare, and Maputo, large segments of the urban population reside in informal areas that are excluded from formal planning processes and basic services (Satterthwaite et al., 2020). Effective DRR in these settings requires inclusive governance mechanisms and participatory approaches that involve communities in decision-making and risk mapping.

11.8.3 *Climate Change and Urban Infrastructure*

Southern African cities are on the frontline of climate impacts, particularly flooding, drought, and heatwaves. Infrastructure in cities like Johannesburg and Gaborone is increasingly threatened by extreme weather events (Simon et al., 2018). Green infrastructure, nature-based solutions, and ecosystem-based adaptation strategies are gaining traction but need to be scaled up.

11.8.4 *Community-Based Resilience*

Community-based adaptation and grassroots innovations offer scalable and sustainable solutions. Cities such as Durban and Harare have benefited from partnerships with civil society, which have led to practical interventions in settlement upgrading, flood mitigation, and public education (Leck & Simon, 2013).

11.8.5 *Policy Coherence and Global Frameworks*

While most cities reference global DRR and resilience frameworks in their policies, practical implementation remains uneven. Integration with the

Sendai Framework, SDG 11, and the New Urban Agenda is evident in planning documents, but translation into practice is limited by funding and institutional constraints (UN-Habitat, 2020).

11.9 Conclusions

Urban resilience in Southern Africa remains a pressing challenge amidst rapid urbanisation, climate vulnerability, and persistent inequality. This chapter has examined how cities across the region—Durban, Johannesburg, Maputo, Harare, Lusaka, Gaborone, and Windhoek—have responded to disaster risks through urban planning frameworks, with varying levels of success. Some cities, like Durban and Windhoek, demonstrate leadership in integrating DRR into city-wide plans and institutional innovations. Others, such as Harare and Maputo, face structural and political barriers that impede risk-informed development. The uneven capacity to address disaster risks reflects broader governance, resource, and institutional issues within the SADC region.

To enhance DRR integration in urban planning, the following recommendations are offered:

1. **Strengthen Local Government Capacity**: Municipalities need technical, financial, and institutional resources to conduct risk assessments, enforce planning regulations, and respond to emergencies.
2. **Mainstream DRR into Urban Planning**: DRR principles must be embedded in spatial development frameworks, infrastructure investment decisions, and land use policies.
3. **Invest in Informal Settlement Upgrading**: Risk reduction must address the needs of vulnerable populations in informal settlements through inclusive planning, tenure regularisation, and basic services.
4. **Enhance Multi-level Governance**: Coordination between national, regional, and local governments must be improved to ensure policy alignment and efficient resource use.
5. **Promote Community Participation**: Resilience building is most effective when local knowledge and capacities are incorporated into planning and implementation.
6. **Leverage International Support and Knowledge Sharing**: Partnerships with international organisations, academia, and peer cities can provide technical assistance, innovation, and policy learning.

While significant progress has been made in some cities, systemic challenges remain. Integrating DRR into urban planning is essential to achieving sustainable development and protecting lives and livelihoods in the face of escalating disaster risks in Southern Africa.

References

Andersson, K., Dzikiti, S., & Mager, S. (2019). *Urban resilience and adaptation in Africa*. Routledge.

Archer, D., Macgregor, H., & Boamah, N. (2014). Shelter in the storm: Understanding the impact of climate change on informal settlements. *Environment and Urbanization, 26*(1), 147–162.

Botswana Government. (2020). *National Development Plan 11*. Ministry of Finance and Economic Development.

Chigudu, S. (2020). *The political life of an epidemic: Cholera, crisis and citizenship in Zimbabwe*. Cambridge University Press.

Christelis, G., & Struckmeier, W. (2011). *Groundwater in Namibia: An explanation to the hydrogeological map*. Ministry of Agriculture, Water and Rural Development.

Erastus, I. M., Mwazi, F., & Keulder, C. (2019). Informality and the urban poor in Namibia: Challenges and opportunities. *Journal of Namibian Studies, 25*, 35–52.

Frantzeskaki, N., McPhearson, T., Collier, M. J., Kendal, D., Bulkeley, H., Dumitru, A., et al. (2019). Nature-based solutions for urban climate change adaptation: Linking science, policy, and practice communities for evidence-based decision-making. *BioScience, 69*(6), 455–466.

Jenks, M., Burton, E., & Williams, K. (2019). *The compact city: A sustainable urban form?* Routledge.

Kamhinya, B., & Makajuma, G. (2020). Assessing urban planning capacity for climate change resilience in Lusaka, Zambia. *Urban Forum, 31*(2), 203–220.

Keitumetse, S. O. (2016). *African cultural heritage conservation and management*. Springer.

Leck, H., & Simon, D. (2013). Fostering multiscalar collaboration and co-operation for effective governance of climate change adaptation. *Urban Studies, 50*(6), 1221–1238.

LuWSI. (2021). *Lusaka Water Security Initiative Annual Report 2020/21*. LuWSI Secretariat.

Makoni, F. S., Manase, G., & Ndamba, J. (2018). Patterns of governance and water access in Zimbabwe's urban settlements. *Water Policy, 20*(1), 62–77.

Manzungu, E., & Chioreso, M. (2012). Governance of urban water: Unravelling the challenges in the city of Harare, Zimbabwe. *Journal of Environmental Studies, 11*(2), 77–89.

Mercer, J., Kelman, I., Taranis, L., & Suchet-Pearson, S. (2014). Framework for integrating indigenous and scientific knowledge for disaster risk reduction. *Disasters, 34*(1), 214–239.

Muchadenyika, D. (2015). Slum upgrading and inclusive municipal governance in Harare, Zimbabwe. *Habitat International, 48*, 1–10.

Mulenga, M. (2003). Water and sanitation in peri-urban areas: How informal service providers fill the gap in Lusaka. *Environment and Urbanization, 15*(2), 161–178.

Pelling, M., & Dill, K. (2010). Disaster politics: Tipping points for change in the adaptation of sociopolitical regimes. *Progress in Human Geography, 34*(1), 21–37.

Pelling, M., & Holloway, A. (2006). *Legislation for mainstreaming disaster risk reduction*. UNISDR.

Pelling, M., & Wisner, B. (2009). *Disaster risk reduction: Cases from urban Africa*. Earthscan.

Pelling, M., Leck, H., Pasquini, L., Ajibade, I., Osuteye, E., Parnell, S., et al. (2018). Africa's urban adaptation transition under a 1.5°C climate. *Current Opinion in Environmental Sustainability, 31*, 10–15.

Republic of Botswana. (2017). *National Disaster Risk Reduction Strategy 2017–2021*. Office of the President.

Republic of Namibia. (2011). *National Climate Change Policy*. Ministry of Environment and Tourism.

Roberts, D. (2010). Prioritising climate change adaptation and local level resilience in Durban, South Africa. *Environment and Urbanization, 22*(2), 397–413.

Roberts, D., & O'Donoghue, S. (2013). Urban environmental challenges and climate change action in Durban, South Africa. *Environment and Urbanization, 25*(2), 299–319.

Satterthwaite, D., Archer, D., Colenbrander, S., Dodman, D., Hardoy, J., Mitlin, D., & Patel, S. (2018). *Responding to climate change in cities and in their informal settlements and economies*. IIED.

Satterthwaite, D., Mitlin, D., & Bartlett, S. (2020). *Urban development and climate adaptation: Lessons from the global South*. Routledge.

Simon, D., Arfvidsson, H., Bazaz, A., Bazaaz, A., Buckley, M., Chikulo, S., et al. (2018). Developing and testing the Urban Sustainable Development Goal's targets and indicators—A five-city study. *Environment and Urbanization, 30*(2), 539–558.

Sutherland, C., Roberts, D., & Douwes, J. (2015). Constructing resilience at three different scales: The 2009–2011 drought in eThekwini Municipality, South Africa. *Environment and Urbanization, 27*(2), 1–18.

Tibaijuka, A. (2005). *Report of the Fact-Finding Mission to Zimbabwe on Operation Murambatsvina*. UN-Habitat.

Tjipueja, M. (2016). Informality and resilience in Namibian urban planning. *Namibia Planning Journal, 6*(1), 15–27.

UNDRR. (2015). *Sendai Framework for Disaster Risk Reduction 2015–2030*. UNDRR.

UNDRR. (2019). *Cyclone Idai: Recovery and Resilience*. UNDRR.

UNDRR. (2020). *Namibia Risk Profile Report*. UNDRR.

UN-Habitat. (2017). *New Urban Agenda*. UN-Habitat.

UN-Habitat. (2019). *State of African Cities Report*. UN-Habitat.

UN-Habitat. (2020). *World Cities Report: The value of sustainable urbanisation*. UN-Habitat.

Van Niekerk, D. (2021). *Disaster Risk Reduction: A development approach*. Springer.

Watson, V. (2020). African urban fantasies: Dreams or nightmares? *Environment and Urbanization, 26*(1), 215–231.

Zulu, N. (2022). Durban floods expose gaps in South Africa's disaster planning. *Mail & Guardian*, April 2022.

CHAPTER 12

Pathways to Sustainable and Resilient Urban Futures in Southern Africa

12.1 Introduction

As the twenty-first century progresses, cities in Southern Africa stand at a decisive crossroads, facing mounting pressures from rapid urbanisation, climate change, economic instability, and weak governance structures. Urban centres like Johannesburg, Harare, Lusaka, Maputo, and Gaborone are expanding at unprecedented rates, often without the necessary planning frameworks to guide sustainable and resilient development. The region's urban landscape is increasingly defined by informal settlements, overstretched infrastructure, and social inequality, all of which amplify vulnerability to disasters (Parnell & Pieterse, 2014; Satterthwaite et al., 2020). In the previous chapters of this book, we explored the dynamics of disaster risk reduction (DRR) and urban planning, highlighting how fragmented governance, poor land use practices, underinvestment in resilient infrastructure, and insufficient community engagement have hampered efforts to build sustainable cities in the region. Drawing on global lessons, case studies from Southern Africa, and critical theoretical insights, this book has demonstrated that integrating DRR into urban planning is not merely a technical necessity but a moral and developmental imperative.

This concluding chapter synthesises the key findings from the preceding chapters and proposes strategic pathways to guide urban development in Southern Africa towards a more sustainable and resilient future. It

F. Mangara, N. Dorasamy, *Sustainable Urban Development in Southern Africa*, https://doi.org/10.1007/978-3-032-08286-2_12

begins by summarising the dominant challenges and lessons discussed across the book before moving into a forward-looking discussion on how cities can reorient planning and governance to mitigate risks, adapt to changing climatic conditions, and foster inclusive development. It identifies five critical domains for intervention: policy integration, infrastructure planning, land use management, institutional reform, and community participation.

The chapter also proposes a research agenda and policy recommendations to inform urban resilience programming and investment. It emphasises the need for multi-level and multi-stakeholder engagement in urban development, arguing that sustainable urban futures cannot be built by planners or technocrats alone. Resilience must be co-produced with communities, informed by local realities, and backed by institutional and financial commitments at all levels of government (UN-Habitat, 2020; Wisner et al., 2004).

The pathway to sustainable and resilient urban futures in Southern Africa is both complex and urgent. As climate extremes intensify and urban populations grow, the costs of inaction are likely to be severe. Yet, within these challenges lie profound opportunities—opportunities to rethink urban governance, invest in transformative infrastructure, and embed equity and sustainability at the heart of development. The time for action is now.

12.2 Synthesis of Key Findings

This section consolidates the central insights from Chaps. 1 to 11, identifying common themes, regional patterns, and lessons that inform the broader trajectory of sustainable urban development in Southern Africa.

12.2.1 Urban Vulnerability and Structural Risk Drivers

Southern African cities face overlapping and systemic vulnerabilities rooted in historical, socio-economic, and environmental conditions. Across various chapters, one recurring theme has been the colonial-era spatial planning legacies that continue to shape urban morphology, producing fragmented, exclusionary, and inefficient cities (Parnell & Pieterse, 2014). Post-independence development trajectories in countries like Zimbabwe, Namibia, and Mozambique have often failed to reverse these patterns, instead perpetuating marginalisation through unplanned urban growth and informalisation.

Informal settlements, home to over 60% of urban residents in many Southern African cities, are typically located on hazardous sites such as floodplains, unstable hillsides, or areas without drainage infrastructure (UN-Habitat, 2020; Satterthwaite et al., 2020). These residents face acute exposure to fire outbreaks, landslides, flooding, and communicable diseases due to the lack of adequate shelter, sanitation, and access to services. The COVID-19 pandemic further exposed the fragility of urban health systems and the socio-spatial inequalities within urban centres (Wilkinson, 2020). Additionally, the lack of updated data and hazard mapping contributes to poor risk knowledge, which in turn affects land allocation, building control, and emergency response systems (Douglas et al., 2008; Van Niekerk, 2014). These vulnerabilities are exacerbated by limited municipal capacities, weak enforcement of development controls, and poor coordination between urban planning and DRR institutions (Mercer et al., 2012).

12.2.2 Planning Gaps and Fragmented Governance

Governance challenges form another layer of risk. Multiple chapters pointed to the disconnect between different sectors—urban planning, environmental protection, infrastructure development, and emergency management—which often function in silos. This fragmentation results in disjointed urban responses, missed synergies, and duplicated mandates (Cirolia et al., 2016). Decentralisation policies have attempted to empower local authorities in countries like South Africa, Zambia, and Botswana. However, in practice, local governments often lack the financial autonomy, technical staff, or legal mandate to effectively plan and manage urban risks (Dodman et al., 2017). National policies are frequently outdated, and municipal development plans rarely integrate climate change projections or hazard exposure data.

Moreover, intergovernmental coordination mechanisms between national ministries, city councils, and disaster management units are either absent or dysfunctional. Institutional turnover, lack of training, and inadequate legal frameworks further weaken the implementation of resilience strategies (Van Niekerk, 2020; Aitsi-Selmi et al., 2016).

12.2.3 *Case Study Insights: Local Innovations and Emerging Practices*

Despite these challenges, several innovative practices have emerged across the region. In Durban (South Africa), the municipality has adopted an ecosystem-based approach to climate adaptation through initiatives like the Buffelsdraai Reforestation Project and the Durban Adaptation Charter (Roberts & O'Donoghue, 2013). These initiatives show how integrating green infrastructure with urban development can enhance both ecological and community resilience.

In Maputo (Mozambique), participatory enumeration and risk mapping exercises led by civil society have enabled informal residents to identify local vulnerabilities and co-design solutions with government stakeholders (Brown et al., 2014). Similarly, Harare's post-2008 cholera outbreak catalysed the creation of integrated urban health and sanitation response strategies that connected spatial planning with public health. These examples reinforce a key message from the book: resilience must be locally grounded, participatory, and context-specific. Cities that have made progress on resilience have done so by embedding DRR in broader development strategies and prioritising inclusive governance.

12.3 Strategic Pathways to Resilient Urban Futures

Moving from analysis to action, this section presents strategic pathways for embedding resilience in urban development. It builds upon the patterns, practices, and policy failures identified in earlier chapters to propose integrated, evidence-based solutions for Southern African cities.

12.3.1 *Integrated Policy and Planning Frameworks*

A key barrier to effective resilience is policy fragmentation. To address this, governments must establish integrated urban resilience frameworks that harmonise disaster risk reduction, land use, infrastructure development, and climate change adaptation. This can be operationalised through national urban policies that include resilience indicators and require local authorities to embed risk considerations into their municipal development plans (Carmin et al., 2012; UN-Habitat, 2020).

Policy integration should be both vertical (across levels of government) and horizontal (across sectors). For example, South Africa's National Development Plan and the Climate Change Bill illustrate how national policies can embed localised resilience goals, but more robust enforcement and municipal-level planning are needed (Republic of South Africa, 2011). Countries like Rwanda and Mauritius have gone further by mainstreaming DRR into land use frameworks and capital budgeting processes (Republic of Rwanda, 2011; Government of Mauritius, 2013). A regional resilience protocol under the Southern African Development Community (SADC) could provide coherence and technical support across countries.

12.3.2 *Infrastructure Investment and Risk-Sensitive Design*

Infrastructure sits at the heart of urban resilience. Roads, drainage systems, public buildings, transport, and utilities must be designed with risk and climate stressors in mind. Southern Africa continues to suffer significant economic and human losses due to infrastructure failure during disasters, particularly in urban poor areas. Cities must adopt risk-sensitive infrastructure planning, involving hazard assessments, environmental impact analyses, and long-term maintenance models. Incorporating nature-based solutions such as urban wetlands, bioswales, green roofs, and permeable pavements can reduce surface runoff and cool urban microclimates (Kabisch et al., 2017). Cape Town's water-sensitive design and green infrastructure pilots following the 2018 drought offer instructive models (Armitage et al., 2014). Infrastructure resilience must also consider social equity. Investment should prioritise underserved informal settlements, with retrofitting programmes for roads, sanitation, and stormwater systems that also generate local employment (Douglas et al., 2008).

12.3.3 *Land Use Management and Spatial Justice*

Spatial planning is a powerful tool for resilience but remains underutilised across Southern Africa. Risk-informed land-use planning involves mapping hazard zones, enforcing building regulations, and guiding urban growth away from high-risk areas. This requires up-to-date geospatial data, clear land tenure systems, and community buy-in. Tools such as GIS, participatory mapping, and scenario modelling can support planners in balancing development needs with environmental constraints (Moser &

Satterthwaite, 2008). Urban growth boundaries, no-build zones, and incentive schemes for compliance can curb the expansion of informal settlements in high-risk locations. Achieving spatial justice also involves upgrading existing informal settlements with infrastructure and security of tenure, an approach supported by UN-Habitat's Participatory Slum Upgrading Programme (UN-Habitat, 2017).

12.3.4 *Institutional Reform and Capacity Building*

Even the best policies and plans will fail without institutions capable of implementation. Governments must invest in institutional reform and capacity building for DRR and urban planning functions at both local and national levels (Van Niekerk, 2014). This includes hiring and retaining skilled urban planners, engineers, and risk analysts within municipal governments; developing disaster management curricula in universities; and strengthening data and early warning systems. Institutions must be structured to promote coordination through multi-agency task forces, joint funding mechanisms, and interdepartmental working groups. The case of Lusaka's integrated city resilience office, supported by international donors and embedded within the planning department, demonstrates how institutional innovations can be locally adapted and effective (World Bank, 2020).

12.3.5 *Community-Based Resilience and Participatory Governance*

Lastly, resilience must be socially embedded. Communities possess invaluable knowledge about local hazards, vulnerabilities, and coping mechanisms. *Participatory governance* mechanisms such as ward committees, community mapping, and public hearings can democratise planning and enhance legitimacy (Wisner et al., 2004; Brown et al., 2014). Cities like Kisumu (Kenya) and Durban (South Africa) have institutionalised community engagement within DRR planning, facilitating the co-design of infrastructure projects and inclusive early warning systems. These approaches not only improve effectiveness but also foster civic responsibility and social cohesion. Resilience is not merely a technical end-state; it is a dynamic process grounded in relationships, equity, and trust.

12.4 Research Priorities for Evidence-Based Urban Resilience

Robust, context-sensitive, and disaggregated data remain some of the most critical enablers of effective disaster risk reduction and urban resilience in Southern Africa. Although some countries have begun establishing national risk databases and early warning systems, most urban areas still suffer from a lack of current, accurate, and accessible information. This section proposes key research areas that should guide both academic inquiry and policy experimentation in the region.

12.4.1 Urban Risk Profiling and Hazard Mapping

Detailed, city-level risk profiles are urgently required to inform land-use planning, building codes, and emergency response strategies. Many urban areas operate without updated floodplain maps, landslide inventories, or exposure models for critical infrastructure. Furthermore, risks in informal settlements are poorly documented, despite being home to a significant portion of urban populations (Satterthwaite et al., 2020; UN-Habitat, 2020). Collaborative risk assessments integrating local government, universities, and communities can generate high-resolution data tailored to each urban context. Innovations such as drone mapping, remote sensing, and participatory GIS can improve data quality and community ownership.

12.4.2 Climate Scenario Modelling and Urban Impacts

Understanding how future climate extremes will affect Southern African cities is essential. This includes not only temperature and rainfall projections but also indirect effects such as heat-induced migration, water scarcity, and urban heat island effects. Research must localise global models, incorporating variables like topography, socio-economic inequality, and infrastructure quality (IPCC, 2022). Scenario modelling can help cities anticipate compound hazards such as flooding during pandemics or droughts during power shortages and make long-term investments accordingly. Partnerships between meteorological agencies, universities, and planning departments can build predictive capacity at the local level.

12.4.3 *Institutional Performance and Governance Metrics*

Effective governance is a cornerstone of resilience, yet there is little empirical work assessing how institutions perform in implementing DRR policies. Researchers should develop metrics to evaluate coordination, responsiveness, accountability, and transparency across institutions involved in urban planning, emergency services, and climate adaptation (Van Niekerk, 2020; Aitsi-Selmi et al., 2016). Longitudinal studies that track how policies are implemented across cities—what succeeds, what fails, and why—can offer valuable policy insights and foster cross-learning.

12.4.4 *Innovative Financing for Resilience*

Urban resilience requires sustained investment, but traditional public budgets are often insufficient. There is a growing need to investigate alternative financing mechanisms, such as municipal bonds, climate adaptation funds, green infrastructure banks, and public-private partnerships (UNEP, 2016). Research should assess the feasibility, risks, and governance of these instruments in contexts marked by fiscal austerity and weak institutions. For instance, how might a green bond be structured for a mid-sized Southern African city? What accountability mechanisms are needed for transparent fund use?

12.4.5 *Digital Technology and Smart Resilience Systems*

Digital innovation presents immense opportunities for transforming urban risk governance. The use of Internet of Things (IoT) sensors, mobile applications, AI-based flood forecasting, and real-time data platforms can enhance early warning, infrastructure monitoring, and disaster communication (Aitsi-Selmi et al., 2016; World Bank, 2020). Future research should explore how digital technologies can be scaled and democratised in resource-constrained urban environments, ensuring that they do not deepen the digital divide but rather empower communities and improve decision-making at all levels.

12.5 Policy Recommendations

Building on the findings and strategic pathways elaborated in this chapter and throughout the book, the following policy recommendations are proposed for national, sub-national, and local governments, as well as regional institutions and civil society actors across Southern Africa. These recommendations aim to transform current urban development approaches into inclusive, risk-informed, and future-proof systems.

12.5.1 Mainstream DRR Across Urban Policy and Planning Instruments

Governments should ensure that all urban development policies, national urban policies, municipal integrated development plans, spatial development frameworks, and infrastructure investment guidelines explicitly include disaster risk reduction provisions. This includes:

- Mandating hazard assessments before any urban expansion or major construction.
- Including resilience indicators in municipal performance contracts.
- Aligning urban policies with climate change adaptation frameworks and sustainable development goals (UN-Habitat, 2020; UNDRR, 2015).

Legislation must be revised to give legal weight to DRR considerations in spatial planning and construction regulation.

12.5.2 Invest in Resilient and Inclusive Infrastructure

Priority must be given to infrastructure that both serves essential needs and enhances resilience. This includes flood-resistant roads, decentralised energy systems, multi-purpose public spaces, and climate-smart housing. Governments should:

- Incorporate resilience standards into public infrastructure procurement processes.
- Offer incentives to developers for building green and risk-compliant structures.

- Allocate capital budgets to upgrade infrastructure in informal and underserved communities (Douglas et al., 2008; Kabisch et al., 2017).

Infrastructure finance mechanisms, such as resilience bonds or blended finance models, should be developed at the regional level through SADC or development finance institutions.

12.5.3 *Build Institutional Capacity at Local Levels*

Urban resilience depends heavily on the operational capacity of local governments. Policies should:

- Increase the budgetary share for urban planning and disaster management departments.
- Establish training programmes for urban practitioners in risk-sensitive planning, climate adaptation, and participatory governance.
- Create interdepartmental coordination units for integrated urban management (Van Niekerk, 2014; Dodman et al., 2017).

These reforms require political commitment at the national level, as well as support from universities and development partners.

12.5.4 *Enable Community-Led Resilience Action*

Policy must go beyond consultation and support genuine community leadership in DRR. Governments and NGOs should:

- Institutionalise participatory planning methods in municipal procedures.
- Fund community-based risk mapping, upgrading, and monitoring initiatives.
- Recognise and support informal governance structures, such as savings groups and traditional authorities, as resilience actors (Brown et al., 2014; Wisner et al., 2004).

Urban policy should be rights-based and equity-oriented, ensuring that vulnerable populations are not left behind.

12.5.5 Foster Regional Collaboration and Peer Learning

Finally, Southern African cities can benefit enormously from *regional knowledge sharing and collaboration*. SADC, the African Union, and continental platforms such as the African Cities Research Consortium should:

- Facilitate regional urban resilience dialogues and benchmarking.
- Develop a shared urban resilience framework tailored to African priorities.
- Support cross-border infrastructure and climate adaptation programmes (Carmin et al., 2012).

Through cooperation and solidarity, cities can overcome common challenges and scale proven solutions.

12.6 Conclusion

Southern Africa's cities are undergoing rapid and irreversible transformations. As they grow, they also accumulate risks, both old and new, stemming from spatial inequality, weak governance, climate stress, and fragmented infrastructure systems. Left unaddressed, these risks threaten not only lives and livelihoods but also the economic and developmental gains made over the past decades. Throughout this book, we have examined how the integration of disaster risk reduction (DRR) and urban planning offers a viable pathway to more sustainable and resilient urban futures. We have explored international best practices, local innovations, structural barriers, and policy gaps. We have shown that resilience is not a fixed end-goal but a continuous process of adaptation, learning, and transformation.

This concluding chapter has synthesised the key lessons from the preceding chapters and charted strategic pathways for action. From policy integration and infrastructure investment to land use management, institutional reform, and community participation, we have highlighted the multidimensional nature of resilience-building. The recommendations outlined are not exhaustive but form a strategic agenda for reform, investment, and experimentation. Crucially, resilience must be underpinned by a new urban social contract—one that centres equity, empowers local voices, and aligns short-term recovery efforts with long-term development goals. Cities must evolve from being passive recipients of risk to active agents of transformation. They must become spaces where innovation meets inclusion, where growth is tempered by sustainability, and where planning is informed by both data and local knowledge.

The road ahead is undoubtedly complex. Financing constraints, institutional inertia, and political volatility remain significant obstacles. However, these challenges should not obscure the opportunities. Southern Africa has vibrant civil societies, rapidly advancing technologies, decentralisation reforms, and a growing pool of urban professionals. These assets must be mobilised deliberately and urgently. As climate change accelerates and urban populations continue to rise, the stakes are high. But with coherent strategies, collaborative leadership, and an unwavering commitment to inclusive development, the cities of Southern Africa can become global exemplars of resilience and sustainability.

> *The future is not predetermined; it is planned, built, and sustained. Let that planning begin now.*

References

Aitsi-Selmi, A., Murray, V., Wannous, C., & Dickinson, C. (2016). Reflections on a science and technology agenda for 21st century DRR. *International Journal of Disaster Risk Science, 7*(1), 1–29.

Armitage, N., Vice, M., Fisher-Jeffes, L., Winter, K., Spiegel, A., & Dunstan, J. (2014). *The state of water-sensitive design in South Africa*. Water Research Commission.

Brown, D., Smit, W., & Pieterse, E. (2014). *Urban infrastructure in Sub-Saharan Africa: Harnessing land values, housing and transport*. Cities Alliance Working Paper Series.

Carmin, J., Nadkarni, N., & Rhie, C. (2012). *Progress and challenges in urban climate adaptation planning: Results of a global survey*. MIT Global Sustainability Project.

Cirolia, L., Berrisford, S., Cavernelis, Y., & Smit, W. (2016). *Urban infrastructure in Sub-Saharan Africa—Harnessing land values, housing and transport*. African Centre for Cities Working Paper.

Dodman, D., Leck, H., Rusca, M., & Colenbrander, S. (2017). African urbanisation and urbanism: Implications for risk accumulation and reduction. *International Journal of Disaster Risk Reduction, 26*, 7–15.

Douglas, I., Alam, K., Maghenda, M., Mcdonnell, Y., McLean, L., & Campbell, J. (2008). Unjust waters: Climate change, flooding and the urban poor in Africa. *Environment and Urbanization, 20*(1), 187–205.

Government of Mauritius. (2013). *Mauritius climate change adaptation framework*. Ministry of Environment.

IPCC. (2022). *Sixth assessment report*. Intergovernmental Panel on Climate Change.

Kabisch, N., Korn, H., Stadler, J., & Bonn, A. (Eds.). (2017). *Nature-based solutions to climate change adaptation in urban areas*. Springer.

Mercer, J., Kelman, I., Taranis, L., & Suchet-Pearson, S. (2012). Framework for integrating indigenous and scientific knowledge for disaster risk reduction. *Disasters, 34*(1), 214–239.

Moser, C., & Satterthwaite, D. (2008). *Towards pro-poor adaptation to climate change in the urban centres of low- and middle-income countries*. International Institute for Environment and Development (IIED).

Parnell, S., & Pieterse, E. (2014). *Africa's urban revolution*. Zed Books.

Republic of Rwanda. (2011). *Green growth and climate resilience strategy*. Government of Rwanda.

Republic of South Africa. (2011). *National Development Plan 2030: Our future—Make it work*. National Planning Commission.

Roberts, D., & O'Donoghue, S. (2013). Urban environmental challenges and climate change action in Durban, South Africa. *Environment and Urbanization, 25*(2), 299–319.

Satterthwaite, D., Archer, D., Colenbrander, S., Dodman, D., Hardoy, J., & Patel, S. (2020). Building resilience to climate change in informal settlements. *One Earth, 2*(2), 143–156.

UNDRR. (2015). *Sendai framework for disaster risk reduction 2015–2030*. United Nations Office for Disaster Risk Reduction.

UNEP. (2016). *The adaptation finance gap report 2016*. United Nations Environment Programme.

UN-Habitat. (2017). *New urban agenda*. United Nations Human Settlements Programme.

UN-Habitat. (2020). *World cities report: The value of sustainable urbanization*. United Nations Human Settlements Programme.

Van Niekerk, D. (2014). A critical analysis of the South African Disaster Management Act and policy framework. *Disasters, 38*(4), 858–877.

Van Niekerk, D. (2020). Urban risk governance in Africa: Challenges and pathways. In S. Patel & I. Parnell (Eds.), *Urban risk and resilience in the global South*. Routledge.

Wilkinson, A. (2020). Local response in health emergencies: Key considerations for addressing the COVID-19 pandemic in informal urban settlements. *Environment and Urbanization, 32*(2), 503–522.

Wisner, B., Blaikie, P., Cannon, T., & Davis, I. (2004). *At risk: Natural hazards, people's vulnerability and disasters*. Routledge.

World Bank. (2020). *Resilient cities in Africa: Building forward better*. World Bank Group.

Index

F. Mangara, N. Dorasamy, *Sustainable Urban Development in Southern Africa*, https://doi.org/10.1007/978-3-032-08286-2

FSC
www.fsc.org
MIX
Papier | Fördert
gute Waldnutzung
FSC® C083411

Kolibri 360 GmbH
Ferdinand-Jühlke-Straße 7
99095 Erfurt, Deutschland
produktsicherheit@kolibri360.de